From Willard Straight
to Wall Street

From Willard Straight to Wall Street

A MEMOIR

Thomas W. Jones

Cornell University Press / Ithaca and London

First published 2019 by Cornell University Press

Printed in the United States of America

Library of Congress Cataloging-in-Publication Data

Names: Jones, Thomas W. (Thomas Wade), 1949– author.
Title: From Willard Straight to Wall Street : a memoir / Thomas W. Jones.
Description: Ithaca [New York] : Cornell University Press, 2019. | Includes bibliographical references.
Identifiers: LCCN 2018047984 (print) | LCCN 2018053867 (ebook) | ISBN 9781501736339 (pdf) | ISBN 9781501736346 (epub/mobi) | ISBN 9781501736322 | ISBN 9781501736322 (cloth : alk. paper)
Subjects: LCSH: Jones, Thomas W. (Thomas Wade), 1949– | African American capitalists and financiers—Biography. | African American executives—Biography. | Wall Street (New York, N.Y.)—Biography.
Classification: LCC HG172.J66 (ebook) | LCC HG172.J66 J66 2019 (print) | DDC 332.1092 [B]—dc23
LC record available at https://lccn.loc.gov/2018047984

This book is dedicated to my life partner, Adelaide Knox Jones, who has shared my life journey for forty-four years. Her love has lifted my spirit and been the wind beneath my wings. This book is also dedicated to our parents, Lt. Colonel George Knox and Yvonne Wright Knox, and Reverend Edward W. Jones and Marie Carter Jones. I thank God for their lives, their faith, and their commitment to their children. Finally, this book is dedicated to our children, Victoria, Evonne, Michael, and Nigel. I pray that they will know God's love and grace in their lives, as have Addie and I.

Contents

Acknowledgments

I am grateful to Dean Smith, Director of Cornell University Press, for nurturing this project over three years. When he reviewed my first draft manuscript, Dean told me that it wasn't good enough to publish, but it had the potential to be an interesting book. As I worked to produce subsequent drafts Dean always invested the time to read them and explain their deficiencies, and always encouraged me by saying my project had high potential and my story was important to tell. Dean eventually suggested that I should work with Emily Hopkins to produce a polished manuscript. Emily spent many hours talking with me to understand the nuances of my story, and she interviewed ten of the people mentioned in my manuscript to gain insights through the eyes of others who experienced the events I described. Emily skillfully edited and rewrote my manuscript so that it was transformed from my "business memo" style into a more engaging story dialogue, and I thank Emily for her good work. I also thank my friends and colleagues who took the time to be interviewed by Emily. Finally, I'm very appreciative of the skilled professionalism that the Cornell University Press team brought to this project. This includes Ange Romeo-Hall, Managing Editor, who coordinated the editing and production; Martyn Beeny, Marketing Director, and his team; Amanda Heller, who provided skillful copyediting to polish the manuscript; and Scott Levine, Art Director, who designed the interior and the cover.

From Willard Straight
to Wall Street

Guns at Cornell

One of the astonishing things about 1968 was how quickly each
shocking, consciousness-altering event succeeded the last, leaving
no time for people to reorient themselves.

—Bob Herbert, *New York Times, January 1, 2008*

My homemade war club, studded with nails, dangled from my belt,
hitting my right thigh. There was also a butcher knife tucked into
my waistband. This was not what I had expected from college, not
at all. Someone down the darkened hall coughed, and I picked up my rifle
by its strap and slung it across my shoulder. Guns, knives, a two-day standoff
with the university authorities. I hadn't really slept in forty hours, and now it
was morning again. I was nineteen years old.

I stood near the ground-floor rear entrance of Willard Straight Hall,
the five-story student union building on Cornell University's campus. The
electricity had been turned off, but the white light of a cold, overcast April
day shone in through the tall windows. Outside, dozens of police waited, and
hundreds more armed sheriffs, as many as four hundred, we'd heard, were
amassed downtown, ready to move in on us. The rumors were nonstop. We
couldn't know for sure what was true and what was a lie, a fantasy, or a hys-
terical guess. Below, circling the building, was a growing gaggle of reporters
from local and national newspapers. My mind raced to put the situation into
perspective.

If we are attacked either by those police or by more vigilantes, I'll fight,
I decided. That will make for some surprising news: Parents' Weekend 1969,
dozens of armed black students at an Ivy League school fighting for educational relevance, giving their lives just to have black history and culture claim
its rightful place in the curriculum.

I thought I might be killed if we fought, but I wasn't afraid. In fact, the idea of my own death, as I stood there not knowing what would happen next, struck me as a sacrifice I had to be willing to make. Hadn't I often mused that if I had been born in slavery, I would have tried to start a slave rebellion? Or if I had been born in 1845, I would have tried to join the Colored Troops in the Union Army to fight for my freedom on Civil War battlefields in the face of cannon and rifle fire, and I likely would have died? If I had been born in 1925, I would have wanted to fight on the battlefields of World War II against the Nazis. Now, since I was the perfect age for it, I might soon be drafted into the U.S. Army to join other young black soldiers who were dying in disproportionate numbers on battlefields in Vietnam.

But it was more than a romantic daydream, the idea of my own death right there on campus, maybe right in this big, cold building. Just fourteen months before, thirty unarmed black students had been shot by police during a demonstration at South Carolina State University, and three of them had died of their wounds. Two years earlier, during the "long, hot summer" of 1967, there were race riots (also called "armed uprisings") in over one hundred U.S. cities; hundreds of people were killed, and thousands were injured. And, in the most recent months, we had witnessed the assassinations of Martin Luther King and Robert Kennedy, the protests and violence in Chicago at the Democratic National Convention, and more riots, including one in Washington, D. C., where marines with machine guns were positioned on the steps of the Capitol building. In 1969, I lived in a violent world. I was comforted by the thought that at least I was choosing my own cause to die for, and that it was a good and just cause. The fight for black freedom and equality in America had already claimed many lives and would likely claim many more. I was fully committed to the fight.

But it was pure irony that I was there in that position at all, occupying a university building in protest, instead of watching from the outside and preparing for graduation.

Freshman Year

Nearly four years earlier, in 1965, my parents had driven me to Cornell on a cloudless Saturday afternoon in September. It was the first time any of us had been to Ithaca or to Cornell University, whose campus is built on a hill overlooking a glacial valley and Cayuga Lake, thirty-five miles long and almost five hundred feet deep. Ithaca was a sleepy town, we could see, segmented by dramatic gorges and surprising waterfalls tucked here and there, appearing suddenly when you rounded a corner.

In the flats below the university lay the little town, a nothing-much place with modest houses built for mill workers, a small downtown where there was a men's clothing store, a Rothschild's department store, some restaurants, four movie theaters, a drugstore, some churches, the Selective Service draft office, and the courthouse. Outside of town was farmland and smaller towns.

I had applied to three schools—Penn State, Ohio State, and Cornell. Cornell appealed to me because it was in the Ivy League and in New York State. I missed New York City, where I'd enjoyed being a public school student for six years, from third to tenth grade. But my Ohio high school guidance counselor steered me away from urban schools, thinking I was too young to navigate city life and college at the same time. Fine, I thought, but it's still New York.

I knew that at college, nobody would know I was only sixteen. (I'd skipped two grades.) It would be a huge psychological weight off my shoulders, not always having to be on my guard against guys eager to put me down and gain advantage over me because of my age. It was going to be real liberation, I thought, not having to prove that I was not a person you wanted to mess with. People's ignorance of my birthdate would even the playing field.

Our peripatetic living pattern—we'd moved three times in eight years because of my father's work, from Baltimore to New York to San Diego to Ohio—had two indelible effects on me. The first was that I became self-contained. I was perpetually the new kid on the block, and other kids were sometimes friendly and welcoming and sometimes not. This uncertainty taught me to be content with friendships that were offered, and indifferent to those that weren't. The second effect stemmed from my experience in New York City public schools, which at that time practiced a policy of "accelerating" the best students (in contrast to current educational philosophy, which emphasizes "enriching and deepening" the educational experience). I scored 150 on an IQ test and was an excellent student, so I was accelerated past fourth grade and then again past eighth grade. I had no difficulties with this academically, but it exacerbated and reinforced my inclination to be guarded. I entered high school at age twelve, the youngest in my class. Some classmates admired me for this; others thought it was an opening to put me down and try to belittle me.

I remember very clearly my conscious decision one day on the playground at P.S. 15 in Queens, when some older boys were trying to bully me, that

I wouldn't allow others to diminish my self-confidence or self-esteem, as though I had something to be ashamed of for being accelerated academically. I will always define myself, I decided, and never allow others to define me. Put-downs and hazing would not make me feel diminished. They would not make me feel anything. This was the origin of what became my lifelong tendency to be a maverick. And because of this decision, I simply didn't need a lot of approval from my peers, and yet I always seemed to be popular. In my one year at Abraham Lincoln Senior High School in San Diego, I was elected to the high school student representative position on the city board of education, and in my one year at Newark Senior High School in Newark, Ohio, I was voted "Most Likely to Succeed" by my high school senior class.

I leaned my head against the car window in the backseat and looked at Cornell. I could see the McGraw Hall clock tower piercing the sky, and a long stone building with a breezeway and columns. I was stunned. I think my parents were too. What a magnificent campus! We drove slowly down West Avenue, following temporary signs that pointed arriving freshmen to the dorms, and we could see Libe Slope rising from the street out the driver's side window. It was a steep grassy hill, smooth as a vertical golf course, crisscrossed by walkways and dotted with cherry trees. At the top of the slope stood grand university buildings, including the library that gave "Libe" Slope its name, and the hub of student life, Willard Straight Hall. The buildings above us at the top of that slope stood stark and imposing against a blue sky. I thought, "Man, this is what I'm talking about: *college.*"

It had rained earlier that day, leaving the grass fresh and the pavement dark, but now the sun was out. Orientation staff wearing special white straw hats directed us and the hundreds of other families where to park, where to bring our trunks and suitcases, which doors to use to enter the buildings.

The dorm I was assigned to wasn't grand. It was one of the nondescript University Halls, room 5208. When we got to my room, I was surprised by how small it was. But what did I know about dorm rooms? I didn't have anything to compare it to but my expectations. The room had two beds and two desks, and so I guessed that someone else would arrive soon. I started to unpack my things. Mom and Dad lectured me gently, reminding me I'd have to work hard. They said they were proud of me and expected the best. My mother kept looking out the window and exclaiming how beautiful the place was. I half-listened to them.

I was one of only thirty-seven black students in a freshman class of 2,600. This was a fact that must have weighed more heavily on my parents' minds

Figure 1 / *Tom, age three months, with his father*

than it did on mine. They were both from the South, from poor families that had struggled under the boot of Jim Crow, and they had both escaped those constricted circumstances by getting college educations and moving north. But like most black people of their generation, they remained wary, careful.

My father's carefulness manifested itself in his formality. He was one of the most formal, gracious men I've ever met, polite in the extreme, controlled and correct, deferential. He called everyone "sir" or "ma'am." Before any significant car trip, he called us all to bow our heads and pray together for God to watch over us. We had prayed that morning in Ohio before we set off for Ithaca.

Born in 1909, my father, Edward W. Jones, started life with two strikes against him: he was a dark-skinned and heavyset Negro in a color-conscious world, and he came from a poor, broken family. His hometown, Charlotte, North Carolina, had two major train lines running through it—the Seaboard Airline Railroad, with its brick and stucco passenger station, and the Southern Railway on 4th Street in downtown Charlotte. When I listen for the soundtrack of my father's childhood, I hear those trains, clacking in and out of the city, hissing and groaning, their rhythmic noise becoming the beat of escape. And most of those trains coming in and out of his city, day and night,

Figure 2 / *Tom's father in 1957*

included Pullman cars, on which worked Pullman porters, the first group of black workers in America to successfully organize in a labor union and consequently the most revered blue-collar workers in the wider black community. Porters were respected for the dignity they'd demanded for themselves and for the hard work and long hours they put in and got paid relatively well for.

Despite his circumstances growing up in a poor family, my father willed himself to find a way forward, to build a meaningful life worthy of praise. In high school, when his family broke up, he took a room in a boardinghouse run by a relatively well-to-do black woman named Stella Watson. She must have seen that my father was serious and intelligent, because she pushed him to apply to the Johnson C. Smith Theological Seminary in town, a black college, which he did. He earned a master of divinity degree there, and then a master's in physics from Indiana University. He entered the ministry first, because that was the primary path of opportunity open for black men in the South in the 1920s and 1930s. During World War II, he served as a captain in the U.S. Army Chaplain Corps. After the war, he became a minister in the Presbyterian Church in Hillburn, New York. Finally, in the late 1940s, as racial discrimination softened somewhat, he began to get work as an engineer, using his technical skills in the defense industry. He also passed the licensing examination and became a licensed professional engineer. He was working at Picatinny Arsenal when I was born in Philadelphia in May 1949. His career really accelerated in 1957, when he was hired to work on the Atlas missile program at American Bosch Arma Corporation in the New York City suburbs on Long Island. This opportunity followed the Russian Sputnik launch, which galvanized America into a space race with Russia.

Whenever the Lionel train company, which made lifelike toy replicas of real trains, would come out with a new car or engine, my father didn't delay. "Sons," he would say to me and my two brothers—especially to me and my oldest brother Ed—"shall we go to the train store this weekend?" In our basement he had set up a waist-high table with intersecting loops of tracks that filled an entire room measuring twenty feet by twenty feet. There were mountains and valleys, bridges and trestles, a brickyard and a little village and a passenger station, towns, and a church. Down there in the train room, putting together the necessary electronics, carefully wiring the miniature lamps and train signals, making adjustments to the tracks and the cars—it was when my father was most relaxed, most happy.

My mother, Marie Carter, was born in 1911, in Martinsville, a small town in southern Virginia with an economy driven by cotton, tobacco, and furniture making. Like my father, my mother had a difficult childhood but found a way forward through education. She earned an associate's degree from Barber Scotia College in North Carolina and found employment as an elementary school teacher in the 1930s. (Thirty-five years later, she completed a bachelor of arts degree at Muskingum College in Ohio.) In 1938, my mother and father were married. I was the youngest of four children: my sister Marie was born in 1940, my brother Edward Jr. in 1941, and my brother James in 1945. My dominant memory of my mother is that she was always there for me. In many ways she seemed to live her live vicariously, taking to heart her children's successes and failures, rather than focusing on her own needs and desires.

"Do you think you guys should head back home, soon, sir?" I said, after we'd sat and talked a while as the whole glorious Cornell campus beckoned to me through the second-story window and I could hear conversations drifting in from the hallway and outside.

"Yes, I suppose so," he said, sighing and pushing himself off the little chair by the desk with some effort. He straightened his tie and reached for his hat. Mom stood too and picked up her purse.

My roommate arrived, a white boy from upstate New York. He was in the agriculture college. I think he wanted to be a farmer. He was fine, but we weren't going to be close, I could tell. We had nothing in common. I would have to look farther afield than my own room for friends.

Later that day, after my parents had left, I met Skip Meade, whose room was directly above mine, on the third floor. We started talking and I liked him right away. I thought, "Here's a black student in my dorm and he's just like me." I felt a rush of relief, the lifting of a worry I hadn't even been conscious of harboring. Skip, who seemed to be from a family much like mine, hailed from Madison, New Jersey, a suburb of New York. "Skip" was his nickname. His real name was Homer, after his father. He was outgoing, confident, and funny. He was a guy who had seen a million movies and read many books. And like me, he was excited to be at Cornell and seemed happily dedicated to the pursuit of a good time. As we walked through the dorm, people he must have met earlier in the day called out to him. It was the first day of school and already he had friends and seemed to be popular.

On the first day of classes, Skip and I were walking along the wide promenade in front of Willard Straight Hall when we spied three black guys standing there, sizing us up. The steps of the Straight was the place to see everybody, and they were there to see what girls might show up and what other black students might have arrived on campus for the new school year. We introduced ourselves and talked for a bit before moving on. As it turned out, these three sophomores would later become some of my best friends at Cornell: Charles McLean, Milton Fleming, and Greg Grant. Years later, Charles told me that when Skip and I left, he turned to the others and said of me, "Oh, this guy is going to be a factor," indicating that I was going to be credible competition for girls. "We decided to enlist you," he said. "Easier to have you *in* the tent than outside the tent."

Students had been assigned mailboxes, and I found in mine a surprising invitation that first week. It was signed by a Ms. Gloria Joseph in the Dean of Students' office, and she was welcoming me as a member of the COSEP class. I was hereby invited to attend the first COSEP meeting of the year. COSEP, which I had not been aware of during my application process, was the acronym for the Committee on Special Education Projects, an initiative launched by Cornell president James Perkins to increase the number of black students at Cornell. Apparently the thirty-seven of us black students in the class of 1969 represented a marked increase in diversity over previous years. In President Perkins's first year in office at Cornell, just two years earlier, there had been only six black students in the entire student body at Cornell—a shameful example of discrimination at a school that had, in the 1920s, a much more sizable black population and had even been the birthplace, in 1906, of America's first black intercollegiate fraternity. Why, during the civil rights movement, had the black population dwindled to almost zero at a school whose motto was "I would found an institution where any person can find instruction in any study"? President Perkins recognized the hypocrisy and the opportunity to make a positive change, although this wasn't something I appreciated fully until years later.

On orientation day, there were dozens of tables and booths set up in front of the freshman dorms and around Willard Straight Hall, along the big patio in front of the building. The booths were manned by staff and upperclassmen. Here were all the activities and groups you could become involved with: intramural cricket, polo, the football team, which had open tryouts, the campus Democrats, religious groups, student government, and so forth. I loved football and had played in high school in California and Ohio, but I hadn't been able to be a star. I was an excellent athlete, but my classmates' two-year advantage over me showed in their physical development and experience, so I knew that it wasn't realistic for me even to try to join the team at Cornell now.

But how am I going to be somebody on this campus, I wondered? One of the tables offered information about running for class office. I walked up to it.

"What's this about?" I asked. The table was manned by two white upperclassmen, Dick Balzer and Elliott Fiedler. I liked them both immediately—the way they talked, their coolness, a certain cockiness that felt familiar to me. They reminded me of my Jewish friends from seventh and ninth grade in Junior High School 59 in Queens, when I'd gone to public school. Their attitude was "If you want to be a bumpkin, go hang out with those other people."

What were the responsibilities of the class officers? Nothing significant, I learned. There was basically no reason to have a freshman class president.

Dick said, "Why don't you run?" and I said, "Well, maybe I will."

To run for freshman class president, one had to submit a short application and then sit for an interview with a student government committee whose job it was to weed out weaker candidates. Only candidates approved by that committee advanced to the actual ballot. A few days after my interview with the committee, a list of accepted candidates was posted on a sheet pinned to the bulletin board in Willard Straight Hall and my name was nowhere to be seen. I thought back to my interview and wondered what could have gone wrong. Or, I wondered, maybe it was a color thing?

Before I could even think much more about it, Dick and Elliott found me in the dining hall. They were smiling, excited. "Why not run anyway? Those guys are bozos," they said, referring to the election committee that had eliminated me from the running. "We'll mount a write-in campaign."

I agreed. Sure, why not? It would be a good way to raise my profile in the class, meet more people. Dick and Elliott made signs that read "Don't listen to the election committee, listen to yourself." I liked the boldness of that. I thought it was fun—the attention, the interest these older students showed in me—but at the same time, I was amazed. Look at all this stuff that's happening for me! This is like a dream. My name on posters in the hallways. I myself campaigned quietly, person to person, keeping a low profile. And then election day dawned and I wrote in my name, as a write-in candidate. How many of my new classmates will also write in my name, I wondered?

To everyone's surprise, I won the election and was the first black class president in Cornell's history, thanks, really, to the machinations of Dick and Elliott, who I think got a kick out of integrating the student government and being power brokers behind the scenes.

Elliott Fiedler recently wrote the following recollection of these events:

> When I heard about what happened to Tom I was not only concerned that a very capable candidate had been excluded from being on the ballot but also believed that racial bias (either conscious or unconscious) might have been one of the factors in the decision. I decided to engage a few good friends/other student leaders in a plan to help Tom as a write-in candidate. We came up with a plan to print his platform as a flier that we distributed to all freshman dorm rooms the night before the election. It was a brilliant but flawed plan. While we accomplished the "undercover" mission between 2 and 4 a.m., we did not realize that we had broken a newly instituted rule forbidding the passing of campaign materials under doors in the dormitories.
>
> One election day, Tom won 48 percent of the vote. But then all hell broke loose. The Elections Commissioner disqualified Tom for rules infraction. Tom appealed that decision to the Student Government Executive Board (of which I was the president), and at a packed open meeting the election results were thrown out and a new election ordered. Tom won again as a write-in candidate with 64 percent of the 1320 votes cast.

My first-semester classes included psychology, American history, French, calculus, and computer science. I was a student in the College of Arts and Sciences. I didn't know yet what I wanted to be, professionally. The sky was not the limit, in those years, for a black man, but I felt pretty confident nonetheless. There were still whole fields absolutely closed to nonwhites, and others that promised to be nearly impossible to enter, especially in the business world. Those were the days when there were only two black people starring on television, Bill Cosby and Diahann Carroll, and five black people in all of Congress.

Much more culturally crucial than student government was the Greek system of fraternities and sororities. People today may not understand or remember how big the religious distinction (and discrimination) was in those days, but the WASP fraternities didn't want Jewish students in them. In fact, some national charters explicitly forbade the religious or racial integration of fraternities. Although Cornell was the birthplace of the first black intercollegiate fraternity in America, there were no black fraternities or sororities at Cornell by the time I was there.

Dick and Elliott were members of the most prestigious Jewish fraternity, Zeta Beta Tau. My chance meeting with them at the election table during orientation opened up a relationship for me with that whole side of Cornell—Jewish students and the ZBT fraternity.

Rushing was allowed in the second semester of freshman year. That semester, only ten to fifteen of the thirty-seven black freshmen were rushed by fraternities or sororities, and only six to eight ended up joining one. By my calculations, over three-quarters of the black students were consequently excluded from the heart of social life at Cornell. It was a major exclusion that would have far-reaching effects on the racial climate and on many black students' feelings of marginalization.

But I was rushed by five or six fraternities. The process went like this: You got a call, or a visit to your dorm room, with an invitation to attend one of their mixers. Skip and I were both invited to the first ZBT mixer, held at their beautiful frat house on Edgecliff Place, an old stone mansion perched on the edge of the gorge.

We wore jackets and stood around talking with the various ZBT brothers. This was a test of your conversation skills, your level of sophistication, how much you knew. Were you funny or sharp? I felt completely at home and was pleased to be asked to join in the middle of the semester, which I did. Skip also joined. The next year, we both lived in that grand mansion on the edge of the gorge and enjoyed the sounds of birds singing in the tree branches just outside my window. I enjoyed fraternity life and liked my fraternity brothers. I developed close friendships with three in particular—Andy Chodorow, Bart Lubow, and Jay Levine.

Although I was a member of a mostly white fraternity, and had good friendships there, my closest group of friends were black—Charles McLean from Ithaca College, and from Cornell, Milton Fleming, Greg Grant and Warren Barksdale, both from Harlem, Les Hutchinson, and Skip Meade.

We were all city boys. Ithaca was a small town in the middle of nowhere, more than an hour from Syracuse, and it was what we called a cow town. Charles McLean called it "basically Appalachia." We had grown up, all of us, in or near that pulsating, integrated, bustling heart of America that is New York City. When he was as young as nine, Charles had sometimes used his pocket money after school to take a train from Long Island into Manhattan, where he liked to buy steak sandwiches for ninety-nine cents at a place right by the Penn Station subway stop. He'd polish off his sandwich standing on the sidewalk, strangers hurrying past him on every side, then get back on the train and ride home. His parents never even knew that he'd been in the city and had a meal, nor would they necessarily have cared, as long as he was home and at the table for dinner.

The best aspect of my own youth had been the good fortune to live my most formative years, from ages eight to fourteen, in New York City. Subway and bus fares were only fifteen cents, and Yankees bleacher seats cost only a couple of dollars, so my allowance for cutting the lawn and other odd jobs enabled me to explore and enjoy a broad swath of the city. I roamed from Yankee Stadium in the Bronx to Coney Island in Brooklyn, where I liked to buy a hotdog and sit on the boardwalk watching people. Then I'd go on the rides, especially the two giant wooden rollercoasters built in the 1920s, the Cyclone and the Tornado. I would go to the Central Park Zoo, where there were cheerful penguins, monkeys, and noisy parrots. I fully appreciated the wondrous good fortune of living in a city where one minute you could be walking on Fifth Avenue and the next minute you could walk through a big park with a zoo, wild animals chattering and cawing. It was another reason to love the place—the stark contrasts. And I frequented the museums in Manhattan and the New York Public Library, a cavernous, limitless place, intensely American and democratic, where they had every book ever written, it seemed to me, and every type of patron you could imagine, from hobos to society ladies with smooth hair and flowery perfume. I never felt any sense, as a boy, of threat or danger because of my race. I never felt unwelcome or watched as I roamed the city and soaked it in. The place was mine as much as it was anyone's.

New York City at that time was in its peak years of public educational excellence, including its highly regarded tuition-free public college flagship institutions, Hunter College and City College of New York. Middle-class families of all races were attracted to the quality of New York City public schools, and I received an excellent education in integrated schools.

Charles told me that when he arrived as a freshman at Ithaca College in 1964, his assigned roommate came into the room, threw down his duffle bag, allowed Charles to shake his hand, and then excused himself, saying he'd be "right back." Half an hour later he returned, grabbed his bag from the floor, and left without a word. It took them weeks to finally find Charles a replacement roommate, even though, like Cornell in my freshman year, Ithaca College was overenrolled and had a crowding problem. The guy must have gone straight to the housing office to complain about having a black roommate.

The replacement roommate turned out to be something of a character, who Charles sometimes told us about. One night the roommate announced that he was going to do a thousand sit-ups in the hallway. "It went on for hours and hours," Charles reported to us.

On one of his first trips downtown, to window-shop, Charles had stopped in at the men's clothing store on State Street, only to have the staff approach him and start speaking a loud, careful pidgin English to him. "Help with clothes? Shirt, pants, shoes?" When Charles replied in his perfectly fluent Long Island English, the clerks "recoiled," he said, as if in shock. "There were more students from Africa than there were American blacks. The expectation in Ithaca was that if you were black, it was more likely you were from overseas."

There *were* some black townies, though, and my friends and I wanted to meet them, mostly because we wanted to find black women to date, and there were so few black women on the campuses. Sometimes we'd go to the Elks Club downtown, the only gathering place for blacks. When you needed a haircut, you went there, because they had someone cutting hair a couple of days a week. They had a bar and, periodically, little dances and parties. It was a totally unsophisticated place, and the first few times we went there, there was some antipathy from the townies. They didn't want college guys competing with them for the girls.

That year, several of my friends went down to the draft office on Cayuga Street and signed up. It was a rite of passage, and it afforded you a draft card, which let you drink at bars at a time when the legal age in New York was eighteen. Although I was in the ROTC program at Cornell, I was only seventeen at the end of freshman year, so I made myself a fake ID.

I loved everything about my freshman year, including the ritual of trudging up Libe Slope on Saturday morning for 8 am classes. I had made friends early and I was well known and popular. I rarely missed dances or parties where the pretty black student singer Sonye Edwards, who sounded like a cross between Diana Ross and Aretha Franklin, was performing with her band. I chased girls. My favorite was my fellow black freshman Joyce Shorter, but she wasn't interested in me. She wanted to date upperclassmen athletic stars instead. But Joyce and I became friends and maintained that friendship over the years.

On the evening of March 19, 1966, most of us, the black college students in Ithaca, crowded around a television set in a dormitory common room to watch Texas Western College square off against the Kentucky Wildcats in the NCAA finals. As the announcer talked, the starting players for the Texas team arrived, one at a time, at center court to be announced. The first player there, the point guard, black. The next player, also black. And so on until the full squad of five stood there in a line, all black. It was the first time in American history that a coach had started an all-black squad in a championship game. Then it was the Kentucky team's turn to gather at midcourt, and since they were an all-white team (they wouldn't have their first black player until three years later, in 1969), the game began as a tense matchup of white against black.

We sat shoulder to shoulder on the sofa, some of us on the floor, and we leaned forward, holding our breath. "The tension was so great anytime a black person was on the TV," Charles recalled to me recently. Looking back on that night, we realized it was maybe the last time that all the black college men in Ithaca could gather together in a single room. By the next fall, it would be impossible. Or if not impossible, at least very unlikely.

At the end of the semester, rather than go home for the summer, I stayed at Cornell and worked a summer job as a waiter at Johnny's Big Red Grill in Collegetown. I never again went home to live with my parents.

Sophomore Year

I lived in the Zeta Beta Tau house sophomore year. It was easy and comfortable for me, I found, to live in two parallel worlds—the white fraternity world with Skip and my white friends, and also the black student social and political world with Skip and a group of black friends. I was active in student government and continued to be happy at Cornell. This was where I belonged. But the intensity of debates at the Afro-American Society (AAS) meetings, and the urgency of the national civil rights movement, gradually pulled me deeper into racial issues.

In our sophomore year, an unprecedented number of black students arrived in Cornell's freshman class because of President Perkins's COSEP initiative. There was something different about the new freshman class. Whereas the black students in my class had almost all come from within fifty miles of New York City, many of these new students were from Detroit, Cleveland, Texas, Arkansas, from ghettos and from largely black high schools. Many were southern and rural, and they arrived on campus with something we hadn't come with: an already partially developed sense of militancy born of grievances, an impatience to reform the world, to get rid of injustices they had felt more keenly that we had. We rubbed each other the wrong way from the start.

The first time I met John Garner was at an Afro-American Society meeting in the fall of 1966. My first impression was that he perceived and interpreted every event through very different eyes and different sensitivities from mine. He didn't seem to enjoy Cornell in the least, or relish the good luck of being there and the chance to take advantage of all that it offered us. How completely alienated he seemed from all things Cornell—the classes, the professors, the conversations and obsessions, the fashions and the amusements. I wondered why he had come to a place where he seemed so uncomfortable. But here he was, and he was the leader of this disaffected cohort of black students in the class of 1970. He set the tone of "black consciousness."

I tried to be friendly toward every group of black students, but Garner and company quickly evinced intense dislike of me and Skip Meade. Just hearing us talk, it seemed, angered them, or seeing that we were comfortable wherever we went. Skip and I, they said, were "not really black." What? I thought. This idea of "blackness" being defined solely by one's adherence to a strict class compartment or to a revolutionary idea caught me off guard. It was a familiar cancer, though, one I'd first encountered when older boys wanted to put me down for skipping grades in elementary and middle school. "It's not black to be smart" was the message. Similarly, Garner's crowd's message was "It's not black to be middle class" and "It's not black to fit so comfortably into the white Cornell scene." I believe that this cancer exacts an enormous toll on the black community in the form of educational underachievement, as so many black children are implicitly steered away by their peers from trying to excel academically, because academic excellence "isn't black." The resulting lack of educational achievement reverberates through diminished career opportunities and income for many black families. In my opinion, this cancer is a major reason for the perpetuation of the black underclass and arguably, in the current era, robs black people as surely as racism and discrimination do, contributing to the inferior condition of blacks in America.

This idea that Skip and I and our friends weren't black enough infuriated me, especially when I thought about what I knew of my own family's history. I knew that my father and mother had been born in poverty in 1909 and 1911 in North Carolina and Virginia, respectively, in an era of harsh racial discrimination. They had managed—against long odds—to become educated and lift themselves from poverty into the middle class by building successful professional careers. Was it my parents' fault, or my fault, that more black families had not achieved comparable success? How could it be?

My father's success flowed from his faith in God, his belief in the value of education, and his commitment to hard work. On many nights in my childhood, I would say good night to my father knowing that it would be hours before he allowed himself the luxury of sleeping too. No, he had work to do, at his big wooden desk at home, after a full day at the office. Late into the night he studied and wrote, drafting important scientific papers on electronics, or weightlessness in space, and design guidelines for thermal environments in space. Science didn't care about color; it cared about relevance, research, breakthroughs, truth. My father put in the long hours needed to publish numerous papers in top scientific journals, an achievement no layoffs or racist slights could take away from him.

Dad was rarely unemployed, and he was fairly well compensated, but he lived at a time when blacks were last hired and first fired. As defense contractors won new business in the 1950s and 1960s, his skills were in demand, and he secured good employment. But every time the contracts ended, Dad's position was invariably eliminated. He was never included in the ongoing core company teams. This meant that our family relocated frequently as my father moved from job to job.

I enjoyed an important six-year period of stability while my father was employed at American Bosch Arma Corporation in Garden City on Long Island, working on the Atlas missile guidance system. His position was senior engineer, Missile Guidance Systems, Product Reliability Department. This unusually good job resulted from the Russian Sputnik launch in 1957, which spurred the United States to ramp up spending on missile technologies and the space race. After that job, we spent a year's sojourn in San Diego, California, in 1963–64, for my junior year in high school, where my father worked at General Dynamics on the Centaur missile system. Then, a year in Newark, Ohio, where he worked at the U.S. Air Force Instrumentation Laboratory in the position of physicist, Mechanical Standards, Calibration and Metrology Division.

And it wasn't just his intelligence and hard work that had gotten him and us to where we were. It was also, I knew, his faith in God. When I thought of his humble, rock-steady faith, and his late nights of toil, I couldn't square it with the sneering disdain the "black vanguard" had for me and my friends and our families.

It could be that part of why the newer crop of black students didn't love us was that we were so dedicated to living the good life. And we were not, as first-semester sophomores, strongly focused yet on social justice and racial equity. For example, one weekend, when Smokey Robinson and the Miracles were scheduled to play a concert in Barton Hall, we hired some freshmen to go early and save good spots for us right up by the stage. While they stood for hours there and the crowd filled in behind them, we had a small, elegant dinner party for our girlfriends at Charles's apartment on Seneca Street, with a piano in the front room and big windows in the back looking out onto a lush garden. We did the cooking. Then, when our dinner was over, we took our dates to Barton Hall, an old airplane hangar turned into a field house and the largest concert venue on campus. When we arrived, we took the freshmen's place down front and sent them to the nosebleed seats, seconds before Smokey Robinson took the stage.

Another day, we challenged the younger crowd to a game of flag football, which could be a very aggressive, physical game. You could knock people down; it was organized brawling. They accepted our challenge and said they'd meet us for the game the next day, on the quad for the women's dormitories. Charles, who had played quarterback in high school and who was and remains today one of the biggest sports fans I've ever met, rubbed his hands together happily and said, "If we can run the ball up their throats, we'll take their hearts."

We devised some plays. And we choreographed some showboating inspired by the Dallas Cowboys, which had become a franchise a few seasons earlier and had a way of shifting that was new: they'd call a number and then readjust, in unison. "That was a very sexy, attractive thing to do," as Charles put it later. When we borrowed that move on game day, surrounded by a decent crowd of casual onlookers—girls—we were rewarded with a collective murmur of surprise and appreciation from the crowd. We went on to dominate the other team with our plays, too, and the opposing team slowly shrank in numbers as, one by one, their players slunk off. The game did not improve relations between us and the younger men, either. There's a tendency to attribute serious philosophical or political motives to events of the past, but sometimes animosities grow out of simpler things . . .

Whenever we found ourselves in the same room, John Garner and I would argue at length. On two occasions our verbal confrontations deteriorated into physical fights triggered by name-calling. How dare he think he was blacker than me? I had good friends like Warren Barksdale and Greg Grant who came from Harlem, so I didn't perceive my clash with Garner to suggest any sort of economic class conflict. I saw him as a guy who just didn't like me for his own reasons. As always, I resisted—with the weapon of indifference. Unless you act like their opinion matters to your perception of yourself, your enemies can't get any satisfaction.

Like most other black students, I went to hear the black speakers who were visiting our campus and introducing us—passionately and influentially—to contemporary black thought. People like James Farmer (CORE/Congress of Racial Equality), poet LeRoi Jones (aka Amiri Baraka), Black Panther leader Bobby Seale, Stokely Carmichael from SNCC (Student Nonviolent Coordinating Committee), and Malcolm X from the Nation of Islam (Black Muslims). We heard them all and were electrified by their words.

John Garner and his friends aspired to be part of the "black revolutionary vanguard," in the footsteps of Malcolm X, Carmichael, Huey Newton, and Seale. In contrast, they labeled me and my crowd "mainstream Negro integrationists," in the mold of Dr. Martin Luther King Jr., Roy Wilkins (NAACP), and Whitney Young (National Urban League). I could feel the tension growing between the self-styled "revolutionaries" and the "integrationists," a tension that mirrored the same divides in black communities across America. The broader black community was torn between those who advocated nonviolent protest and civil disobedience in pursuit of integration and civil rights, versus those who advocated armed self-defense, self-determination, and black separatism.

I was converted slowly, to an extent that surprised me. Exposure to my student peers, visiting campus speakers, and my own immersion in the literature of the movement gradually caused me to question my thinking as a "Martin Luther King integrationist." I read hundreds of books on black history, slavery, African colonialism, sociology, and civil rights in America. At the same time, the Watts riots in 1965 and the Newark and Detroit riots in 1967 created an impression that black America was on the verge of outright rebellion or armed insurrection. In 1968, when riots erupted in Washington after the assassination of Martin Luther King, the U.S. military positioned marines with machine guns on the steps of the Capitol building and in front of the White House. I had to pick a side.

I had joined army ROTC as a freshman mostly because my father was an army veteran and my oldest brother had been in ROTC at Hampton Institute, but in my sophomore year I dropped ROTC. An unfair percentage of American casualties in Vietnam were black men. Black men, with a much-reduced chance to get an education exemption or a cushy assignment in the National Guard, were being used and they were dying. Suddenly I didn't feel like being seen in a uniform that symbolized that.

I was thirsty for knowledge about the story of my people. I learned to understand the significance of language, and I embraced the Malcolm X–inspired "language of self-definition and self-determination" which was crystallized in the terms "Afro-American" and "black," in preference to the terms "Negro" or "colored," which are associated with colonial exploitation and slavery. The need for a black studies curriculum that would enable black students to learn more about ourselves became, for me, the most important political issue on campus. Knowledge is power. People who are ignorant of their history are psychologically crippled.

Even though I did not personally like most of the "John Garner group" of students, I was influenced by their arguments to think more deeply about the place of blacks in America and the political implications of our historical subjugation and oppression. While I rejected their criticisms of my "bourgeois" background, I understood that my family history and personal life experiences were not representative of the realities that confronted most blacks in America.

Junior Year

My junior year was absorbed by a deep dive into reading about sociology, anthropology, economics, and politics. Black students had succeeded in securing a few black studies courses, and I enrolled in most of them. I drifted away from my white friends, and my ties to ZBT weakened. Near the end of my junior year, in April of 1968, the Reverend Martin Luther King Jr. was assassinated, and the ensuing widespread black inner city riots (or insurrections, depending on one's perspective) crystallized my thinking. Black America might be evolving toward armed revolution. If that day arrived, I thought, my place would be fighting next to my black brothers and sisters for freedom and respect.

Garner and his friends espoused a "revolutionary dialectic," in which the "revolutionary vanguard" engages in political demonstrations and confrontations to expose the inherent contradictions and injustice of the prevailing power structure. The demonstrations and confrontations would raise the political consciousness of followers and "educate the masses." In practice, this meant that Garner and his friends were the cutting edge in three major political events that shaped the tone of Cornell's campus and led directly to the Willard Straight Hall takeover.

The first significant political event came in the spring of 1968, when Garner, Bert Cooper, and Robert Rone initiated demands to fire visiting professor Michael McPhelin for racially insensitive remarks in an economics class they were taking, and subsequently led an occupation of the economics department offices in Goldwin Smith Hall. The second major political event occurred in December 1968, when the same group of five or six black students engaged in disruptive actions in support of securing a black studies program. They hadn't—and wouldn't—come to the AAS beforehand to propose taking this sort of action, of course; they just went off and did it, rogue, creating a situation in which less politicized students had to "raise their consciousness" to support them. In this way, some black students were being manipulated into backing tactics that they wouldn't otherwise have endorsed.

It was AAS's vision that Cornell launch a black-run, academically autonomous black studies college. The Garner group's demonstrations attempting to force this issue included brandishing toy guns in the Day Hall administration building, dancing on tables in the dining room at Willard Straight Hall, dumping books from shelves in Olin and Uris libraries, and disrupting an intercollegiate varsity basketball game at Barton Hall. All the AAS negotiations thenceforward intertwined two issues—the internal judicial review and possible punishment of students involved in those disruptive demonstrations, and a black studies program. What had been a political fight over black studies was, in effect, partially co-opted into a fight about sanctions against individual students.

On April 4, Skip and Charles and I were riding in Skip's VW bug. I remember that we were by the girls' dorms on campus. The radio was on. Maybe they were playing "You're My Everything" by the Temptations, or "Ain't No Mountain High Enough" by Marvin Gaye and Tammi Terrell. The music stopped abruptly and an announcer came on. The Reverend Martin Luther King Jr. had been shot in Memphis. We looked at one another. Skip slowed the car but did not pull over. Devastation. Heartbreak. Fury. Black revolutionaries at Cornell and in black communities across America nodded knowingly, saying, "I told you so. America is hopeless and cannot be redeemed."

After King's assassination, it appeared to us that America was on the brink of revolution. In fact, it was. Riots in over a hundred cities. In June 1968, the Democratic presidential candidate Robert F. Kennedy was gunned down and killed. And in August 1968, massive daily antiwar protest marches at the Democratic nominating convention in Chicago erupted into severe police repression and violence. It seemed like America was coming apart at the seams, and we black students at Cornell subsequently initiated self-defense measures by gathering firearms at our 320 Wait Avenue headquarters.

One of the new black freshmen was Stephanie Bell from the Bronx. She was beautiful and had a toughness and swagger I liked. She was passionate about the arts, a free spirit who had close friendships with both white girls and black girls. A New Yorker through and through, she'd already marched against Vietnam while still in high school in the city, and had hung out with Stokely Carmichael, a friend of one of her older sisters. Stephanie was a talented painter. We became friends, although she later admitted to me that she hadn't liked me when she first met me; she thought I was too square, too straight. But we quickly grew close, and Stephanie would tell me stories about all the other guys who were trying to date her, pestering her. Her mother had warned her against having anything to do with men at college.

I was Stephanie's first lover. She got pregnant almost immediately. She didn't know she was pregnant until she complained to her mother about feeling sick all the time and her mother took her to the doctor. She was terrified. A baby had not been in her plans, nor in mine. She was still a freshman. Back in the Bronx, a high school friend had gotten an illegal abortion and died. There was, she told me, an underground network at Cornell that all the women knew about. If you became pregnant, this network would help you buy a plane ticket to London for an abortion.

We decided to get married.

I hadn't lived with my parents since entering college, but they consented to host our wedding at their home in St. Albans, in Queens. We were married in August of 1968 by my father, followed by a small reception at my brother Ed's place in Hempstead. I wore a traditional African tunic to our wedding, to my parents' consternation. My father didn't especially like Stephanie, I could tell, because he didn't approve of our situation, but I didn't need him to love her.

Senior Year

Senior year was dominated by the ongoing reverberations from Dr. King's assassination the previous April, the assassination of Robert Kennedy in June, and the bloody confrontation in August between police and antiwar demonstrators at the Democratic National Convention in Chicago.

Cornell campus politics were dominated by the continuing black student demands for a full-fledged black studies program and amnesty from judicial sanctions for the John Garner clique of students who had conducted disruptive demonstrations. The dominant strand of politics in the Cornell black student community was reflected in the evolution of our student organization's name from the Afro-American Society to the Black Liberation Front (BLF).

Senior year, John Garner left campus, dropped out of Cornell for good, to do community organizing work. I had the feeling that he had given up too soon, without really accomplishing anything. The AAS was badly split between Garner's group and people like me.

Another significant political event on campus happened in February of my senior year, in 1969, when Eric Evans, Gary Patton, and Larry Dickson—part of Garner's clique—interrupted and then physically manhandled President James Perkins, lifting him by his collar to remove him from his place at the podium at a symposium on South Africa. They, and many other students in the audience, were there to demand that Cornell University's endowment divest investments in South Africa. This physical confrontation spurred demands on campus for strong judicial proceedings and sanctions against disruptive students.

The cross-currents and tensions culminated eventually in the April 1969 black student takeover of Willard Straight Hall. The night before the takeover, black students convened an emotional all-night meeting at our Wait Avenue headquarters. Accompanied by the beat of bongo and conga drums, we danced war dances and sang war chants to prepare emotionally and psychologically for the coming confrontation. At dawn, we marched across campus and seized Willard Straight Hall.

The Straight takeover started early Saturday morning, April 19, of Parents' Weekend. I was not one of the planners of the takeover. Nor was I a member of the Afro-American Society leadership committee in the early stages of the plan. In fact, when the idea to take over the building came to a vote the day before, I voted against it. It didn't seem like a good idea to me. Hadn't we already won the university's agreement to launch a black studies program, and wasn't that the really crucial point—more important than some judicial decision against students who had in fact done the things the administration accused them of doing? Their physical confrontations had spurred demands for strong proceedings and sanctions against disruptive students. And hadn't those students engaged in those actions without consulting AAS? But I would go along, I would lend my physical support, because of my commitment to our group solidarity.

Willard Straight Hall is a massive, labyrinthine building made of bluestone. It was commissioned by the widow of a distinguished Cornell graduate, Willard Straight, and it was completed and dedicated in 1925. It is a substantial structure with stone and tile floors, multiple staircases, mullioned windows, and several entrances, the main entrance opening onto a wide plaza that is the main pedestrian thoroughfare of Cornell's central campus. The building's purpose, from the beginning, was to be a student union. And in 1969 it was still the hub of nonacademic student life. There was a stage for theater productions; there were dance studios and music rooms, game rooms, a library. The fourth and fifth floors, though, were used as a sort of hotel for short-term visitors—trustees, alumni, and parents. In the basement was the student radio station, WHCU, in a little office crammed with papers and posters, equipment and chairs.

The night before the takeover, someone set a wooden cross wrapped in fabric afire on the porch of Wari House, the university housing for black women. All night long, fire alarms went off every few hours at residence halls across campus. The night was filled with the recurring sound of sirens as the fire department trucks raced to address the nonexistent fires. Roughly a hundred of us arrived at Willard Straight Hall early that morning and evicted the occupants—janitorial staff, visiting parents—into the rain. We were occupying the building. After we'd been in the building for a few hours, the administration and most of the campus knew what was happening.

At first, the takeover was peaceful. I was playing pool in the Straight game room on the lower level when suddenly I heard a commotion in the hall outside—angry shouting. I couldn't make out the words. I put down my cue and went into the hallway to see what was going on. Events now began to spin in unpredictable and unanticipated directions.

A group of white fraternity guys had gained entry through a window at the back of the building on the ground level. They were arguing with a group of black students, shouting that we had no right to take over the building. I recognized some of them. And as I was standing there in that moment, it just flashed through my mind that whatever I had thought of its merits initially, the takeover certainly was not going to end this way, with a group of fraternity guys from Delta Upsilon throwing us out of the building. I covered the distance between us with a few long strides and went straight to the leader of the DU group. Standing close to him, I said, "We're not talking about this any longer," and I punched him square in the face. Instantly, a brawl ensued—punches, wrestling, rolling around on the ground, shouting. We threw the Delta Upsilon guys out of the building.

Step by step, I was then drawn deeper and deeper into the dynamics of the Straight seizure and our confrontation with the university administration. In the wake of the Delta Upsilon vigilante action, we heard many rumors regarding possible attempts to oust us from the building. Some were rumors of police action. Some were rumors of another fraternity attack. Some were rumors of vigilantes from the rural areas surrounding Ithaca. We made a decision to bring in weapons to defend ourselves.

My mentality was shaped by my deep dive over the past two years into black history and literature. I had come to Cornell ignorant of these topics because they weren't taught in the public schools I'd attended. As I became educated in the true story of the three-hundred-year history of blacks in America, I had become angry. I developed a belief that American slavery and oppression could not have survived for so long without the implicit cooperation of the oppressed. I felt that my ancestors, and the ancestors of most other African Americans, had not resisted slavery and oppression to the extent that they could have and should have. I knew they had been literally beaten into fear and submission, and I believed that overcoming this legacy was the only way to win freedom and respect. Slaves could be tortured and killed for resistance and rebellion, but they became productive economic assets only when they cooperated in submission to the slave masters. I thought, What if my ancestors had simply *drawn the line*? Drawn the line and refused to be enslaved. Drawn the line and refused to be treated as subhuman. I thought that if they had fought for their freedom and dignity, yes, many would have died, but they also would have been free, because a people who refuse to acquiesce cannot be enslaved. Death is not the worst thing that can happen to a person.

The wheel of history, I thought, had turned; my generation were to be the African Americans tasked with the obligation and destiny to finally draw the line and end our oppression in America. In a five-year span, President John Kennedy had been assassinated, Malcolm X had been assassinated, Martin Luther King had been assassinated, and Robert Kennedy had been assassinated. We were in an endless war in Vietnam, where hundreds of black soldiers were dying every month. Riots were raging in cities across America. And our university was dragging its feet on supporting the black studies program and the fair judicial system we deserved. Maybe that meant that the time to act was now, in Willard Straight Hall, at the heart of white power—the Ivy League. As unlikely as it might be, was this idyllic campus in rural upstate New York about to take center stage in America's racial drama? If so, maybe that meant I was in the middle of a historic event. I understood that history is often a series of accidental and unplanned occurrences in which ordinary people must make decisions about what to do. Sometimes they decide to do ordinary things; other times they decide to do extraordinary things. I had also internalized a conviction that one of the necessary strategies to end oppression was to *raise the price* of oppression, and that meant black Americans had to be willing to fight, and die if need be, to win our freedom. This right now, I thought, might be one of those crossroads, and I have to be prepared to do something extraordinary.

Our weapons, seventeen shotguns and rifles, were stored at the AAS headquarters building, on the other side of campus. There were campus police surrounding the Straight, and we knew we'd have to evade them if we were going to be able to leave the building, get the weapons, and manage to bring them inside. I was one of the students who slipped out, with two others, through the same window the Delta Upsilon boys had used to gain entrance. My heart thudded in my chest. The night was cool. There were no police in sight at our Wait Avenue building.

On our way back across campus, we clutched the weapons, wrapped in blankets, under our arms, and we waited, hidden in the bushes near the Straight, for the door to be opened on a prearranged signal. It flew open and we dashed into the building past the startled and unsuspecting campus police. We had enough guns to arm seventeen, but there were nearly eighty of us—men and women—occupying the building. I was armed with a hunting rifle that I owned. I had grown up going deer hunting with my father and brothers, and had been in army ROTC as a freshman. I was an excellent marksman.

Tension was high inside the Straight overnight and into the following morning. They'd turned the electricity off on us, and so the only lights were a few powered by the building's emergency generator, and candles we found in the kitchen. Students sat and lay against the walls, nervous, wondering what would happen next. Some studied. Finals were coming up. "Did you hear . . . ?" and "Well, I heard that . . ." Rumors were flying about impending attacks from more vigilantes, or from a large force of local and state police gathering in Ithaca to move against us. Later it was tension from the reality of weapons on-site, and the unpredictability of what might happen at any moment. I could see apprehension and doubt tinged with fear in the eyes of some black students, especially those without weapons. They seemed stunned by the dramatic escalation of a typical 1960s college building occupation (building takeovers were as common as dirt in those years) into what was now an armed confrontation, something very different.

As I looked into their eyes, it occurred to me that many of the black students had fragile psyches and were not accustomed to confronting, or winning against, white authority. This hardened my attitude, and my emotions swung decisively into an assurance that "we're going to win this, one way or another." I was now fully committed to the fight. And fights are for winning.

Fortunately, the introduction of weapons seemed to galvanize the university administration into a sense of urgency about ending the takeover. They seemed to fear, and were probably correct in doing so, that events could rapidly spin further out of control. They were probably most concerned that the police forces gathering in downtown Ithaca might decide to end the occupation by force. The possibility of gunfire ringing out on campus, of students being shot dead, of a SWAT team storming the building and taking it back by force . . . these images were in everyone's mind, theirs and ours.

By Sunday afternoon, April 20, the university administration negotiated a settlement with us, in which the most important point was that the administration committed to convene a faculty meeting on Monday, April 21, and request nullification of the judicial reprimands against the black students. And so it wasn't a total victory for the AAS/BLF but a temporary victory,

Figure 3 / *Tom exiting Willard Straight Hall at Cornell University, April 1969 (By permission of Steve Starr, photographer, AP).*

contingent upon the faculty's voting to give us, finally, what we demanded: not only a black studies program but also a clean slate for the protesters.

Over the phone, we agreed to leave the building, but we refused to disarm first. No, we will march out with our weapons, we said. In the end, the administration sent representatives over to us. They would exit the Straight with us. Their presence would protect us from being fired upon, and it would also show that we had reached an agreement together.

I would bring up the rear, I decided. "We should take the rear," I told Skip. He understood the symbolism immediately: we were the rear guard, and we were the ones most prepared for a fight. Skip looked like a gunslinger in a Clint Eastwood western—floppy hat, woolen poncho he had made from drapes in the Straight, cigar between his lips, rifle at the ready resting in the crook of his arm. Skip, like me, had grown up hunting and knew how to handle a rifle. When we opened the double doors and stepped out into the day, we were met with the chants of Students for a Democratic Society (SDS) supporting us, by stony silence and stares from parents and some of the faculty, and by the clicking of camera shutters. We marched across campus toward our headquarters building in military formation. Armed black male students were in front and in the rear and on both flanks; in the middle, women and other unarmed students.

I felt a sense of pride in this display of solidarity and courage, and its implicit repudiation of hundreds of years of American history of blacks cowering in fear. I was quoted in a contemporaneous interview saying:

> We marched out in military formation. We had the sisters in the middle. The brothers with guns were on the outside. We were strategically placed. Different calibers of guns were at different points in the procession, because at all times we were ready. The maxim applied: "If we die, you are going to die" . . . That moment was a moment in history—armed black people marching out of the student union at Cornell University in military formation! That was a moment that galvanized black people across this nation! . . . We'd taken pains to make sure that the cartridges weren't in the breeches. Uh-huh, I'll admit they were within a flick of being in the breech.

That night, my brother Ed called me. At eight years my senior, he was a twenty-seven-year-old Vietnam veteran and an executive at New York Telephone Company. He told me that our parents were besides themselves over the takeover and my role in it. He said, "Police have guns! Don't make me have to drive up to Ithaca and track down the person who shot you."

On Monday afternoon, April 21, the university faculty voted against the negotiated settlement to dismiss the judicial reprimands, condemned the seizure of Willard Straight Hall, and condemned the presence of weapons on campus. The formal resolution on which the faculty voted included conciliatory language "expressing sympathy for the problems of the black students in adjusting themselves to life at Cornell," and invited AAS representatives to meet with the Faculty Council the following day.

Reports and rumors were that the faculty resistance was led by a core of conservatives from the government and history departments. I was a government major and personally knew many of the leading faculty members of those departments. In their classes I had debated the role of race in American history and government, and I had emphasized the importance of Negro slavery to produce tobacco, cotton, and sugarcane as cash crops that were a key pillar of early American economic growth and capital formation. In their classes I had argued that cheap Negro slave labor had enabled the accumulation of substantial pools of capital, and that these "excess profits" from slavery had propelled America's rapid economic growth from the mid-1600s to the mid-1800s. Unfortunately, I had learned in their classes that the ravages of slavery and the story of blacks in America did not figure very prominently in the versions of American history and government taught by faculty icons such as Walter Berns and Allan Bloom. I knew that we were essentially invisible to them.

On Tuesday, April 22, we ignored the invitation to meet with the Faculty Council. I argued with the BLF leadership committee that we needed to shift our strategy from acting alone to engaging more actively with white students to form an alliance that could defeat the faculty conservatives. My stance was controversial in BLF because the prevailing "Black Power" sentiment and rhetoric was for black self-determination and complete independence from "honkies" and "white devils." Eventually I secured grudging approval to engage with the broader white student community. I thought that I could work effectively with the white students because I was well known and familiar to them from my history as freshman class president, student judicial board member, member of the Quill and Dagger honor society, and member of Zeta Beta Tau.

My first initiative was an interview early Tuesday evening, April 22, on radio station WHCU, back in the basement of the Straight. The host asked me questions and I gave answers calculated to be harsh, frightening. I escalated the fight with the conservative faculty, calling them out by name. I said that the faculty vote placed black students in a position where we had to choose whether to possibly risk our lives to defend our principles, or bow to the faculty position. I said that I had made my choice, and I would fight for my principles. Then I said that what was different this time from American history, where blacks had done all the dying, was that now the faculty conservatives would also have to decide if the principles they were espousing were worth the possibility of risking *their* own lives. They couldn't just decide that blacks might have to suffer in a fight over principles, but they had to face the same question for themselves.

When I named specific faculty members and administrators, I warned that their names and addresses had been given to people who would ensure that they and their families met the same fate as me and my family. When the interviewer asked if there was anything that Cornell could do, I ended by saying, "I would suggest that the faculty have an emergency meeting tonight and, if they can do so by nine o'clock, nullify this decision. After nine o'clock it's going to be too late. Cornell University has three hours to live."

I left the basement radio station office and went to the meeting SDS had convened to decide how to support AAS. It was scheduled for 7:30 pm in Bailey Hall, which had a capacity of approximately two thousand seats, but so many students turned out that the meeting was moved to Barton Hall. When I arrived at Barton, where we'd seen so many concerts and basketball games, and where my ROTC drill practices had been held my freshman year, there were approximately six thousand students in attendance. Black students owe an enormous debt of gratitude to David Burak and the SDS leadership for not letting us be isolated and alone in our fight. SDS maintained a vigil outside Willard Straight Hall during the takeover, and SDS organized this student rally which would decisively shift the dynamics of our confrontation with the faculty conservatives.

Six thousand students: it was the largest crowd I'd ever faced, a sea of mostly white faces. I didn't think it was likely that black students alone could achieve a mutually acceptable compromise with the conservative faculty, but I knew that if I could get those white students on our side, we would win. I stepped up to the mic and gave a speech in which I explained to the white students why the black students' struggle was important in the historical context of slavery and racism, and I explained the principles underlying our fight for black studies and against the judicial board's sanctions. I understood how to reach the white students by appealing to their sympathies on the one hand, and appealing to their fears on the other hand. I concluded by asking them to support AAS, and asked for a show of hands. The response was overwhelming. At least four thousand hands shot up. And a few hours later, this new entity, this crowd of students that became known as the "Barton Hall Assembly," declared that they were occupying a building too, Barton Hall, in support of AAS and in support of faculty nullification of the judicial reprimands.

As word spread around campus, the "Barton Hall occupation" swelled to ten thousand students. My mission was accomplished. I didn't think the hardcore faculty conservatives would bend in the face of potential physical harm to black students, but I knew they weren't prepared for a confrontation with ten thousand white students.

The next day the university faculty convened again and this time voted to nullify the judicial sanctions. I spoke again to the Barton Hall Assembly and told them, "That faculty decision to nullify was made right here. They didn't make any decision; they were told from this room what to do. The old order has ended, and this is the new university community."

When I eventually called my parents a week after the takeover, my father was too upset to talk. "I'm praying for your safety" was all he could say. Mom got on the phone and said that Dad thought I had destroyed my future and would likely be gunned down by police sooner or later. She cried and kept saying, "I don't understand what is happening! Why are you doing this, son, why?" Because, I said, I was caught in an important historical moment, and I understood what it meant, and I had to do what that historical moment required. I called again a couple of weeks later to say that I expected to graduate at the end of May but they shouldn't come to Ithaca because I was not going to participate in the graduation ceremony.

After the Takeover

I was not surprised when John Garner dropped out of Cornell before Willard Straight Hall. I was also not surprised when Ed Whitfield, who had led the takeover and the negotiations with the administration, dropped out after Willard Straight Hall, along with other Garner sidekicks. They were going to work on founding Malcolm X University in Greensboro, North Carolina. It seemed to me that they had been alienated from the Cornell experience and what the university had to offer from the first day they arrived on campus. I thought they were heading into a dead end by leaving Cornell without completing their undergraduate degrees, and it was fortunate that more Cornell black students did not follow Garner's and Whitfield's examples. Their whole line of thinking was flawed, I thought. Rather than distancing themselves, black Americans desperately needed the commitment and support of elite higher education institutions to provide educational opportunities for the black community, and to provide national leadership in changing the prevailing racial climate in America.

One thing that especially turned me off about Garner and Whitfield was that while they criticized and complained constantly about various campus issues, they rarely engaged constructively with the university administration. They rarely participated in any of the various committees, commissions, or study groups that the administration organized to address the issues black students raised. And they would often accuse the black students who *did* participate of being "co-opted." I began to suspect that these aspiring black revolutionaries feared constructive solutions arrived at through engagement. They were more interested in exposing "inherent contradictions of the power structure" and "raising the political consciousness" of the black community than they were in fixing things and really arriving at practical solutions. Their approach meant that they never took responsibility for actually getting anything done. In contrast, even during my most "angry militant" phase, my nature was to be a problem solver, and I was a leading participant in most of the university study groups, commissions, and committees that addressed black student issues.

In the spring of 1969 I was the lead AAS negotiator on the final agreement with Vice Provost Keith Kennedy to establish the black studies program as an "independent center" outside of any academic department, and with an initial budget of $250,000 (equivalent to several million dollars today). I was also heavily involved in the recruitment process that identified Professor James Turner and recruited him to Cornell as the founding director of the Africana Studies & Research Center. I knew that nothing gets done in large bureaucratic institutions like Cornell unless there is a determined "champion" to drive the process, and I suspected that the departure of Garner, Whitfield, and their "revolutionary" clique might tempt some administrators and faculty to try to "reshape" the Africana Center agreement through bureaucratic maneuvers and delays. Not on my watch, I thought. So I stayed at Cornell for three more years to champion the administrative processes of getting the Africana Center up and running successfully. Education, I knew from my father's life, was the way out and the way up—education combined with hard work. I stayed at Cornell because I believed deeply in the educational importance of a strong black studies program, and I thought it would be shameful if nothing of lasting significance and value emerged as our legacy from the black students' struggle which culminated in the Willard Straight Hall takeover.

I received my draft notice from the Selective Service in the spring of 1969. I was to report to the U.S. Armed Forces station in Syracuse, New York, for my pre-induction physical examination. My medical history included a heart murmur from birth, but it had never impaired me or limited me physically in any way, and I doubted it would be sufficient to justify a medical deferment. The odds were high that I would be drafted immediately after graduation in May. This was typical for college seniors approaching graduation and the end of their student deferment. The Vietnam War was extremely unpopular, and antiwar protests on college campuses and in major cities were in the news daily. Outside the White House, demonstrators chanted, "Hey, hey, LBJ, how many kids did you kill today?" Many of my college-age peers were agonizing over what to do about the draft, and some chose to flee the country to Canada or elsewhere. Some applied for conscientious objector status, and risked potential criminal charges if they were denied CO status and refused to be inducted. Some became active draft resisters who refused to comply with the draft and faced criminal prosecution. And some went, as ordered, and shipped out to Southeast Asia, where they found themselves immediately in grave danger, slogging through swamps in the jungle, raising their M-16s above their heads to keep them dry, tiptoeing through minefields, killing, being shot, blown to bits by mines, ambushed, or taken prisoner.

When I reported for my pre-induction physical, I was directed to a large waiting room with many other pre-inductees. After sitting and waiting for half an hour, I lay down across several chairs and closed my eyes. The soldier at the desk in front of the room walked over and told me to sit up. I opened my eyes, looked at him, ignored him, and closed my eyes again. Many of the other pre-inductees started laughing. The soldier left the room and returned shortly with an officer. "Tom Jones? I'm going to be conducting your interview. Come with me," he said. I got up and followed him back to a small office. When we were seated across from each other, with his desk between us, the officer (probably a psychologist) asked me how I felt about the possibility of being drafted. I said, "I think the war is wrong, and is primarily residual imperialism against Vietnamese nationalists who are fighting for freedom from French and American colonialism. I have no fight with them, but if I have to go, I'll go. I'm not going to give you an easy way to get rid of me by jailing me for draft resistance. And I'm not going to leave the country and give you that easy way to get rid of me. I figure that my fight is to organize young black men to fight for civil rights and freedom from American oppression, and I can just as well do that in the army, where you have plenty of young black men who need leadership. So I'll continue to do what I'm already doing, but I'll just do it in the army."

The outcome was that I received a 1Y classification, which meant I would be drafted only in the event of a national emergency. In the twisted logic of the era, the country was fighting a major war in Vietnam but had not declared a "state of national emergency." Consequently, I was never drafted and never served in the military. I was fortunate because my fate in the military might have been similar to my black Cornell classmate Larry Dickson's, who was drafted in 1969 and died shortly afterwards in what the army claimed was a training accident at Fort Dix in New Jersey.

I wasn't headed for the army or the war, but I didn't have a plan for what to do or where to go. I was emotionally and psychologically drained and exhausted from the events of the previous months. My personal life was in turmoil. I had no income to support a wife and child—Stephanie had given birth to our son Nigel in January, just a few months before the Willard Straight takeover—and I was teetering on the brink of emotional collapse from stress. I went to the university's Gannett Medical Clinic for help, and was admitted for observation. In hindsight, I think I was experiencing what was then called "combat fatigue," which today is known as post-traumatic stress disorder (PTSD). At that critical juncture in my life, Professor Barclay G. Jones, chairman of the Department of City and Regional Planning, offered me late admission to Cornell's master's in regional planning program in the College of Architecture, Art, and Planning, plus a fellowship and stipend to pay my tuition and living expenses.

For some reason, I had liked Professor Jones from the start. I met him in my sophomore year. He taught city planning courses and historic preservation and was a world authority on earthquakes and the prevention of earthquake damage to buildings and historic sites. During World War II, he had been taken prisoner by the Germans. He'd been a professor at Cornell for only eight years, but he was already a beloved mentor to many, including me. He seemed always to be in his office—especially late at night—listening carefully and calmly to whatever you had to say.

After the takeover, I got into the habit of frequently stopping by his office late at night to talk. He was interested in me, and not judgmental. He wanted to know my thinking. Why had I done what I'd done? What did I think about the various student and faculty positions on the controversy?

Professor Jones's decision to admit me to the graduate program was not popular in some campus circles. But he nonetheless extended his hand and picked me up. He gave me critical time to clear my head and plan a way forward with my life. It was something he did not have to do, and I appreciated him for it very much. We became friends, and shared many thoughtful and wide-ranging conversations stretching deep into the night in his office at Sibley Hall. Professor Jones, in his bow tie and tweed jacket, personified the teachers who shape students' lives because they take the time to care.

With time to decompress and reflect, I pondered the reality that many of the "black revolutionary" students, especially those who had left Cornell, harbored levels of animosity toward me which at times seemed like borderline hatred. They called me "Uncle Tom Jones" to disparage my family background and my friendships with whites. It's just as likely, I thought, that I'll be assaulted or shot by one of these self-styled "black revolutionaries" as it is that I might be attacked by white hillbillies or a county sheriff on some back road.

Conversely, there were whites at Cornell who extended friendship to me and helped me at critical junctures. I also believed, more broadly, that the history of America abounds with many white Americans of conscience and goodwill who fought alongside blacks to overcome America's racial history and to create a better country. Recent examples that were fresh in my mind included SDS and the white students who occupied Barton Hall to support AAS against the conservative wing of the faculty; the large numbers of white participants at the March on Washington in 1963 and the Selma, Alabama, voting rights march in 1965. There was the courageous example of Cornell's own Michael Schwerner, class of 1961, who was murdered with Andrew Goodman (the son of Cornell graduates) and James Chaney by the Ku Klux Klan for registering black voters in Mississippi in 1964.

These reflections, and my feeling of relief during my long talks with Professor Jones, my relief in getting back to studying, led me to conclude that I wanted to return to my roots. And my roots were faith and optimism. My parents' lives were stories of hope and optimism. Our Christian religious faith is also a message of hope and optimism at its core. My formative childhood years in New York City had afforded me very positive interracial experiences, and a very optimistic sense of what was possible in America. I wanted to return to this sense of optimism and lead a positive life trying to build for the future. I did not want to be mired in anger and complaint, victimhood and self-imposed segregation.

When I wasn't studying or spending time with my young family, I enjoyed the sense of achievement that came from being instrumental in the creation of the Africana Studies Center, and from completing the job of getting it up and running. I recognized that an ingrained sense of optimism, a positive outlook, is who I am in my core. And so, yes, I returned to my roots determined to align my life with people who share my fundamental moral values and principles, regardless of race or socioeconomic status. To paraphrase the famous words of Dr. Martin Luther King Jr. at the 1963 March on Washington, I decided to select my friends and associates on the basis of the content of their character rather than the color of their skin.

I also concluded that I was deeply proud that we Cornell black students had put our lives on the line at Willard Straight Hall. I had no regrets for the role that I played. I nurtured the idea that this glimpse of the "black intelligentsia" at an elite university arming in self-defense might shock American thought leaders and institutions into more energetic efforts to improve opportunities for black America. And I looked forward to a day when our action might be interpreted as an important historical statement that blacks in America were no longer willing to be passive, frightened victims of injustice. I thought it was possible that what we'd done might contribute to galvanizing a national sense of urgency that America was at a critical crossroads in race relations—the metaphorical fork in the road being either the "right fork" to political suppression and oppression or the "left fork" to political, social, and economic reform and inclusion.

After leaving Cornell upon graduating with a master's degree in 1972, I never again associated with people or organizations that might be inclined to express the view that I was "not really black," whatever that means. I was simply no longer willing to have any tolerance for those who thought they were endowed with the insight, wisdom, and moral authority to make such a judgment.

By the time I left Cornell, the Africana Studies & Research Center was established and operating successfully. Mission accomplished. But my marriage to Stephanie Bell did not survive the stress and turmoil of those years, and we divorced in 1972. Stephanie completed her Cornell degree and subsequently remarried. Our son Nigel lived with Stephanie during his younger years before coming to live with me in his teenage years.

I was impressed with America's passage of important civil rights legislation such as the Civil Rights Act of 1964 and the Voting Rights Act of 1965, President Lyndon Johnson's commitment of federal government resources to the "War on Poverty," and the growing efforts to promote affirmative action to accelerate black economic progress and social integration. It appeared to me that America was taking the "left fork" in the road toward political and social reform and economic opportunity and inclusion, and I wanted to participate in this "new America." A new battleground was opening for my generation to seize opportunities that had never been available to any prior generation of Afro-Americans. I was determined to master the anger I had internalized at Cornell, and to convert it to positive energy to pursue those new opportunities.

1970s: Getting Started

From the beginning, the South End's urban renewal plan
contained an unresolved tension. On the one hand, it pledged to
"protect and expand the city's tax base, arrest economic decline,
and, by stabilizing property values, protect private investment."
On the other hand, it promised to ensure "the availability
of standard housing at rentals that all displaced low-income
residents wishing to remain in the South End could afford" . . .
By June 1973, many South Enders had plainly concluded that
those two ends could not be pursued simultaneously.

—J. ANTHONY LUKAS, *Common Ground, 1985*

Stephanie took Nigel with her when she moved back to her mother's
apartment in New York. Now I was alone again and, as always, ambitious. My brief attempt to start family life with as much effort and
good faith as possible had sputtered out in under a year, during which time
we realized we just weren't that compatible. Much later Nigel would say of
us, "Mom and Dad are oil and water," and he was right.

One day in graduate school, I saw a job notice pinned to the bulletin
board in the hallway outside the department office. The NY-PENN Health
Planning Agency (NY-Penn) in Binghamton, New York, a small city about an
hour away from Ithaca, was looking for a planning analyst. I was hired by the
president, Richard Landis, and I worked for him for two years while finishing
up my degree coursework. This was in the early days of Health Maintenance
Organizations, and during my tenure with the agency, I got a deep education
in the philosophy, economics, challenges, and benefits of HMOs. I helped
NY-Penn develop Binghamton regional health demographic data, service
provider network data, and medical cost data. I also assisted in outreach and
networking with local medical providers.

I worked hard and did a good job, and Richard took an interest in me
both professionally and personally. This was the beginning of a pattern that

recurred throughout my career. I am not sure if it is possible to rise far, in fact, without the presence of interested and well-placed mentors along the way.

When I completed my master of regional planning degree in 1972, I wanted to leave upstate New York and move to a more cosmopolitan area. I had been in Ithaca, and then Binghamton, for a total of seven years and was ready to live in a city.

Abt Associates, a leading social science research and consulting firm in Cambridge, Massachusetts, came to my attention through a Cornell friend who worked there. Abt had opened just a few years earlier, in 1965, with thirty employees, and the idea of Boston appealed to me as an attractive place to live—larger and more sophisticated than Ithaca but not as expensive and overwhelming as New York City. Abt had recently won a federal government contract for research related to health maintenance organizations, and my HMO experience in Binghamton made me a good fit for its contract research staff. I succeeded in securing a job there and drove off with all my things packed in boxes in the trunk and backseat of my car. My Boston apartment was a comfortable one-bedroom in the South End; not yet the upscale area it has become, it was the best neighborhood I could afford at the time. On my first night in my new place, I called home and spoke to my parents. Then I called the two Cornellians I knew in Boston and made plans to have drinks with them later in the week.

Abt was in a squat glass building on Wheeler Street in Cambridge and was full of fairly radical recent college graduates—policy wonks and idealistic young scholars with a social work bent. I was not the only associate there who had been involved in a nationally covered student revolt on a college campus. Men and women came to work in sandals, with their shirts open one too many buttons down. Most of the black people at Abt—and it was a markedly diverse group for Boston—wore their hair in big afros. In comparison, I practically looked like a Wall Street banker, according to my colleagues' teasing. Well, the way I dressed and carried myself was just a reflection of how serious I was and how hard I worked. Within one year, I was promoted to contract manager.

One day in 1973, my old boss Richard Landis from NY-Penn called to ask if I would be interested in working for him again, this time at Arthur Young & Company (AY), where he was the new co-head of a health industry consulting practice based in Washington, D.C. I told him I liked living in Boston and wasn't interested in relocating, but would consider an opportunity if something was available in Arthur Young's Boston office. Landis arranged for me to be interviewed by Arthur Young executives in Boston and the national office executives in the New York headquarters.

That first glimpse of the Arthur Young & Company offices made a strong impression on me. The elevator opened onto a plush waiting room with deep carpets and big windows that looked out onto Boston Harbor and the financial district. Everything gleamed. People practically whispered. The art on the walls was beautiful and lit from above as in a museum. I announced myself and was asked to take a seat. As always, I was extremely well prepared and confident, but as I looked at the water below and the tugboats silently inching across the expanse of blue, I felt a pang of even stronger yearning than usual. This was the kind of place where I wanted to be. This was the pinnacle, one of the leading accounting and consulting firms in the country, and even though I didn't yet know the ins and outs of that excellence and what made it possible—that it was built on pride and a culture of high standards and long hours—I could feel it, just sitting there.

I received an offer to join Arthur Young as a manager in the health industry consulting practice, based in Boston, and I started work in September of 1973. The Boston office had approximately 250 professionals, which was mid-sized for AY offices. My initial reception was decidedly cool—not overtly hostile but distinctly wary. I realized that I didn't fit the mold of the other professionals in the office, most of whom were accounting or business majors with significant corporate business experience. Also, stories about guns at Cornell and my "black militant" past circulated around the office. Someone would tentatively ask me to explain my role in the takeover, or ask me if it was true that I was a Malcolm X devotee or what did I think of the current busing crisis in Boston, in which white families were stubbornly fighting the court-ordered integration, via busing, of Boston public schools. (I supported the push to follow the law and end school segregation based on race, but I wasn't about to enter into such a discussion at work for the titillation of white colleagues.) It was clear that many of the professionals in the Boston office thought that I was some sort of alien aberration who would probably not survive for long. Fortunately for me, my childhood experiences of frequently being the new kid on the block and youngest in the class had inoculated me, I think, to social isolation. I didn't crave peer approval and support. In fact, the coldness and the questioning looks pushed me deeper into my favorite mode of operation: keep your head down, work harder than anyone else, stay smart and alert and as correct as possible, and, finally, don't let anyone else's vision of you, or their dismissal of you, chip away by even a millimeter at your sense of self-esteem.

AY had three business practice areas—audit, tax, and management services (consulting). Audit was the core business, and AY was the independent public auditor for many Fortune 500 and other major companies. AY was a partnership consisting of several hundred U.S. partners, and the partners were extremely proud of the firm's professional reputation and stature. All partners were certified public accountants, and they were intensely protective of their reputation for being one of the highest-quality public accounting firms in the world. Partners were generally well compensated (typically several hundred thousand dollars annually in 1973 dollars, approximately $1.5 to $2 million today), and were able to support comfortable lifestyles. I was impressed with the long workdays and working Saturdays, which was the norm during the busy season—the year-end audit and the months leading up to Tax Day on April 15—and the personal satisfaction that most of the partners seemed to derive from their work. I felt that I had found my people, in a sense.

But as the first few months passed, I began to perceive with a growing certainty how different AY was from any environment I had experienced previously and how difficult it would be for me to be promoted along to the next level. At Abt Associates, I had stood out as an anomaly—more serious and focused than most of my peers. But here at AY, everyone was working their tails off, and nearly everyone around me seemed highly intelligent, too, and most had gone to top-tier colleges. All that was left was for me to focus my energies on the things I could control and forget about everything else. I decided that what I could control was my attitude, my demeanor, my effort, and the quality of my work. So I always maintained a positive attitude in the office, and I avoided any negative exchanges even if I perceived slights or provocations as intentional.

I also showed a talent for developing new business. In early 1974 I wrote a proposal that won a $250,000 consulting contract from the federal government—the Boston regional office of the Department of Health and Human Services (HHS)—for work on HMO projects in New England. A quarter-million dollars was significant money in 1974 (my salary was only $25,000), and my ability to be a rainmaker and bring in substantial revenue finally managed to set me apart from the crowd.

I began to attract the attention of senior executives at AY after winning the HHS contract. I wasn't aware of it at first, but there were occasions when I was giving presentations and a senior partner would just happen to be in town to sit in on the meeting. My most frequent senior-level interactions were with Len Miller, the eastern region managing partner for management services from the New York headquarters. He was a gregarious man from California, with a great sense of humor paired with an underlying seriousness, which I liked. Len ultimately adopted me and became my friend and key senior management mentor. I also attracted attention from Arthur Koumantzelis, Boston office managing partner, who also became my friend and mentor.

My mentors usually began by engaging me in one-on-one conversation over coffee or lunch, and always with a focus on work—my projects, clients, revenues, and so forth. Over time, these conversations would broaden to include my family background and career aspirations, and in turn I learned about their personal and career backgrounds, about the paths they'd traveled to success. The third stage—and I outline this for the benefit of young people reading this book, wanting to know how fruitful mentorships grow, and how they can be fostered—was social engagement, usually in the form of an invitation to dinner with their spouse or significant other. Now, if the social invitations were repeated and made known to the office by the mentor (never by me, of course!), then it was the equivalent of a public declaration by the mentor that I was one of his people. Sometimes the social engagements with my mentors and their wives went beyond dinner—for example, theater weekends in New York and ski weekends in Maine.

These two mentors, Miller and Koumantzelis, were critical in providing me with promotions, compensation increases, and psychological support during my years at AY, from 1973 to 1981. They also protected me from people who didn't like me and would have done me harm. The best mentor relationships are usually reciprocal, and I made them look good by bringing in new business every year that was a multiple of my compensation. I later came to understand that the most successful senior executives in large business organizations are often like coaches for sports teams. They are always scouting outstanding talent to bring onto their team, because in business as in sports, the team with the best talent usually wins. I attracted their attention because I had a knack for generating revenue, which is highly valued in professional services businesses, and clients were pleased with my work. I also eventually developed friendships with Richard Myers and Ron Mastrogiovanni, my Boston office colleagues who were computer systems consultants in management services. Having two friends in the office was a critical ingredient for workplace satisfaction, and I grew increasingly comfortable and enjoyed working for AY.

I was twenty-five years old. I dated many women and had a large circle of friends I socialized with, many of whom lived within blocks of my apartment in the South End. "Tom, why don't you bring over your latest lady and join us for dinner Saturday," Flash or Charles or Aggrey might say. "Flash" (Fletcher) Wiley was a new friend from my year at Abt Associates, where he and his wife, Bennie, also worked. Flash was a recent joint-degree graduate of Harvard Law School and the Kennedy School of Government, and Bennie was a graduate of Harvard Business School, and they introduced me to the black social world that revolved around Harvard. Charles McLean was my good friend from Cornell, who had also moved to Boston. Aggrey Mbere was also a Cornell friend, a refugee from South Africa active in the African National Congress's fight against apartheid, who had been a graduate student in the history department at Cornell and was now teaching at Roxbury Community College in Boston.

Some of the women I dated were black, some were white, but most of my friends—some of whom were single like me, others in relationships or married—were part of a new breed of Bostonian: black, well educated, ambitious, and not willing to settle for old limitations placed on people on the basis of race and background and neighborhood. Boston was a city that seemed to want to cramp and squeeze blacks away in a corner, separate from most of the city. The South End was very diverse, but mainly the city was starkly segregated by race. There were neighborhoods where it wasn't safe to go if you were black. My friend Charles worked for a time at the Suffolk County House of Corrections, and he was on very good terms with his boss, an Irish Catholic guy. The boss said to him one day, "This is such a horrendous thing that I can't invite you over for dinner at my house. It wouldn't be safe for you, and it wouldn't be safe for me either."

Charles had a girlfriend who was a teacher at a school in Charlestown, one of those neighborhoods where it wasn't safe for black people to go. He would drive her there and, he told me, "as soon as I cross the bridge into Charlestown, I've got this whole group of Charlestown Marshals on my tail!" The Charlestown Marshals were a vigilante group of white supremacists who were monitoring the racial situation to ensure the so-called integrity of their community. Every weekday, Charles's day started with this scene of major tension, a whole cavalcade of white people following him. On his way back out of Charlestown, they kept close to his bumper, but they'd turn around as soon as his car passed over into Middlesex County.

The Elma Lewis School of Fine Arts, founded in 1950 by a woman who would go on to win a MacArthur fellowship and the Presidential Medal for the Arts, was a jewel in black Boston society. The school offered instruction in painting, acting, music, and sculpture. Elma Lewis also founded a black theater production company that put on plays in Franklin Park in the summers, and she founded the National Center of Afro-American Artists in 1968.

Her eponymous school's annual fund-raiser was an important event where you could rub elbows with the city's most prominent black people, both artists and the philanthropists who supported their work, and many of my friends were planning to attend the gala, so I thought I'd go too. But who would I take as a date? This wasn't a function to which I could or would want to take a white woman, and I didn't have in mind any serious black girlfriend I could go with that month. But I knew who to ask: Flash Wiley. Flash and his wife were my good friends, though seven years my senior. Flash was now a lawyer in a prominent Boston firm and a transplant from Indiana, where I knew he had traveled in the best circles of black high society. Flash was the kind of person who knows everyone.

"Well, sure, how about Addie Knox?" he said, a smile in his voice. I had called him at work and at that moment he just happened to have a certain Addie Knox, a twenty-four-year-old woman from his hometown, sitting in his office with her mother. They had just arrived in Boston to install Addie in her brother's apartment. The brother, George, was attending Harvard Business School, but was lending the apartment to his sister for the summer while he was away.

"I think I'd have to meet her first," I told Flash, much to his amusement. I drove a hard bargain for a man begging for a date. And so he invited me over to dinner. When we got off the phone, Flash told Addie and her mother about me—that I was a straight arrow who would be a suitable escort for Addie.

That night, I arrived at Flash and Bennie's house with a bottle of wine, and there, sitting on the sofa smiling, was Adelaide Emma Knox. I was immediately struck by her deep, reflective eyes, which I thought seemed to have a clarity and purity that must be reflecting the soul of a very good person. This is what songstress Erykah Badu meant in her lyric "I see God in your eyes." Having just finished graduate school at Southern Illinois University, she had moved to Boston to look for employment. She was very quick to laugh, strikingly beautiful, and very easy to talk to. And I liked her impeccable personal grooming; her manicured and polished fingernails matched her toenails.

Addie and I went to the Elma Lewis event. I picked her up at her brother's apartment and she came to the door wearing a green "pilgrim dress," nearly floor-length, with a broad Quaker Oats white collar around her neck. Her brown shoes were clunky and reminded me of something a nun might wear, or a schoolteacher. Interesting choice, I thought, for a high-profile gala! I myself was dressed to the nines, very fashionably, in a white suit with red patent leather shoes.

We went to dinner at the best black restaurant in Boston at the time, Bob the Chef in Roxbury, where we talked so much that our food got cold on our plates before we remembered to keep eating. Then, artistic performances and dancing at the gala. Afterwards, we went to a party hosted by some of my friends. In the early hours of the morning, I drove her back to her brother's apartment.

Every day for the next twelve days, Addie and I went out together. Charles, who had helped me move out of the apartment I lived in on West Canton Street and move into another apartment in the next building, carrying boxes and individual items up flights of stairs—items like a giant two-hundred-pound abstract sculpture made by my Cornell friend Reginald Bradford, who had needed to sell some art to support his family and found a willing art collector in me—was shocked to learn the next week, from a mutual friend filling him in on the latest gossip, that I was seriously dating a new woman. "How did that happen?" Charles asked, incredulous. "I just saw him!" But two weeks was enough. Neither of us had ever felt so comfortable with someone or had so much fun talking. Addie had practically moved out of her brother George's apartment and into my new one on the top floor of a South End brownstone. We had enormous fun playing games such as cribbage, gin rummy, and chess with each other. And we enjoyed playing card games such as pinochle and bid whist with our friends.

I enjoyed the unusual perspective Addie brought to life. On the one hand, it was a global, sophisticated view, but one that included the insight gained by living in a predominantly black community in Alabama in the 1960s, during the racist reign of Governor George Wallace. You didn't have to go far from the town where Addie had lived to meet black sharecroppers, victims of terrible racist abuse, but she had also grown up surrounded by black scientists, black scholars and lawyers and poets and socialites.

Figure 4 / *Tom and Addie's wedding, June 1975*

Addie's father was a Tuskegee Airman, one of a group of black aviators sponsored by Eleanor Roosevelt. They broke the U.S. Air Force color barrier and became fighter pilots in World War II. Later in his career, her father held the rank of lieutenant colonel and headed the air force ROTC program at Tuskegee Institute in Alabama, until he died there in an accident in 1964. As an air force brat, Addie had lived in interesting places, including Japan and Alaska, but her most formative years were spent in the strong and supportive black professional community built around Tuskegee Institute, where her mother continued to live and work after Addie's father's death. That environment is what shaped her as a confident, educated, and socially graceful black woman. I thought that I was very fortunate to meet her, and fortunate that she saw good things in me. (I now know, because she has since confessed it to me, that what she saw in me was maturity. I think she saw a young guy who was really a man, someone serious about trying to do something with his life. And she liked that I was serious. When Flash showed her the photograph of me armed with a rifle and knife, standing on the steps of Willard Straight Hall, she liked that too.)

Addie and I were married at St. Andrew's Episcopal Church in Tuskegee on June 14, 1975, one year and one day after we first met. My groomsmen included Flash Wiley as best man; my two brothers, Edward and James; and two Cornell friends, Aggrey Mbere, who had been in the doctoral program in history at Cornell, and Tim Weldon, my classmate in the city and regional planning master's program.

My wedding toast, which I was told later held the room spellbound in mingled admiration and surprise (at its length and thoroughness), went as follows:

In thinking about this wedding toast, I thought about this morning. Despite the bachelor party last night, I rose early this morning and was sitting outside at 7:00 am . . . I was thinking that I only had three wishes for today.

My first wish has been realized at 5:00 pm today. I've been made whole by the honor of marrying my bride and friend Addie. The minister gave me the opportunity to salute Addie physically, and now I'd like to salute her verbally. So I raise a toast to Addie, because in my eyes she is the essence of womanhood.

But in thinking about that, I understand that Addie didn't just drop from the sky or spring from the earth. Addie is not an accident, she is a product of a family and a community. So I want to honor those who helped shape Addie. Addie's mother, Mrs. Yvonne Knox, and her oldest brother, George Knox Jr., and as representatives of this community, Paul Wall and Pauline Punch. I don't want to slight anyone, but I know Paul and Pauline because I'm staying at Paul's house and Pauline fed us last night! They represent how much this community loves Addie, and how much this community has given to make this day possible for Addie. So I toast Addie and her family and her community. Addie is a product of this family and this strong black community, and I'm grateful to them. Addie is a product of many people working to guide her and direct her.

Last but not least, I also want to pay tribute to my mother and father. If something makes it possible for me to be a man, and to say that I love Addie, and I want to marry Addie, and I'll take care of Addie, it originates with my mother and father. My parents come from the South. My dad was born in Charlotte, North Carolina, and my mom was born in Martinsville, Virginia. They haven't lived in the South for thirty or forty years. I wanted today to be a triumphant return to the South for them. In my eyes, the woman that I love had to come from the South. She had to come from this soil, and this community, and this people and so in a way I feel that wedding Addie makes me more one with them.

Finally, I think Addie and I have a union of love, and we have a community of friends who also love one another. What Addie and I need is the spiritual strength to love one another and to serve one another as long as we live. And we need our friends and our community to have the strength to love one another and to serve one another. So I ask you to bear with me as I ask my father for a prayer that we have the strength to love one another and serve one another all the days of our lives. Dad, would you make a prayer?

"You were sure going to let every person in that room know that Addie had selected the correct groom," Flash teased me later.

We honeymooned in the Bahamas, with the Wileys, who had introduced us, after all, and who were our closest friends. One day on the beach, Addie and Bennie lay on towels sunning themselves, two brown-skinned beauties. The water was impossibly blue, the sky wide. There was a gentle breeze and it seemed that everything was right in the world. Two locals approached Flash and me and said, "Whatch ya doin' wasting your time with these black women? There's beautiful white women just down the beach!" and Flash and I looked at each other and laughed. We knew we were already with the two most beautiful women within thousands of miles.

The honeymoon gave me a chance to relax and take careful stock. I told Addie that even though I was doing very well at Arthur Young, I didn't think I had the training, skills, and credentials to sustain success over the long term. I told her that I needed to attend business school to get an MBA degree, and I needed to acquire strong accounting and finance skills. "What I'd like us to do," I told her, "is try to live on one salary even though both of us are working. That way, we can save the second salary to build investment capital."

Addie agreed readily to both proposals, my enrolling in business school and our saving one salary with the idea of using it to buy real estate later, or invest it in a company, whichever looked best to us when the time came. While her acquiescence might seem inevitable in hindsight, my proposals actually entailed considerable sacrifice. I was proposing to get my MBA by using Arthur Young's tuition reimbursement program for part-time college enrollment, so that my tuition would be paid and I could continue to work and generate income. This meant that I would be working full-time, and going to school most nights and weekends. Living on one salary meant we couldn't afford the vacations, nights out on the town, or clothes that our peers enjoyed.

I enrolled in the evening MBA program at Boston University Graduate School of Management starting in September 1975, three months after our wedding. I selected Boston University because the more prestigious business schools at Harvard and Massachusetts Institute of Technology did not offer part-time evening programs. "What do you expect to do with a business degree from Boston University?" my older brother Eddie (a 1973 Harvard Business School graduate) asked me, laughing.

"As far as I can tell," I replied, annoyed at the sneering tone in his voice, "the primary difference between BU and Harvard seems to be that your professors are more famous than mine. But I'm not going to be competing against your professors; I'm going to be competing against people like *you*."

My radio alarm clock went off at 5:45 am, as it did every morning, and I reached over and shut it off with the palm of my hand. Addie stirred next to me but did not wake. Time to get up and start what I knew would be a very full day. There was getting to the office by 7:00 am, meetings, the work of completing consulting engagements or auditing a business's books. I would be one of the first people in the Arthur Young offices. If I happened to walk by the big windows looking out onto the city, I would see the sky go from dark gray to blue. Then, at around eight, others would start to arrive, getting coffee from the break room, greeting one another, pausing outside my office to say a quick good morning. At 5:00 pm I would be one of the first to leave, which was always a bit nerve-wracking in an office whose culture prized long hours so highly. But I'd put in my hours, and I had a train to take and class to get to. Each class met twice a week, for three hours at a time, from 5:30 to 8:30. After class, another train ride home to our apartment and to Addie. We'd trade accounts of our day before I would retreat to my desk in the dining room to hit the books for another hour or two of study before bed,

Figure 5 / *Nigel and Addie on a Bike Vermont vacation, August 1976*

while the new material was fresh in my mind. If there was an extra exercise or study test in the textbook chapter, you could be sure that I would take it. My goal: to know the material as well as anybody possibly could. Then, on some weekends, Nigel, who was in the first grade during my first year in business school, would visit, and we would take him to a children's museum or the library or a theater performance, and go for long walks in the Back Bay and Boston Common and along the Charles River.

Boston University Graduate School of Management was the first time I had ever approached school with really serious purpose and focus. I took two courses each fall and spring semester, and one course in each of the two summer sessions. To concentrate on accounting and finance as much as possible, I frontloaded my curriculum with those courses, while deferring distribution requirements in areas like marketing and organizational behavior. I attended classes and studied with purpose and passion. For the first time, I discovered the difference between working hard and working to full capacity. I did this day after day, for three years, between 1975 and 1978.

I learned that, like most people, I had rarely exceeded a 95 percent level of effort before, probably because most of us are socialized to think that 95 percent is an A, and an A is the best grade, isn't it? But I didn't have to stop at average or above average. I could work nearly every waking minute, and it felt good. I had the energy for it. I never stopped at 95 percent anymore, and the resulting gap between me and my peers who were top performers drove much of my subsequent career success.

The five points separating 95 and 100 don't seem like much—and they aren't, on any given day, or any given test or work assignment. But it's a lot when those five points are compounded every day, week after week and month after month. Over the span of five years, it becomes an enormous gap in effort and achievement. When you do it—push yourself to the 100 percent mark— over the course of a forty-year career, as I learned to do, you can lift yourself to an elite level. But what's most fulfilling about giving 100 percent commitment is the resulting feeling of self-actualization, meaning that you've achieved your highest potential, which is all that any person can do—regardless of whether you eventually "win" or "lose" the worldly "prize" you seek. This is a spiritual gift you can give to yourself, and you guarantee yourself a spiritual "win" when you achieve your highest potential—whatever that may be.

I never received less than an A-minus grade in any finance or accounting course (and only one A-minus at that). At the end of the second summer session in August 1978, I completed my MBA degree and enrolled immediately in a certified public accounting licensing examination preparation course. I sat for the three-day examination in October 1978, passing it on my first attempt, and became a licensed CPA in the Commonwealth of Massachusetts.

"Let's play tennis," Addie said to me one day as we watched the U.S. Open on our little television set in the kitchen. A dashing Spanish player, Manuel Orantes, upset Jimmy Connors in a thrilling final, and earlier in the week, Chris Evert had won her fourth Grand Slam title by defeating an Australian woman, Evonne Goolagong Cawley.

We signed up for private lessons at a nearby tennis club, and before long, we were not terrible. In fact, since we played every Saturday, and sometimes more than once a week, we got better and better. (Our weekly tennis tradition continues to this day, over forty years later.) We also played card games and board games together and with friends, and we hung out with young black professional couples in Boston and Cambridge. We also socialized regularly with my Arthur Young friends Ron Mastrogiovanni and Dick Myers and their spouses. Dick was a white man from Texas, about my age, with a strong southern drawl and very good manners. It was Dick who, in one of my first weeks at AY, had stopped by my office and leaned in to invite me to join him and some others for lunch at a restaurant. I had just been about to bite into the sandwich Addie had made for me, but put it back down and wrapped it back up in its foil. "Sure, let's go," I said, and that was the beginning of a friendship that would last for decades.

Addie and I also spent time with my AY mentors Len Miller and Arthur Koumantzelis and their wives. Addie's graciousness and positive relationships made a significant contribution to my career success. I loved to look over at her and see her laughing easily, saying something kind and interesting to my friends, listening intently. While she's not a person who tries to gather people around her, people are attracted to her nonetheless, simply because she is gentle and confident and an engaging conversationalist. But she has always been just as happy to be solitary as to be in a crowd of friends, and that's a quality that we share.

Addie and I were, in short, simpatico on all the topics that mattered— friends, work, recreation. And we were successful with our savings and investment plan too. After saving Addie's salary for two years, we had amassed a nest egg of $25,000. We hadn't gone out to eat much; we hadn't bought much meat at the grocery store. We had instead perfected a small set of bean dishes from a book that compiled bean recipes from various cuisines—Moroccan, Mexican, Israeli. We had become bean connoisseurs. One time when Addie's brother George was over at our apartment, she offered him something to drink. "I have tap water or chilled tap water from the fridge," she said, informing him of his beverage options. It would become a story he liked to retell later, evidence of our extreme frugality in those early days of marriage.

In the fall of 1975, I saw an ad in the *Boston Globe* inviting bids to redevelop derelict residential properties seized by the city. "Addie, I think I've found our investment," I told her. We submitted an application to the Boston Redevelopment Authority (BRA) to acquire two adjoining abandoned brownstones at 325 and 327 Columbus Avenue near Dartmouth Street, a short walk from where we lived in the South End. The buildings were burned out and derelict. One had almost no unbroken windows left; the other's front door had been replaced with plywood, which was covered with halfhearted graffiti. But we thought the location was near enough to Copley Square in the Back Bay that it could be viable as an apartment rental property. Living just a few blocks from the burned-out buildings, we were familiar with the

Figure 6 / *Boarded-up brownstones purchased from the Boston Redevelopment Authority, October 1976 (front view)*

Figure 7 / *Boarded-up brownstones purchased from the Boston Redevelopment Authority, October 1976 (back view)*

neighborhood and believed that it was probably in the early stages of an urban renaissance. Rents were inching up, and more and more professionals, black and white, were moving in.

In the weeks that followed, I wondered how many other applications they'd received, and how stiff our competition would be to win the bid. But then the call came. It turned out that our application was the one and only indication of interest the BRA received on those buildings. As we worked through the application process, a friendly BRA official suggested that we consider also applying for Section 312 Housing and Urban Development mortgage funds, which were currently available but, with the related budget authority, close to expiring. The primary attraction of Section 312 financing was its 3 percent interest rate, which compared favorably to then prevailing 6 to 7 percent commercial bank mortgage interest rates. We quickly assembled and filed the Section 312 mortgage application and retained an architect to prepare building renovation plans.

By a stroke of very good luck, our South End apartment landlord just happened to be Mark Goldweitz, a leading real estate developer in the residential brownstone rehabilitation and reconstruction renaissance that was then in its early stages in Boston's Back Bay and South End. He was a graduate of the Harvard Business School, where he'd also served on the faculty during the Vietnam War. More than one case study given to business students at Harvard bore his name, including one titled "Gentrification: The Mark Goldweitz Case."

Mark was my type of man—vigorous, no-nonsense, busy, and ambitious. He was thirty when I met him. He'd grown up nearby in Natick, gone to Harvard, bought his first apartment building when he was twenty-three, and now he owned half a dozen buildings (and would go on to be one of the primary real estate developers, managers, and investors in Boston). I had rented an apartment from him on West Canton Street in the South End when I first moved to Boston in 1972. We had become friends. Mark liked Addie and me, and regarded us as the kind of people who could help make the South End an attractive and stable neighborhood. When we started our development project, Mark helped us by recommending excellent architectural and legal professionals whom he used on his own projects, and by encouraging those professionals to accept us as clients.

By early summer 1976 we had completed architectural plans to combine the two Columbus Avenue buildings into a single ten-unit rental property, our Section 312 mortgage application had been preliminarily approved, and the BRA had granted us "preliminary redeveloper status." It was exciting—and uncharted. We were still in our twenties, were black in a city with almost no black people in high positions in business or philanthropy, and had only moderately well-paid positions. But we'd planned and saved and done our homework. The next step was a public hearing process, since the BRA was proposing to sell public properties. I did not anticipate any problems. Why would there be? Ours was the only proposal the BRA had received on the buildings.

The first BRA hearing was held at the South End community center in a drab room with linoleum floors and folding chairs set up in tight rows, crowded with folks from the neighborhood. I was very surprised when community activists, organized as the South End Political Action Committee (SEPAC), stood and announced to Addie and Flash (our attorney) and me that they would oppose our project unless we designated some of the rental units for low-income occupancy. The idea had occurred to me before this meeting, of course, but I had considered and rejected it. I refused to accept their terms, reasoning that the economics of a ten-unit building could collapse quickly under the weight of rent and occupancy restrictions. Addie and I would be personally liable for the full mortgage obligation, and we would be legally liable for paying operating expenses—such as property taxes, insurance, utilities, and repairs—from our personal funds if the building failed to generate sufficient cash flow to cover those costs. We were already making a significant contribution to the community by taking abandoned, uninhabitable buildings and converting them into taxpaying property, and attracting tenants who would improve neighborhood stability and add to the economic activity for neighborhood businesses.

The activists were true to their word. Just as they'd threatened in the first public hearing, they formally opposed our application in the subsequent BRA community hearings that followed weeks later. Those hearings were crowded too, because the word had got out that rich developers (Addie and me!) were coming to exploit the community. Flash anticipated all of this and made the rounds, quietly, in advance of the hearings, speaking to key community members about us and our plans. "This young couple," he told them, "are just the kind of people that we should be supporting, not fighting." And then, when the neighborhood residents who attended the hearings had a chance to see and listen to Addie and me for themselves, they were impressed that a young black couple was trying to do a building redevelopment project. In the end, we won approval from the community review hearing process.

The SEPAC newsletter contained the following article under "Neighborhood Notes . . . More on 312 Loan":

> Luxury developer Thomas Jones is scheduled to receive $200,000 (1/6 of all funds available to Boston from the federal government) in 312 Loans for two buildings at 325–327 Columbus Avenue, next to Chandler's, according to BRA officials. Jones' application was processed in record time after he was granted final ownership by the BRA over SEPAC objections. SEPAC objected because there was not enough time to verify whether Jones would commit to provide some low rent units in the 10-unit development.
>
> SEPAC's long-standing policy has been that developers who benefit from large public subsidies (such as reduction in building acquisition costs from the BRA) should take steps to address public needs, such as low rent apartments for long-term South End residents.
>
> Robert Kenney of the BRA justified the unusual action on the designation so that Mr. Jones would have an advantage in applying for the 312 Loan. If approved by HUD, the 312 Loan will enable Jones to get an additional $200,000 bank loan for the rehabilitation project. Even with the federal subsidy, Jones' apartments will rent in the $350–400 range for a one bedroom unit.
>
> The Jones incident points out the longstanding dilemma faced by low and moderate income homeowners who have tried to get 312 Loans in the past with little or no success. Hence, luxury developers or affluent homeowners have benefited most from the program because they had the resources to hire the attorneys or architects to assist them in making their way through red tape, credit checks, and processing deadlines put up by HUD and the BRA.
>
> Most recently, for example, HUD released funds to the South End on June 1, leaving only ten weeks for people on the BRA's waiting list to complete their applications. Along with rigid credit requirements, this tended to weed out many applicants in favor of those with better technical or financial resources.

I was alienated by SEPAC's opposition to our efforts. It tasted like other conflicts from my past, and reminded me of my alienation from the Cornell black students who had criticized me as being "not really black." Just like those bitter students at Cornell who seemed to cling to a mentality of victimhood, the SEPAC activists wanted to equate our success to our betrayal of them. We were taking something away from the community, they suggested, and therefore owed them an allocation of low-income units in return. But we weren't taking anything away from "the community," and we didn't have to apologize for being prepared.

My maverick inclinations made me indifferent to—or rather affronted by and resistant to—the psychological intimidation. I wasn't trying to win a community popularity contest, and yet they seemed to hope that their disapproval would sting, would sway me. It did not. I thought SEPAC could have better spent their efforts in organizing a cooperative to bid on development opportunities and provide legal and architectural assistance to low-income residents, rather than attacking people like us.

The purchase price was $6,000. Now that we owned the buildings, we needed to fix them. Our final step with the BRA was to complete a public construction bid process compliant with BRA regulations, since we were acquiring Boston city property and using federal mortgage funds. The low bidder on our project was Powell General Contracting, owned by Eric Powell, a West Indian who had a good business reputation. His bid price was approximately 20 percent below the bid from our preferred builder, Ben Polishook, whom we had invited to bid on the basis of Mark Goldweitz's recommendation.

"He's not going to be able to do it at that price. Not well and not on time, at least," Goldweitz and Polishook both warned us. But my conscience obliged me to give Powell a chance. I met with him to discuss the details of his bid, and I told him that unnamed experts were warning me that he had underbid the project and wouldn't perform. "Listen, Mr. Powell," I said to him carefully, "my wife and I will be carrying these costs out of our own pockets, so finishing it on time is critical. We have a certain amount of money and no more, and so if you mess this up, we could be ruined financially, do you see? We can only afford very modest schedule slippage or cost overruns. It's going to be tight." Finally, I implored him, "Please decline this project unless you are one hundred percent confident you can deliver. And if you're not one hundred percent confident, please withdraw your bid and we'll work with you on our next project when we're stronger financially." He had been silent all this time, and now he looked me square in the eyes and said, "You can trust me. I'm one hundred percent sure I can do this at this price on time."

We were in a tight spot. Our $25,000 nest egg had been completely consumed by purchasing the buildings and paying the architectural and legal fees. We would have to pay the monthly debt service for the construction loan out of our salaries during the construction period.

I was worried, but I could not in good conscience deny the project to a black man who had a good reputation and had built a successful construction business and seemingly won the bid fairly. So we signed a contract with Powell General Contracting. I made this decision with my heart rather than with my head, and I never again made this mistake in my business career.

Powell started the project very strongly in the first two months of what was scheduled to be a six-month project, but then started sending only skeleton crews to maintain a presence on the job. When I complained, he said he was "encountering unanticipated difficult construction conditions and building deterioration" which would require additional funds. I was furious, thinking that the only reason he had been the low bidder was that he had failed to make reasonable estimates for "unanticipated difficult construction conditions and building deterioration." It was clear that he thought he had me trapped because he had started the project and had builders' liens in place on the property. But he didn't know me. Reasoning that I probably had only one chance to get the project completed before my funds were exhausted, I took an unexpected tack. I simply wasn't going to trust him with a second chance.

Quietly, I lobbied BRA officials to cooperate with me to terminate Powell for nonperformance. I approached Polishook General Contracting for an updated "as is" construction bid to complete the building. And I sought Mark Goldweitz's advice regarding the best law firm to quickly and effectively navigate the legal landmines of terminating Powell, clearing his builders' liens, and hiring Polishook to replace him. When everything was lined up, I pulled the trigger. Powell didn't know what hit him. Within one month, his contract was terminated and his builders' liens were lifted, with the help of BRA affidavits that Powell had abandoned the project and had been paid in full for all work performed. Polishook was under contract and working on the building the next week. We were two months behind our original construction schedule, but we were moving forward with reasonably good odds of completing the project on the revised budget and schedule.

The delay threatened to leave Addie and me homeless, though. Our lease on our apartment was up in June, but the renovations on the buildings we'd purchased wouldn't be done until the fall. We started to look for short-term leases nearby, but there didn't seem to be any, and anyway we were close to broke. No amount of bean eating was going to put much cash in our pockets now.

Our friend Aggrey Mbere lived a few blocks from us in a large three-bedroom apartment, secured with the plan to have a wife and maybe

Figure 8 / *Tom on brownstones construction site, March 1977*

Figure 9 / *Addie's cousin, Tom, and Addie (left to right)*
in front of brownstones nearing completion, fall 1977

even a family soon to fill the space. But he was still single, and so he graciously offered us a room for three months. All our friends were following our journey closely, cheering us on. I called Stephanie and Nigel and explained our vagabond status. "But when you visit in the fall, son," I told Nigel, "you'll have a new room in the new building. It's going to be beautiful."

My widowed mother wanted to help us too. She loaned us her last $10,000 certificate of deposit (equivalent to approximately $50,000 today) to use as working capital. Polishook completed construction on time and on budget, and delivered an attractive ten-unit building.

Before anyone—us or any tenants—could move into the building, it had to pass city inspection to earn a certificate of occupancy. Polishook, the architect who'd drawn the plans, Mark Goldweitz, and I met the inspector one crisp September morning. I stood on the sidewalk next to them looking up at what we'd done. In my mind's eye, I could see clearly what had been there before—blight, disrepair, plywood, and dark windows. And in its place, we had put this gleaming, attractively appointed, solid red brick dwelling, where dozens of people would live in comfort.

"Very nice fixtures," the inspector noted, as we looked at the first apartment's bathroom. He was right. We had done good work, with the long term in mind.

Addie and I moved into a two-bedroom apartment on the top floor with a roof deck overlooking Copley Square in early 1978. We soon had the other nine units rented, and the building was cash-flow positive by early 1979. That same year, Arthur Young promoted me to principal in the firm. It was a key distinction I had fervently sought.

To celebrate our success and reward ourselves for our years of beans and rice, Addie and I went on a three-week American Express "European Grand Tour" summer vacation in 1979. Charles agreed to stay in our apartment while we were gone, to keep an eye on things. Neither Addie nor I had ever been to Europe, so together we experienced the highlights of London, Paris, Normandy, Monaco, Rome, Florence, Venice, Munich, Zurich, and Amsterdam. And so it was with a mood of elation and pride that we strolled the Champs-Élysées, floated down the canals of Venice, and sat at a café in Rome, sharing a light breakfast of bread and coffee as men on Vespas zoomed past us too fast over cobblestone streets. Our travels were a special growth experience, resulting from our shared efforts.

I grieved that my father was not there to enjoy our success. In January 1976, seven months after Addie and I were married, I got a call from my mother to come home to St. Albans, Queens. My father had died.

He'd been in the basement that night, in his train room for hours. Then he climbed the basement stairs around nine o'clock and collapsed at the top of the stairs. The heart attack killed him before the ambulance that was carrying him reached the hospital.

He was only sixty-six years old. I couldn't believe that my father, that towering exemplar of diligence and correctness, faith in God, and grace, had left us. I thanked God that Dad had lived long enough to meet Addie and participate in our wedding. He thought Addie was very special, and I could see that he hoped my relationship with her meant that I was finally beginning to get my life on the right track.

Figure 10 / *Tom's mother, Addie, and Addie's mother (left to right) in renovated apartment, October 1978*

Figure 11 / *Tom's mother, Charles McLean, Nigel, and Tom (left to right) in renovated apartment, October 1978*

My father's devout spirituality is reflected in an undated letter—likely written a year or two before Nigel was born in 1969—that he kept tucked in his Bible. It read:

Dear Children,

Again it is Christmas.

I want you to know that thru you, I have come to know more of the depths of love of God than otherwise would have been possible. My children: Sister [Marie], Eddie, Jimmy, and Tommy. And now, at least at this time, Kim and Wally [Marie's children]. God bless you all, now and evermore.

Remember Christmas at Montclair? Sister's feigned nonchalance over the record player? Eddie's glistening eyes, Jim's broad grin, Tom's simple delight over the bicycles? Please let Christmas live forever in your hearts, and in the hearts and minds of your children.

Oh yes, we must always remember that in this planetary frame of reference, we measure entities in terms of length, mass and time. But in the Eternal frame of reference, planetary standards are not valid. So, when for me, the curtain falls, I want no tears. In fact, at any possible earthly service, I want only three items:

1. The 23rd Psalm
2. The Hallelujah Chorus from Handel's Messiah
3. Recitation by my children of the Lord's Prayer

No obituary. No Eulogy. No tears.

Love,
Dad

$$\boxed{3}$$

1980s: Climbing Higher

Such a perfect black couple that it seemed as though they might
have come from central casting at the CIA.

—CLIVE BARNES, *New York Times dance critic, describing us
in a story about Boston Ballet's China tour, 1980*

The Boston Ballet was founded in 1963 as the Boston Ballet Company, and by the time Addie and I were living in Boston, it had already become one of the best dance companies in the United States. So it was fortunate for us that our friend and former landlord Mark Goldweitz invited us to numerous Boston Ballet events. He was an ardent supporter and always had tickets to special access ballet soirees and mixers with the principals, company founder E. Virginia Williams, donors, and the dashing director and former ballerina, Violette Verdy. Attending the performances and special events with the Goldweitzes, Addie and I fell in love with dance, with the exquisite athleticism and precision of the dancers, the hush of expectation before the curtain's rise, and the social buzz surrounding grand productions. Our growing interest in the company had a side effect of placing us in new social circles. The city's aristocracy, the "Boston Brahmins," were deeply involved in supporting the ballet. If Boston had a caste system, this was its apex. Mark introduced us to people like Mary Ellen Cabot, who was the board chair, and her husband, Louis Cabot, descendent of John Cabot, one of the first Europeans to explore the northeastern coast of what would become America. John Cabot and his son made a great fortune by shipping rum and African slaves. Subsequent Cabots went on to even greater business and political prominence and became one of Boston's leading philanthropic families. I was pleasantly surprised by how welcome they and the other ballet supporters made me feel, despite Boston's reputation for inhospitality toward blacks.

Nigel took the ballet in stride. He was a New York City kid, after all, and by nature cool and unflappable. Because his mother was an artist, married briefly to an actor (with whom she had a second son, Christopher), Nigel was used to being exposed to cultural events. In the winter of 1980, when he was eleven, we took him to *The Nutcracker,* one of Boston Ballet's signature productions, which they've continued to stage every year since 1975. He sat between me and Addie and watched as dozens of little dancers emerged from Mother Ginger's tentlike hoopskirt. He smiled up at me, mildly intrigued at the engineering feat. I looked down at him and was reminded how sharp he was, how little he missed of what was going on around him. He had recently taken an oral placement test to be admitted to a competitive middle school near the United Nations headquarters in Manhattan, and Stephanie had told me how Nigel had known he'd done well even before the results were shared with her because he had been reading the test administrator's notes on his answers, upside down from where he sat, as the administrator jotted them down.

Addie and I liked being parents, even if it was only part-time duty. I had often told Stephanie that I thought it might be a good idea for Nigel to come live with us for his teenage years.

As we became more involved with Boston Ballet, I was asked to join the board of trustees, and then I was elected treasurer. A few months after I joined the board, the company was invited to tour China in the summer of 1980. This was newsworthy during the Cold War years, and it attracted significant press coverage and was regarded as a diplomatic and artistic coup for Boston. The itinerary included Beijing, Shanghai, and Canton (now known as Guangzhou), with entry and exit to and from China via Hong Kong. Board members and spouses were invited to accompany the tour at their own expense, and Addie and I decided to participate. We were among the first Americans to visit mainland China since the Nixon-Kissinger diplomatic breakthrough in the mid-1970s, and our group was afforded diplomatic status. That meant we received official state tours of the most significant Chinese cultural and historical sites, and there were many elegant receptions and dinners with our Chinese hosts and local government dignitaries in each city. Accompanying our delegation was Clive Barnes, an Oxford-educated Englishman and drama scholar who had served as the *New York Times'* dance critic for many years and who described us in comical and flattering terms in his write-up of the tour for the paper. Addie and I were feeling that our life together was on a very nice arc, climbing higher.

The *Manchester Union Leader* was one of the most conservative newspapers in the country, and it was the only statewide paper in New Hampshire. The journalist Hunter S. Thompson called it "America's worst newspaper" and labeled the paper's publisher a "neo-Nazi." When I was assigned to manage the audit of the Union Leader Corporation in Manchester, I was the only minority on the Arthur Young audit engagement team, and there were no minorities in the *Union Leader*'s business office. Meeting me for the first time, the client financial team couldn't conceal their surprise. Their eyes popped open and they seemed too stunned, for a brief moment, to speak. It was as if a black man standing in their midst was as unexpected as an alien from outer space.

Every morning for several weeks, during the fieldwork portion of my assignment, I arrived at their offices early and stayed late. Mindful of American racial history, in which a black man could be beaten or lynched if a white woman complained that he had looked at her or spoken to her disrespectfully, I tried to avoid talking to or looking at the women in the office unless it was absolutely necessary, and I never had lunch or coffee or any remotely social exchanges with the female staff. On the occasions when I had lunch or conversations with the men on the *Union Leader* finance team, I avoided being drawn into political discussions. When someone asked me directly, for instance, "Aren't you the guy from the student revolt at Cornell? What happened there?" I said only, "Yes, but it's a long story and we don't have enough time to go through it," and I would change the topic to Red Sox small talk. I simply refused to engage on any level other than the most polite and superficial, or in my professional responsibilities, which I was diligent in performing. Ultimately, the people at the *Union Leader* never had any cause for complaint. I was their audit manager for three years, and the assignment was a good example of my knack for working well even with difficult clients.

Arthur Young had promoted me to principal in 1979, but my outlook toward the company was altered by two unexpected events. First, my primary mentor, eastern region managing partner Len Miller, died suddenly and unexpectedly. And my other significant mentor, Boston office managing partner Arthur Koumantzelis, retired in 1980. With my original mentor relationship with Richard Landis already disrupted by his departure from AY several years earlier to pursue other opportunities, I was now without any close personal ties to anyone in senior management. The incoming Boston office managing partner, Thomas McDermott, who had transferred from another city to assume the position, was very friendly toward me, and his wife, Maria, was gracious to both Addie and me, and they made us feel very welcome at the firm. But I knew in my gut that it wasn't the same. I also began to consider the possibility that I might not be able to progress higher on the career ladder at AY unless I demonstrated my commitment to the firm by a willingness to transfer to another city, which was a common pattern at AY. I was not enthusiastic about that possibility because Addie and I had built a nice real estate portfolio in Boston, we had a very enjoyable social life, and Addie had a job she liked as director of career services at Harvard's Kennedy School of Government. So I began to think about other possibilities for pursuing my career.

Our phenomenal China experience was equaled in the summer of 1981, when Boston Ballet was invited to tour Russia. Again it was a newsworthy event, and we were met with diplomatic fanfare on each leg of the itinerary in Moscow and Leningrad. We were among the first Americans to have a personal view into Soviet Russia at the height of the post–World War II period.

Moscow struck me as utilitarian and drab. Buildings were gray and square, people were dour, the public landscaping minimal. And every supposedly cold drink we were served was warm.

I jotted down notes and impressions every night of our trip in a journal:

Moscow does not demonstrate much that would appeal to a spiritual person. Buildings tend to be drab . . . virtually devoid of flowers or pleasantly manicured greenery. People are not seen laughing or smiling very often. And even on Sunday afternoon, a very sunny day, we saw very little street play or family fun (laughing, picnics in grassy areas, ball games, etc.). But the people do appear well fed and decently clothed. Perhaps Russia is an economic success and a spiritual failure. These people need more God, love, faith, bright colors, and laughter in their lives. It is almost as though the weight of the system—the struggle to get small things done in everyday life—saps many of their smiles and pleasantness.

Leningrad is architecturally attractive in the center city (Winter Palace, St. Isaac's Cathedral, Nevsky Prospect area), and its artistic heritage per the Hermitage is quite impressive. The people are somewhat more elegant than in Moscow, and the city generally feels more cosmopolitan. But overall, life still appears to be drab and tedious for most people. The main department store is very shabby, with long lines of people at counters which have some particularly desirable item in stock. Usually there were too many people crowded around for us to see what they were after, but once we did glimpse ladies' winter boots. The people wait in line with stoic and weary expressions. They are not accustomed to having very much, or to being served with courtesy and alacrity. It's easy to see how they defeated the Germans—by simply refusing to be worn down. They have a peculiar kind of strength—endurance is probably more accurate.

One of our guides (Nina) seems to go out of her way to be nasty to a Russian lady who attempts to accompany her cousin—a member of our group visiting from the U.S.—on our various sightseeing trips. Usually, since one or more members of our group opt to do something else, an extra ticket is available for the Russian lady. But Nina seems to delight in preventing her from feeling part of us. And the two cousins are only harmless women in their fifties. Nina is probably typical of the manner in which the petty bureaucrats of this society abuse those over whom they can exercise authority—always preferring the option of negativism rather than extending the benefit of the doubt and helping another person. Interesting that people who love to dwell on their history of being abused (the czars, Nazi Germany) are so quick to become abusive. Perhaps they wouldn't be this way if their communist revolution had been more supportive (or at least tolerant) of Christianity.

The subway mosaics in Moscow are beautiful. It is astounding to see such art, including delightful chandeliers, in underground public areas. It reflects well on the people that these areas are spotless, without graffiti or litter. It is almost out of character with the broader impression of Russians—the shabbiness of surface landscaping, and the general drabness of the buildings and the people. Perhaps the explanation is that these are people of a harsh winter climate, and the subway is one of their winter burrows. Surface appearances don't receive comparable attention, perhaps, because they are typically snow-covered more than half of the year? In any event, it is also clear that the extraordinarily deep subways can also serve as bomb shelters. And the newer subway stations have sliding doors in the tunnels to seal the platform (perhaps to seal the station platforms from gas or radiation, or to permit emergency use of the tracks unimpeded by persons getting into the tunnels from the platforms?). These people always seem to bring one back to themes of war!

Went to the circus in Leningrad this evening. The nicest part of it was to see so many Russians smiling and laughing.

After visiting here I am moved to serve my country in some positive manner. Not having been in the military service because of the civil rights and anti–Vietnam War struggles in the sixties, I would like to find a way to perform national service which signifies my love and respect for the USA. The country seems to have put behind and moved forward from the worst mistakes of institutional/systemic racism and colonial war (aka Vietnam), and my generation should acknowledge what appears to be genuine efforts of America to correct past mistaken policies. No person, or nation, can do any more than to attempt to correct past grievances—but none can undo the past. Within this context, it is right and appropriate for people like me to demonstrate our willingness to assume our obligations under the social contract which must be achieved for America to survive and prosper. And the first obligation may well be for people from the most successful strata of society to perform two years of national service.

Russia would make a much nicer impression if the service people extended a modicum of effort to be courteous, pleasant, and helpful. They seem to compete with one another to see how quickly they can interrupt your service request, and point you toward someone else who is allegedly responsible for whatever you are requesting (they seldom are, and quickly point you toward yet another "service person"). This process can transform the simplest request into an agonizing, tiring, and time-consuming ordeal. We have walked back and forth multiple times between foreign currency exchange counters at opposite ends of the lobby balcony in the Cosmos Hotel, as the clerks at each counter continue to chat with each other, and point us toward the opposite counter as the one which is "open for service. We have tried to confirm flights with the Aeroflot representative in the Cosmos Hotel at 1:00 pm in the afternoon, only to be told by her as she sat and chatted with a friend, that she was on her lunch hour and we should return at 2:00 pm. We have stood in a line of twenty persons at the sole open cash register at a Beriozka store (for foreign nationals only, accepting certain foreign currencies but not Russian rubles), as ten clerks stood nearby with arms crossed watching the line but making no move to open a second register. They seemed totally disinterested in whether people were served or put down their intended purchases and departed. The single spark of service zeal we observed was among the clutch of doormen who are assigned to keep non-guests out of hotels (which usually means keeping ordinary Russians out), as they energetically challenge everyone for room registration cards. This they seem to enjoy. To receive such poor service is mind-boggling in a country where most service positions appear to be staffed quite heavily (presumably one of the ways they achieve full employment). But productivity is nonexistent. Perhaps this is the result when people's income is not in any way related to the quality of service they render—the monthly check for most of these workers probably doesn't change one iota as a result of either excellent or poor service on their part.

It seems as though we are reminded several times daily of the tremendous suffering of the Russian people in World War II (twenty million dead, virtually countless injured, and numerous cities destroyed). There are numerous war memorials in Moscow and Leningrad, of which one of the most moving was the cemetery in Leningrad where 480,000 war dead are buried in mass graves. One cannot help but sympathize with the Russian people for this unfathomable suffering, which is so far beyond anything in the American experience. And, to a certain extent, one understands why the war memory is invoked frequently as rationale for Soviet military strength. But there is an important distinction, which we all must learn to identify and observe, between respect for history and entrapment in history. Virtually all nationalities and ethnic groups have suffered some historical tragedy—that is the nature of man's inhumanity to man—and it behooves thoughtful persons to learn important historical lessons from those tragedies. But at the same time, we all need to be capable of "leaving history behind" and focusing our energies on the only time horizon we can actually impact, which is our own lifetimes and the future. I have an uneasy sense that Russia dwells a bit too much on World War II, and I'm instinctively uncomfortable with people who perhaps prefer to wallow in their past suffering rather than focus on moving forward. Has their misery become a way of life? A final observation is that the Russians don't like to discuss the suffering they inflicted on themselves under Stalin. Some historians estimate the toll from Stalin to also be approximately twenty million dead from the upheavals associated with forced industrialization, forced collectivization of agriculture, and consolidation of Stalin's ruling power. When asked about this, the guides say "only a few thousand died under Stalin." The overall impression I'm left with is that it is less the anguish at human suffering which motivates the focus on World War II, and more its utility as a tool for social cohesion by focusing the population on external enemies rather than internal economic and social problems.

Today is Monday June 22 in Moscow. We have been here since late Saturday evening June 20, and we have toured Red Square (Kremlin, St. Basil's Cathedral, and Lenin's Mausoleum), toured the city by bus, and visited the Exhibition of Economic Achievements (forty-odd pavilions devoted to Russian exploits in science, industry, and agriculture). We are learning that Russians have been first or biggest (which is sometimes better than being first!) in just about all spheres of human endeavor, including the first printing press (poor Gutenberg), and that the USA being first to land men on the moon doesn't mean very much because Russia has a much larger lunar rover!

Addie squealed with glee when I came to our hotel room with two Pepsi-Colas and a smug smile of triumph (they were even chilled!). This followed two days of a fruitless quest for cola drinks at all of the bars and service areas in the hotel. And last night we were even defeated in our efforts to obtain a cold beer from any of the hotel bars. But it turns out that there is a "dollar store" in a far corner of the hotel, and it stocks cold colas and beer! I must say that I was thrilled at Addie's joy, and my own sense of achievement. So we are Muscovites—we are weary, we are defeated, and we are hoarding our

Pepsi-Colas with smug self-satisfaction at having "gotten something," however modest it may be. Perhaps, after we rest, we will be ready to engage in the struggle for dinner.

What is good about Russia? The pride and self-respect they have for their culture, history, and their nation. The spirit of service and individual sacrifice for the common good. Their individual and collective will to prevail. The improvement in the economic lot of the common person since the communist revolution. And Russia's ability to harness its vast natural resources and progress toward economic self-sufficiency.

When we returned from Russia, Stephanie called me and said, "I think it's time for Nigel to come stay with you." He was twelve and highly opinionated and independent, and for the first time in his childhood, she was worried she might not have the authority over him to keep him out of trouble. She loved what living in New York City had given him—the great schools and the confidence and sophistication New Yorkers have—but she also remembered, from her childhood in the Bronx projects, that young men without firm guidance could wind up dead. Addie and I were more than happy to welcome him as a full-time member of our household that fall, in time for the new school year. To make room for the change, we moved from our two-bedroom apartment into a large three-bedroom apartment in our Columbus Avenue building. Nigel attended Boston Latin School, which was considered the premier public school in Boston and had a highly competitive admission process.

That winter, Addie learned that she was pregnant, but we decided to wait a few months before sharing the good news with anyone else.

"Oh, you have to hear this," she said to me one night as we lay in bed reading. "Today I told Nigel about the baby."

"How did he take it?"

"Very well, I think. But, listen, he asked me, 'Does my dad know?' As if I would have forgotten to tell you!"

Our daughter Evonne was born on September 19, 1982, at 8:15 in the evening. Charles came to our place to stay with Nigel while we were at the Brigham and Women's Hospital for the delivery. Both Addie's mother and mine came to be with us. The doctors let me into the room for the birth. She was a pretty little baby in perfect health.

Figure 12 / *Tom's mother, Tom, Evonne, Addie, and Addie's mother
(left to right) at Evonne's baptism, December 1982*

Charles was one of our last friends to get married. He stayed single until he was fifty, when he met his wife, Susan, who had also never married before. Maybe because he wasn't wrapped up in a family of his own yet, he occupied a place in our family very much like that of an uncle to my children. For instance, he took Nigel with him on maintenance jobs in our properties, which he managed. "You're my Paint Man!" he said to Nigel. When an apartment or hallway had to be repainted, Nigel would get the job of taping off the baseboards and window trim. Charles was meticulous as a property manager, and proactive in gaining new insights into how we could best maintain the buildings, conserve energy during the winters (during the oil crisis, no less), and in other ways provide the tenants with the best possible home while also watching the bottom line.

Addie and I were unbelievably happy to have shared with each other that enriching cultural and educational experience of travel to Europe, China, and Russia. Our horizons had been broadened, and we began developing a sense that we might be blessed with a very special life together. We also were enjoying Boston, where we had many friends in both the white and black communities. We felt like we belonged and that the city was embracing us.

It was around that time that I came up with and adopted a "rule of three," a practice I have kept and lived by since. As each New Year approaches, I reflect and meditate on potential areas of self-improvement. I select three to focus on and achieve in the coming year—improvement of mind, body, or soul. In 1983, for example, one of my goals was to read the Holy Bible cover to cover, which I did. When our lives were changed by the presence of children, one of my three goals was to become more loving, patient, and gentle with Addie and the children. Over time, I have learned that achieving three important goals every year is an enormously powerful personal discipline that leads to tremendous personal growth.

It was the only time I pursued a business opportunity that I probably shouldn't have. Had I been successful, I think I would have felt slightly uncomfortable about my success, because it would have been the result of the worst kind of capitalism, essentially a seizing of public assets. In 1981 I became aware of an unexpected opportunity to pursue a Federal Communications Commission license challenge for one of the Boston television stations. The incumbent owner had violated certain license provisions, so the license renewal was vulnerable to challenge, if the FCC could be persuaded to follow the strict letter of the law and make no allowances. It was an era of federal government affirmative action, and FCC rules called for additional favorable consideration to be given to minority-controlled applicants. It was a long shot, but I wanted to try for it. I assembled a number of significant investor commitments and founded Atlantic Television Corporation. If successful, I would become owner of the ABC affiliate in one of the largest television markets in the country.

I resigned from Arthur Young & Company, rented an office downtown, and worked full-time for Atlantic for the next year, putting together the license application and visiting Washington, D.C., to lobby for the license. At the end of the year, my television station dreams fell through when the FCC moderated its stance and backed away from imposing severe loss-of-license sanctions on the current licensee.

To hedge my bets, on the side I had also been working to put together another investment in real estate. In May 1981 we invested to purchase a second South End property with eight rental units. This building had already undergone renovation several years earlier, so it required only modest refurbishing. And so, by the end of 1981, we had accumulated a promising real estate portfolio of eighteen apartments in the rapidly gentrifying South End neighborhood at a time when Boston's economy was experiencing a nice upswing, driven by its employment base in higher education, computer technology, medical services, and financial services.

"Come on, son, it's time to walk to church!" I called out from the foyer of our apartment. Addie stood waiting already, with baby Evonne strapped into the stroller and kicking her legs. Evonne loved these walks to Trinity Church in Copley Square, just three blocks from our building. We had recently started attending Trinity because we wanted our family to have a spiritual framework, much like what both of us had had growing up. (Addie was raised an Episcopalian.)

Trinity is an architectural marvel, built in the 1870s and named by the American Institute of Architects as one of the ten most significant buildings in the United States. In our family's life, it certainly ranks as one of the most important too, with its soaring ceiling and massive pipe organs, but also, more important, the role it played in our lives every week.

The Reverend Spencer Morgan Rice, an extraordinarily gifted preacher, was rector of Trinity from 1982 to 1992, and so when we visited the church on the recommendation of Addie's family friend the Reverend Peter Gomes (professor of Christian morals at the Harvard School of Divinity and Pusey minister of Memorial Church at Harvard University), Reverend Rice was newly arrived. But he'd been aimed toward Trinity since he was a young sailor visiting Boston. He'd happened to attend a service at Trinity which so moved him that he felt called to the ministry and vowed one day to return to Trinity as its rector. When his strong voice rang out, intoning lines from the Book of Common Prayer or preaching with vigor and sincerity and heart, I felt transported and uplifted, but also it was a feeling of returning home at last, to the spiritual habit of my youth, directed by my father.

I also found that I enjoyed many of the liturgical aspects of the Episcopal Church, especially the Book of Common Prayer and the way it organizes prayers and meditations around themes people encounter in daily life. There is the prayer for vocation in daily work, for sound government, for church musicians and artists, for prisons, for the good use of leisure. It was easy for me to transfer my religious loyalty from the Presbyterian Church of my childhood.

Reverend Rice's sermons in his first few years at Trinity frequently referenced the book *The Road Less Traveled* by M. Scott Peck, which was published in 1978 and ultimately became one of the best-selling books ever written about love and spiritual growth. I read this book, and it occurred to me that it was also important to read the Holy Bible to further my spiritual growth. I reasoned that the Holy Bible is arguably the most important book in human history, and I felt strong motivation to experience its message firsthand and to reflect and meditate on God's revelations to mankind. I felt such a sense of urgency that I adopted this as one of my three personal goals for 1983. I kept that commitment and read the Bible cover to cover that year, which was one of the most important and satisfying achievements in my life.

Over the years, Addie and I became friends with Reverend Rice and his wife, Harriet. He encouraged me to join the church's governing body, and I was elected to the vestry in 1986. Participating as an insider in the governance of a great church, helping my friend to achieve his spiritual mission there—this was enjoyable and meaningful service.

As I contemplated my next career move in late summer 1982, I was approached by two John Hancock Mutual Life Insurance Company executives who were members of the Boston Ballet company's board of trustees. Philip Saunders and Stuart Yoffe told me that John Hancock was embarking on a strategic initiative to diversify into various non–life insurance financial services businesses and was considering recruiting outside management talent. Would I be interested in discussing possible opportunities at John Hancock?

I was intrigued by their inquiry, as I had long thought that the financial services industry would probably experience a considerable expansion as my demographically oversized "baby boomer" generation moved through its financial life cycle. Demographic forces are extraordinarily powerful and are relatively predictable and foreseeable. It was obvious that America's post–World War II baby boom had had a dramatic impact on K–12 public education across the country in the 1950s and 1960s, and on higher education enrollment in the 1960s and 1970s. It seemed fairly obvious and predictable that successive stages of the baby boomers' financial life cycle would create surging demand for credit products during their young adult years (credit cards, auto loans, mortgages); then savings, investment, and protection products during their midlife years (mutual funds, retirement accumulation products, life insurance); and, finally, retirement income and protection products during their retirement years (mutual funds, annuities, life insurance). I reasoned that there probably would be attractive career opportunities to be found by riding this rising demographic wave in financial services, and it appealed to me to find a way to participate.

In September 1982, I met with Bill Boyan, the executive vice president of John Hancock. We immediately liked each other. He discussed the company's plans for diversification into a broader set of financial services products. Hancock's management tradition, he told me, was to make strictly internal career ladder promotions, but the firm was considering a few external officer hires to refresh and diversify the managerial talent pool. After several interviews, Boyan presented an offer for me to join John Hancock as second vice president in the controller's department. The plan was to use my accounting background as a platform to become involved in various Hancock product diversification initiatives. I accepted the offer and joined John Hancock in October 1982. I later learned that I was only the third external officer hire since the founding of the company in 1862, and I was the first black officer in company history.

My John Hancock years were very enjoyable, and I made rapid progress on the promotion ladder: I was promoted to vice president in 1985, vice president and treasurer in 1987, and senior vice president and treasurer in 1988. My responsibilities were initially budgeting and financial planning; then I became controller of the holding company that owned all of the non-insurance financial services businesses, and then treasurer with responsibility for financial reporting and external rating agency relations. The work habits and quality assurance disciplines I had learned at Arthur Young stood me in good stead. My ingrained habit of 100 percent effort to excel at whatever I was doing really differentiated me from most of my peers in the Hancock environment, which was not as intense or demanding as the AY culture.

Another important factor in my success at John Hancock was my good fortune in having a group of subordinates who really liked me, wanted me to succeed, and took pride in my success. This positive dynamic is not always the case when a young black outsider is brought into an old-line, traditional company and put in charge of seasoned career professionals as direct reports. Two executives in particular earned my gratitude in this regard—Jack Scanlon in the controller's department and Henry Desautel in the treasury department. Both were white men in their forties in management positions, and they could have chosen to resent the young black officer they suddenly found themselves reporting to, but they didn't. They gave me a chance and ultimately came to respect and like me, and even seemed to enjoy my success. I also developed a circle of friendships with my peers in the senior officer ranks, including David D'Alessandro, Judy Markland, Stuart Yoffe, and Phil Saunders. And Bill Boyan became my mentor and senior management advocate. Over the years there, my confidence was growing that I could perform and succeed at a high level in the business world.

My managerial success at Hancock stemmed primarily from my inclination to be a team builder and team leader. I didn't issue orders. I respected people and sought their input on how to solve problems or achieve important objectives. Most people have more to offer than they're given credit for, and most people respond well to being respected. I also led by example, working longer hours than anyone else. When things went well, I always gave public recognition and credit to my subordinates. And when things didn't go so well, I always took responsibility on myself.

You couldn't see the house from the road. It sat beyond an old stone wall topped by a six-foot wooden fence. To see the house, you had to turn into the drive, and then the house became visible, large and gray. It was a Cape Cod, with a garage and a pool equipment shed tucked away at the sides. It had several gables and gave the overall impression, from the outside, of graceful sprawl. Inside, the woodwork was beautiful, the rooms generous and well arranged in relation to one another in a way that produced a pleasant flow. There was a swimming pool out back and room for a tennis court, which we soon built. Two acres for Nigel and Evonne to run around on. After the closing in our lawyer's office, Addie and I went straight to the house and stood together for a moment at the front door, with our backs to the house, surveying our new country life. The town of Weston was one of Boston's prettiest suburbs.

Addie was working as head of career placement services at the John F. Kennedy School of Government at Harvard University, which put her in the midst of enjoyable intellectual and social activities. In the mid-1980s she became head of admissions and financial aid for the international master's in law program at Harvard Law School. Her commute to Harvard Square from our home in Weston was an easy twenty-minute drive door to door. My commute to John Hancock Tower in Boston's Back Bay neighborhood was also very comfortable, in part because the Hancock parking garage was built directly over the Massachusetts Turnpike with interior direct access entry and exit ramps. On most days, barring traffic accidents, I could leave home at 7:30 am and be in my office by 8:00, and I could leave the office at 6:00 pm and be home by 6:30. My standard ten-hour workday was long compared to that of my Hancock peers, and yet on most days I was still home for quality evening family time.

In 1983 Stephanie, who had a nephew at Andover, encouraged Nigel to apply to boarding school. I reserved judgment and drove him to his school visits. We saw Andover and Exeter, two of the most elite boarding schools in the country. But after our visits, and some thought about what the schools offered, I told him he couldn't attend.

We were at the dining room table one night and I explained my thinking: "Those schools won't teach you what you most need to know to succeed as a black man in America, Nigel. Sure, you'd probably be a star at Andover or Exeter, and everybody would love you, and you'd probably be a big man on campus. But the problem is that you'll be getting B-plus grades without even breaking a sweat, and everyone will be telling you that you're doing fine."

He glared at me. Nigel wasn't used to being told he didn't work hard enough, and he didn't like it.

"What I want you to learn in high school is how to dig down deep inside yourself to find out what's there, and what it means to really try hard and give your best efforts, because you're eventually going to need to know how to do that in order to succeed as a black man in America. And the faculty and staff at schools like Andover and Exeter don't train black boys for that."

Nigel pushed back from the table and stormed off. He was upset with my decision, obviously, and he started to rebel. After a week had passed, I wrote him a letter dated April 10, 1983, which read:

Dear Nigel,

I am writing this letter to communicate with you as clearly as I know how in regard to your behavior of the past few days. I am writing while your behavior is fresh in your mind, and in order to give you a permanent record of my position and how I intend to behave toward you.

Let me begin by saying that I am your father, for better or worse. Neither of us can change this fact, even if we desired to do so. Since you can't change it, my advice to you is to be happy and positive—you could be in far worse circumstances. I suggest that you begin to think of your father as a coach. You have learned that the team can only have one coach, and you can't be the coach until you have sufficient experience and knowledge as to be able to give your team good guidance in all situations that arise on the field. The team can't fight the coach and win. The team can discuss strategy and suggest ideas to the coach, but the coach makes the final decisions—who will play, what positions, batting order, etc. As your father, it is my job to coach you to manhood. I will coach you to the best of my ability, drawing on the experience I gained from my coach—your grandfather. I will do my best to train you to be disciplined, hardworking, to strive for excellence, and to conduct yourself in accordance with Christian morality. My father taught me that these were the ingredients of his successful struggle to rise above the circumstances and limitations of his birth as a black man in the rural South in 1909. And I know that these are the ingredients of the success that I have experienced in my life. As your coach, I will do my best to ingrain these qualities deep into your character. And I hope that one day, if you have children and become the coach, you will find that these are the important lessons to be taught and passed on. But you will not and cannot be the coach until you have sufficient experience and, hopefully, the knowledge that flows therefrom. And that is why, at fourteen, you will not make certain decisions which should be made by the coach.

You have given me severe resistance on two occasions this year:

1. In the fall when I put you on a four hours per day study schedule following your worst report card in two years, I told you that you had to learn to really reach inside of yourself and strive for excellence, and that even if you didn't achieve excellent results you would have the pride and satisfaction of knowing that you did your best. And if you did achieve excellent results, you would have the pride and satisfaction of knowing that you earned it and that you could do it again.

You complained bitterly. You complained that the other kids didn't study so hard, and that your cousin didn't study so hard and his mother (your mother's sister) is a teacher and knows what's best. You complained frequently to your mother, who in turn tried to get me to back off, and evidently made you feel that she was very sympathetic to your position because you weren't happy. You and I eventually had an ugly confrontation before you resigned yourself to obeying my orders.

Eventually you discovered that you could achieve at a higher level than ever before, and acquired new depth and capability as a student. In retrospect you recognized how valuable it is to be capable of that kind of academic discipline and effort, and you now do a good job of pacing your own study schedule because you understand what excellence is all about.

2. This past week you resisted me strongly on my decision that you should live at home and attend BB&N [Buckingham Browne & Nichols, a private day school in Cambridge], rather than go away to Andover. I told you that I wanted you to stay home because BB&N was academically equal to Andover and, given equal educational environments, it made more sense for you to be raised by your father rather than strangers.

You argued that Andover has more courses than BB&N; my response was that it didn't matter since, practically speaking, you were going to have little time for anything other than math, English, science, history, language, etc., and that BB&N was equal to Andover in these major subjects. You argued that Andover had better clubs and activities; my response was that having a decent chance to be on athletic teams was an important consideration, and that you had a much better chance at BB&N (250 boys instead of 800), especially since Andover recruits postgraduate athletes for its teams and those guys, who should be playing in college, dominate Andover athletics. You told me all about the famous men who have graduated from Andover (Vice President Bush, Supreme Court justices, etc.); my response was that you should tell me about the famous black men trained by Andover, because the issue is whether the anonymous dormitory counselors can do a better job than me in training you to be successful as a black man in this very tough society. You told me that Andover had more minority students, and a more diverse and cosmopolitan student body; my response was yes, but is this so important that you need to leave home now and spend the next ten years in that type of situation, rather than a last four years at home, to be followed by six or more years of campus living in college and graduate school?

So, son, I weighed all of these considerations and made a decision. You had opportunity for input. But I'm the coach and I make the

decision. You resent it now, but you will eventually grow to appreciate this decision as we live through the various growth crises you
will experience in the next four years. I don't expect you to have that
perspective now, son—you don't have enough experience yet. It's my
responsibility to have that perspective and make the decisions as your
coach.

What I do expect is that you will accept the coach's decision
and execute your assignments to the best of your abilities. I will not
tolerate your rebellion and insolence. And I will not tolerate encouragement of your insolence, and other negative influences, from your
mother or anyone else. It is clear that your mother has encouraged
you to set your heart on Andover, even though she knows virtually nothing about BB&N; she simply knows that Andover is more
famous and "people like Nat Hentoff say it's the best." But these "people" can't possibly have weighed all the subtlety and nuance that I
outlined above.

Your mother must understand that her advice to you must stop
well short of encouraging or condoning the type of resistance you
have given me now on two occasions this year. If this negative influence does not cease, your mother's access to you will be curtailed.

Your mother is well meaning and acts from love for you. I know
that. But I also know that she has no direct experience with the day-
to-day aspects of training a young black man to be successful in this
society. Her father, a dentist, unfortunately died when your mother
was four. Your mother did not grow up in a family or neighborhood
environment which included successful black men. Your mother grew
up in one of the most notorious slums in this country—a place where
black men are more often than not either junkies or criminals by
their late teens. This background is not your mother's fault, and is
certainly not a reason for you to love her any less than you do. But it is
the reason why she is not going to be your coach. She does not really
understand from firsthand experience the subtleties of the training
that I will give you. Your mother means well, but she is not going to
be your coach.

So, son, I am the coach. In order to make my position perfectly
clear, I am taking the following actions.

1. I will no longer pay for your trips to New York to visit your
mother. Since your mother volunteered $3,000 to assist you in leaving

to attend Andover, it is reasonable to believe that she can afford to pay for your travel to New York. This will be her financial contribution to your support. You are free to go to New York one weekend per month and on certain holidays, as long as it does not interfere with your schoolwork. You should obtain advance permission from me, and have your mother send a ticket.

2. I am issuing a warning. If you behave again in the manner you have behaved in the two incidents I have cited, and if I have reason to believe that your mother has encouraged or condoned the rebellion and insolence, I will seek a court order curtailing your mother's access to you. I will file a complaint enumerating her negative influences on your development and I will seek court protection from visitation or telephone contact except upon my permission. This letter will be one of the documents which I will submit to the court.

Well, son, the ground rules are clear. You are going to live with me and be trained by me for the next four years. Neither you or your mother has any choice about this—if either of you thinks you do, we will settle it in court very quickly. Be advised that you or your mother will be hard-pressed to find a judge who will take your custody away from me under these circumstances.

I sincerely hope that these next four years together, probably the last time in our lives that we will live together, will be happy and harmonious. We will make a good team if we both approach our responsibilities in a spirit of love, and if you remember at all times that I am the coach. I love you and, with God's help, I will do well by you.

Dad

The letter had its intended effect. We came to an understanding, and in the end, Nigel stayed with us and attended public school in our neighborhood. It was really our only major conflict in all the years he lived with us.

Addie and I both come from families of four children, and we enjoyed parenting. We were in a good place personally and professionally to expand our family, so in 1987 we adopted our son Michael, who was two years old when he joined us. In 1988 our daughter Victoria was born, and we became a family of six. Addie continued to work at Harvard, but reduced her hours to half-time so she could "manage the affairs," as she jokingly put it, of our high-schooler and three young children.

Figure 13 / *Tom, Evonne, Addie, Nigel, and Michael
(left to right) at home in Weston, April 1987*

Nigel thrived academically and athletically in the Weston school system, and graduated with honors in 1987. The administration and his classmates together selected him to be orator, to deliver the class address for the Weston High School graduation exercises on the Weston town green, a manicured square crisscrossed by gravel walkways and bordered by a profusion of flowers. A large temporary wooden structure was placed in the center of the park as a stage for the graduates. Addie and Evonne and I sat in the second row, along with my mother and Mrs. Knox, Charles McLean, and the Wileys. The graduating seniors formed a sea of white up on the stage, since it was the tradition that the young men wear white jackets and the young women wear white dresses.

The high school principal introduced Nigel, who took the podium. I knew his topic and that his audience was in for a surprise. His delivery of this speech was one of my proudest moments as a father because of his sincerity, the forcefulness and merit of his assertions, and the courage I think it took to say what he said:

Parents, teachers, friends, members of the Class of 1987—
There comes a time in everyone's life when you realize that you must do certain things, even if you know that not everyone, probably

not even the majority, will agree with what you're doing. You do it because you know that it's the right thing to do, and in the end, that's all that really matters. I want to talk to you today about a very difficult aspect of my life that I feel relates to you in a special way—

"Don't apply to any schools that I'm applying to because you're black."

"You just got that grade because you're black."

"You might feel uncomfortable at the Country Club."

"Teachers love you because you're smart and you're black."

When my parents go to play tennis, just like yours, people not only assume my father to be a professional athlete, but come up to him wondering which Celtic or Red Sox player he is.

At Weston High School, I am an enigma. I'm black and I live in Weston. The kids from Boston don't feel like I'm one of them and the kids from Weston look at me as a shooting star, moving quickly through the heavens, leaving a dull, empty void in its path. This is going to be a very difficult thing to say, and I'm extremely hesitant about saying it, but it has to be done. The Town of Weston and its school system pride themselves in being liberal and open-minded and unbiased. I question your definition of open-minded and unbiased.

At Weston High School, prejudice is not overt, and so when I first came to this school system, I was blinded to something deeper and more ominous than overt prejudice that I have only begun to understand this year.

Ralph Ellison's main character in his famous novel *Invisible Man* laments a world where no one will see him purely as a human being, and not as a symbol for this, or a tool for that, or as a means of gratifying one's guilt about how one's life has been led. For many of you out there, and for many of the people behind me, I am invisible. I am a statistic, or a barrier to college admissions, or a symbol of a good black boy. I am anything and everything but a human being, an individual with personal ambitions, emotions, and desires.

"How do I know that I am invisible? When the policeman came to the door, he told my stepmother that he had reports that there had been a black man in a beat-up car sitting in the driveway. He must have seen right through her, not letting her skin color affect his distorted perception of impenetrable class and racial barriers. I was the black man in the driveway. The beat-up car is mine. The driveway is ours. When a black student accidentally walked into an honors class, the teacher told him he had the wrong room, before asking him what section he was in. The teacher assumed that the student wouldn't be taking a difficult course. He saw not a human being, eager for knowledge, but dark skin, and all of the stigmas that his mind attached to it.

What are the reasons for the image that black students have in this town? You can look at the honor roll at the end of each quarter and see that we don't do well academically. But I say to you that if you truly care, and if you don't want to just sit back and tell yourselves how charitable you are and how open you are because the METCO program [enrolling inner-city students in suburban schools] is wonderful and because there are a number of black families in Weston, you will look deeper and ask yourself why there aren't more blacks in honors classes.

Ask yourself why someone complains about a black man sitting in the driveway. Ask yourself why I get stopped and questioned by the police when I walk on the streets after dark. As uncomfortable as it is, just ask yourself. The reason is that we are invisible. Even now you don't see me. You don't see my anguish, and you don't see the deep frustration that I have sometimes felt, and never talked about.

If you really don't care about yourself and about the Town of Weston and the rest of the world, but only about how you are perceived by others, then you'll walk away today and not try to understand. But if you really want Weston to be the open, accepting place that some people seem to think it is right now, then let go of your assumptions and your prejudices and your biases. Look at me, look at all black people as people, as individuals—as you look at your own children. I know that there are few black students in the honors classes. The black students are, as a group, not as academically proficient as the white students. But it's not because of any intrinsic deficiency, as some of the faculty of Weston may believe. If you took any 50 kids from South Boston or Dorchester and placed them in the highly academic environment of Weston High, you would get the same results. It's a socioeconomic problem, not a racial one. If you think that white kids are so much smarter than black kids, send your children to Dorchester High for 5 years and then bring them back to Weston, and see how they do.

The assumptions and biases that I'm talking about are not ingrained in the spirit of any individual, and especially not those in the Class of 1987.

When we leave this town and this school system, we will discover that the rest of the world has made the same unfair judgments that we have. We must be leaders in trying to unlearn the fallacies we have been exposed to. From the friends that I have, and the individual relationships I have had with the members of this class, I know that we can.

I am asking you, the Class of 1987, and your families and friends to really try to make a difference. The problems of class and wealth are too involved for any one person to try to solve. Rather, when you come into contact with a person who has not had the same advantages and the same opportunities, understand that. More importantly, try to see us, to know us as people, as individuals, and not as symbols. I have been invisible for six years now, ever since I started junior high at Boston Latin School, and believe me, it gets very lonely when no one can see you. I want you to let go of your blindness. I want us to make a better town, and a better world. Thank you.

The June 29, 1987, *Boston Globe* published an article titled "Confronting the Unseen," devoted to a summary and analysis of Nigel's remarks and their reception by the people of Weston. "Although fellow students cheered Nigel's speech, the reaction in town has been mixed. 'It almost makes you feel guilty in a sense, but I don't have anything to feel guilty about,' said Richard Murray, chairman of the Board of Selectmen."

Nigel was admitted to Cornell, Harvard, Stanford, and other top schools, and he decided to attend Harvard. He visited Cornell and was impressed, but I didn't try to push him toward my alma mater because I lacked confidence that he would encounter a supportive campus social environment. From keeping up with the *Cornell Daily Sun* student newspaper and talking with friends who were still engaged with the campus, my impression was that black students at Cornell continued to be dominated by "blacker-than-thou" rhetoricians who would probably give Nigel a hard time for being a member of the "black bourgeoisie," just as their predecessors had given me a hard time.

Over the years my attitude had hardened against those in the black community who engage in this rhetorical intimidation. I was more convinced

Figure 14 / *Nigel delivering the senior oration at*
Weston High School graduation, June 1987

than ever that the only viable path to black prosperity, and full political and economic equality in America, is individual commitment to those selfsame so-called bourgeois values of personal moral discipline, hard work, education, and self-improvement. This is the path to success trod by millions of African Americans from many generations, and it is the path trod by my parents to lift themselves from poverty. It is the path I was following in my own life.

When Nigel left home to attend Harvard in September 1987, I reflected on our years together. He had developed into an exceptional young man, and I was sure that part of that was due to the fact that I had been able to give him a spiritual foundation in the church, similar to the one my father had given me. Our family had continued to attend Trinity Church most Sundays from September through May, and Nigel had become Reverend Spencer Rice's favorite acolyte crossbearer, leading the processional and recessional marches of the ministers and choir which opened and closed the worship service. Reverend Rice delighted especially in using Nigel on the most important ceremonial occasions such as Christmas and Easter. Nigel and I often shared the uplifting spiritual experience of participating together in worship services in a church filled with over one thousand people on those Sundays when he served as an acolyte and I served as an usher.

Our South End real estate investments had continued to do well, and the eighteen apartments were always 100 percent occupied, other than during brief vacancy intervals between tenants. We increased rents on every tenant turnover, and we achieved classic real estate positive operating leverage—when debt service expenses are locked in by a long-term fixed-rate mortgage and don't increase each year, and you are able to increase your rents by a higher percentage than the percentage increase in operating expenses such as heat, electricity, real estate taxes, and property maintenance. Thus, net income from our property increased each year.

But in 1985 we experienced an ugly incident that diminished my appetite for the real estate business.

One of our tenants, a single woman in her thirties who worked as a reporter for the *Boston Globe*, lost her job and stopped paying her rent. She started to play the housing code violation game, a scam in which a tenant files a bogus complaint with the municipal building department alleging housing code violations. When the code violation inspection or hearing is scheduled, the tenant cancels at the last minute because of an "emergency" and requests rescheduling. Also, key case documents may disappear from the building department or housing court files or be "misplaced" by clerks who sympathize with the tenant. By law in Boston at that time, an eviction could not proceed if there was a housing code violation complaint still open. A sophisticated person who understood the municipal housing bureaucracy could prolong this process for many months, or even years.

If the tenant had approached me honestly and directly, asking for time— thirty, sixty, or ninety days to pay her rent—I would have felt a moral obligation to be sympathetic and merciful. But since she decided to try to beat me by playing the housing code violation game, I felt no obligations of sympathy or mercy. I refused to play the patsy in this game, and retained a "courthouse dog" attorney who knew the intricacies of the building department and housing court bureaucracies, and knew how to connect with supervisors and judges to keep the process moving. I reasoned that it didn't make sense to be in the real estate business unless I was serious about collecting rents, because if tenants learn that they can skip payments, the landlord may fall to the bottom of their priority list of bills to pay. I also thought that not collecting rent was tantamount to a direct money transfer from me to the tenant, and I was not inclined to run a personal welfare support operation. I was already paying substantial real estate property taxes and personal income taxes, which supported public assistance programs.

When I went to housing court for the final hearing, where the tenant was facing imminent eviction, she shot me a look of absolute hatred. I remember thinking that people don't expect to take food from the grocery store without paying, or clothes from the clothing store without paying, but for some reason some people seem to believe that it's okay to take housing from the property owner without paying. "This is too close for comfort," I thought. "This hatred is directed at me personally, and this woman knows who I am and can easily find out where I live." Perhaps my family could be endangered under some conceivable scenarios. I decided that day that I should either scale up my real estate activities to operate more remotely and anonymously through agents or employees, or I should get out of the business altogether.

From the beginning, I'd considered our real estate development and rental property investments as my backstop to the corporate world, something like an insurance policy I held in case I encountered insurmountable barriers in corporate America. Then, in early 1986, with the sour memory of our rent-dodging tenant still fresh in my mind, federal tax law changes were proposed that would eliminate many favorable real estate tax preferences and negatively impact real estate investment economics. I thought the proposals in Congress had a fairly good chance of being enacted, and would likely have a negative impact on rental apartment valuations, so I decided to get ahead of the curve. I placed our rental properties on the market. We achieved very favorable sale valuations and converted our $25,000 initial savings and subsequent savings and investment in the project into nearly $250,000 net profit. We were out of the market before the federal tax law changes were enacted in late 1986. I was out of the real estate business.

"Mr. Jones, there's a Clif Wharton on the line for you." I knew that my assistant meant Clif Wharton, the CEO of TIAA-CREF. I took the call, of course, and it would prove to be a turning point in my career.

Dr. Clifton R. Wharton Jr. had become the first black chief executive of a Fortune 500 company when he'd been named CEO of TIAA-CREF (Teachers Insurance and Annuity Association–College Retirement Equities

Fund) two years earlier, in 1987. *Fortune* magazine had put him on the cover. But before achieving that historic milestone in business, Wharton had been a philanthropist, an academic, and the first black president of a major university in America, Michigan State University. He was later the chancellor of the entire sixty-four-campus State University of New York (SUNY) system. It was his distinguished career as a university leader that had made him so attractive to TIAA-CREF, which was dealing with something of a rebellion of academics and university staff across the country who wanted more control over their hefty TIAA-CREF retirement accounts. Who better to helm the ship at such a time than a leader famous for his ability to build good relationships with scholars and college staffs?

Wharton was embarking on restructuring TIAA-CREF management to reinvigorate the company. In his autobiography *Privilege and Prejudice: The Life of a Black Pioneer*, Wharton tells the story of how he came to call me on the phone:

> When I asked friends in the insurance business who was the best chief financial officer in the field, one name kept coming up, Thomas Jones. I didn't know him, but soon learned that he was the number two financial officer at John Hancock Mutual Life, in line for the top job within a few years. I also found out that he was Black. Alan Monroe, my friend and Boston Latin classmate, was an officer at Hancock, and he gave Jones a glowing evaluation. So without prior introduction I called Tom up at work, explaining that TIAA-CREF needed a chief financial officer and could we talk? "I get calls from headhunters all the time, and I never respond," Jones told me. "But you're the first CEO to call me directly. (246)

I told him that I was content with where I was at John Hancock, but that I would be happy to meet with him.

That night, I told Addie about the surprising call. "Of course," I said to her, "I'll meet him, because why would I give up the opportunity to develop a relationship with the top black CEO in America? But beyond that, it's really just a courtesy meeting. I love my work, and my prospects for advancement are good at Hancock." My attitude was: "The devil you know is usually better than the devil you don't know."

Addie surprised me. She said, "I don't think you have a chance of becoming president of John Hancock."

"Why is that?" I asked. Addie didn't often express opinions about my career, and when she did, they were almost always positive.

"I know that the top management executives at Hancock like and respect you deeply, but they probably think you should be grateful for what you've already achieved. Steve Brown is Jewish, and is one of the first Jews to break through to the top tier in the Boston business community, right? And that just happened in the last few years! So I don't think Boston is ready for blacks at the top." Addie also said that Steve Brown and my mentor Bill Boyan and others would probably think I hadn't paid my dues sufficiently to become president. She thought I would probably make it one more step to executive vice president and chief financial officer at Hancock, but that would likely be the end of the road. "Just imagine being at a place where Clifton Wharton is around, a living statement that a black man can be CEO. At least in New York, at TIAA-CREF, you'd have the peace of mind of knowing that racism wouldn't block you from a fair shot at the top."

I thought long and hard about Addie's comments and ultimately decided that she was giving me wise counsel.

Wharton and I met for dinner and had a good conversation. He was a soft-spoken, elegant man, with an air of quiet authority and kindness that was attractive. Toward the end of our conversation, when I sensed that he was ready to offer me the job, I said, "You know who I am, don't you?" He looked surprised and asked what I meant, and so I told him about my leading role in the Straight Hall takeover at Cornell in 1969. I could see recognition dawning. Yes, he knew of that historic moment, had seen the famous photographs.

"Does that change your mind?" I asked him.

"No," he said simply.

The world is small, time compresses, and every encounter and relationship can come to bear on events later in time, at unexpected moments. Little did I know that Wharton was a good personal friend of James Perkins, the Cornell University president during my time at the school. So of course Wharton would call Dr. Perkins and check his reaction to this news: "I'm about to bring Tom Jones on as TIAA-CREF's next CFO." He later wrote about that conversation with Perkins. Without pause, Perkins said, "I think that's marvelous."

TIAA-CREF

Tom visibly embodied the intersection of diversity and excellence.
His performance was so first-rate that not a single individual in
the company could call Jones an affirmative-action appointment.

—CLIFTON WHARTON, *Privilege and Prejudice:*
The Life of a Black Pioneer, 2015

In October of 1989 I became the chief financial officer of the $76 billion education pension and insurance system for TIAA-CREF, the largest private pension system in the country. Clif Wharton brought me on to help expand its programs and investment options for its 1 million policy holders. I was the first black person to fill the CFO role in the organization's seventy-one-year history.

My primary focus in the first few years at TIAA-CREF was the challenge of defending the company's investment allocation policy against possible cashing out by frightened customers. The U.S. economy was sliding into a severe recession, which triggered significant deterioration in the performance of commercial mortgage and real estate assets and below-investment-grade corporate bonds. TIAA had heavy exposure to those classes of assets, and was often listed prominently near the top of financial media news stories discussing which companies were most at risk for impaired assets. There was also criticism of TIAA investment policies among the academic economists in our college and university customer base. These atmospherics combined to create an undercurrent of serious concern and uneasiness in the company. TIAA was primarily a fixed-income investment account promising guaranteed principal and competitive current investment yields, with a guaranteed minimum 3 percent interest rate on customer balances. Much of the TIAA portfolio was invested in corporate private placement bonds, mortgage loans, and real estate. TIAA had achieved investment returns superior to competitors' over the years through a combination of astute investment underwriting and greater allocation to relatively illiquid and longer-maturity investments. Bond maturities of one to five years, for example, constituted over 20 percent of average life insurance company bond portfolios but less than 1 percent at TIAA. Mortgages with maturities of one to five years made up nearly 30 percent of average life insurance company mortgage portfolios, but again less than 1 percent at TIAA. Conversely, TIAA had much heavier asset allocations to longer-maturity corporate bonds and commercial mortgages, and equity real estate. TIAA also had substantial exposure to corporate private placement bonds, which were not publicly traded and were very illiquid. In essence, TIAA was taking more investment risk, and being well compensated for that risk.

TIAA could adopt this investment policy because there were significant restrictions on customers' ability to withdraw funds prior to retirement. After being successful for many years, the strategy came under severe challenge in 1990–1992 as the U.S. recession focused a spotlight on financial institutions' exposure to higher-risk assets. TIAA investment professionals were generally first-rate, and their investment underwriting was holding up under the severe stress, but TIAA needed to defuse customer concerns before they morphed into panicky demands for greater withdrawal rights. The many "pension millionaires" among the American professorate were champing at the bit to get at their money. If TIAA was forced to sell investment assets in that recessionary environment, it would incur substantial capital losses.

I proposed that the company seek financial strength ratings from Moody's, Standard & Poor's and A. M. Best, which were the major insurance company rating agencies in the U.S. capital markets. I had been responsible for rating agency relationships at John Hancock, and I was confident of my ability to present TIAA's asset-liability structure in a way that would garner strong ratings. TIAA had not been rated previously, and many company executives thought it was a risky strategy—great if it works, but a potential disaster if the company receives a mediocre rating or worse.

Usually companies that issue large amounts of debt into the public markets are the ones that seek credit ratings. Rating agencies perform in-depth analysis and give their expert opinions on the companies' creditworthiness and ability to pay, especially under adverse stress scenarios. Because insurance companies' long-term financial obligations to policyholders were analogous to long-term debt, rating agencies issued what were called "insurer financial strength" ratings. Dr. Wharton and the board supported my proposal and we engaged with the rating agencies.

I organized extensive preparatory sessions and rehearsals because very few TIAA executives had experience dealing with rating agencies. Even the investment staff, while experienced users of rating agency analytics when underwriting other companies as prospective investments, had little feel for presenting to rating agencies to secure a rating. I laid out the "TIAA story" for each line of business and investment team, and the presentations and supporting materials were polished to a high level as I probed deeply and asked tough questions in our preparatory sessions.

Each major rating agency sent its strongest insurance industry team to the TIAA rating meetings, held in one of our large conference rooms, because TIAA was a major financial institution and clearly had substantial investment portfolio risk characteristics similar to those that had already triggered ratings downgrades of many banks and insurance companies.

For each day-long rating meeting, the rating agency would send four executives—its senior people in insurance industry ratings and commercial credit analysis, mortgage credit analysis, and private placement bond analysis—as well as a senior actuary.

I opened the meetings with a fifteen-minute overview, followed by one-hour slots for each of our major business lines and investment groups—Pension and Annuity Services, Insurance Services, TIAA Mortgage and Real Estate Investments, TIAA Private Placements, Bond Investments, and TIAA Actuarial—to make a twenty-minute presentation, followed by forty minutes of questions and answers.

I knew the people on each rating agency team from dealing with them at John Hancock, and I had correctly anticipated their concerns by reading their reports on other companies, issued during the then widespread downgrading of insurance companies' financial strength ratings.

Dick Gibbs, a vice president and controller who reported to me and served as my right-hand man from my arrival at TIAA-CREF to my departure, put our materials together for the ratings meetings. He'd been with TIAA since joining the actuarial division in 1969 and had steadily earned promotions since, being named a VP in 1981. He was a straight-talking, hardworking guy from Long Island, a graduate of Lehigh with an advanced degree in actuarial science from the University of Michigan. We hit it off from the start and soon were regular golf partners as well as close work colleagues.

The toughest of all the rating agencies was Moody's. The morning of that meeting, we sat on one side of the long conference table and the Moody's team sat facing us. Ken Pinkus, who headed the Moody's group, was a hard-nosed guy. Dick later described him as "persnickety." It soon became obvious that Pinkus was inclined to give us only the second-highest rating, since 50 percent of our investments were in mortgages. I knew this was the time to make a strong argument and not back down. We had the facts on our side and had prepared the evidence carefully. A heated exchange ensued between Pinkus and me, and I stood my ground and pushed home our strong points: I identified and described critical strengths that differentiated TIAA from other insurance companies and banks. I pressed Moody's to adhere to fact-based evaluation and decisions.

The results of our preparation were outstanding. Several weeks after our last rating interview in October, I got the first telephone call with the good news. More calls followed. TIAA had received the highest possible "triple A" financial strength rating from each agency, becoming one of only five insurance companies with that distinction. This success elevated me to superstar status in the company, and Clif Wharton looked prescient for recruiting me.

After the ratings decisions were announced that fall, I commenced a tour of the TIAA-CREF branch offices in Philadelphia, Boston, Denver, Chicago, Detroit, Atlanta, Washington, Dallas, San Francisco, and New York to explain the ratings to our institutional and individual client counselors. I also discussed the best responses to the toughest questions they were receiving from our clients. My tour was so well received that I repeated it each year, and in 1992 added visits to our major institutional clients, including the University of Michigan, the University of Minnesota, Johns Hopkins, Howard University, Duke, Vanderbilt, Emory, the University of Arkansas, Georgetown, Fordham, New York University, Spelman College, Tuskegee, and Wake Forest.

My second area of focus in the first two years was improved financial reporting to senior management and the board. I prided myself on bringing clarity to financial reporting for each line of business and each investment strategy. I believed that true depth of understanding enabled one to present complex and difficult information in ways that could be surprisingly clear and understandable. I thought of this as similar to the knack the best educators have for presenting complex course material in ways that simplify and clarify it to facilitate student comprehension. Improved financial reporting was intended to empower senior management and the board through increased transparency which facilitated deeper understanding of our business and investment operations, enabling them to ask more probing and insightful questions. Clarity in financial reporting is the key to risk management in complex financial institutions. Obfuscation and complexity often suggest that senior management and the board do not truly understand and control company financial risks. Improved financial reporting contributed to positive energy and tension at TIAA-CREF because penetrating and insightful questions from senior management and the board spurred the operating and investment executives to stay alert and on their toes and to be better prepared to explain what they were doing.

I have been asked what my secret has been throughout my career, and in addition to the personal discipline and hard work I've emphasized in this book, the other main attribute that has contributed to my upward rise is my ability to boil complex problems down to their critical elements. The resulting clarity facilitates well-informed and improved decision making.

My third area of focus at TIAA was incentive compensation. It was important to create compensation programs that rewarded executives for creating value for our clients, and for achieving important financial and strategic objectives. TIAA-CREF needed to attract and retain superior professional talent, and improved financial reporting increased the confidence of the board that we could actually identify and weigh important performance metrics. Consequently, the board was supportive of senior management proposals for significant enhancements in incentive compensation tied to critical performance measures.

In his autobiography *Privilege and Prejudice: The Life of a Black Pioneer*, Dr. Wharton wrote about me:

> Tom developed a plan which had an annual individual award and a long-term component. The long-term bonus was especially creative. This bonus was based upon a rolling three-year performance measure, with the creation of summary performance measures for each unit and division to reflect the performance of peers and those who made the company successful as a whole. This collective responsibility for success and dependency upon your colleagues made it clear both conceptually and practically that all persons were part of the TIAA-CREF team, and we were mutually responsible to each other for the total outcome . . . (447–48)

Wharton also wrote about the succession planning process at TIAA-CREF:

> But though I wasn't yet ready to set the cruise control, I thought the time was approaching to begin succession planning. At least once a year I had discussed three topics with the TIAA-CREF boards: the most likely candidate to replace me; my direct reports and their own possible successors; and the top ten mid-level and/or junior officers who showed greatest potential as future leaders. Early in 1992 I began to meet individually with each of the board members to get their perspective on what qualities they were looking for in my successor, as well as their evaluation of inside candidates. For the most part, their views were congruent with my own. Aside from one director, an investment manager, who strongly championed Tom Jones, the overwhelming choice to follow me was John Biggs with Jones as his chief operating officer. (457)

In January 1993, on the heels of Bill Clinton's inauguration as president, Dr. Wharton announced that he was accepting an appointment as deputy secretary of state in the Clinton administration. TIAA-CREF then announced that John Biggs would succeed Wharton as chairman and CEO, and I would succeed Biggs as president and chief operating officer, effective January 26, 1993. Prior to joining TIAA-CREF as president in February 1989, Biggs was chairman, president, and CEO of Centerre Trust Company of St. Louis, and from 1977 to 1985 he was vice chancellor of finance and administration at Washington University in St. Louis (which was a significant TIAA-CREF client). Biggs had been a CREF board member since 1983 and was fifty-six years old. He and I had a friendly relationship, and we both participated regularly in tennis and golf with other TIAA-CREF executives. I felt fortunate to achieve this significant career success, and I felt a large measure of gratitude toward two of my direct reports in particular for the support they had given me as CFO—Dick Gibbs and Richard Adamski.

I was welcomed into the TIAA-CREF presidency with an immediate baptism by fire. The *Wall Street Journal* published an article about me on February 9, 1993, titled "The Ironic Life of a Controversial Cornellian." The article provided a superficial summary of the Willard Straight takeover and the part I played, focusing on the harshness of my oratory that week in 1969, the professors who had left Cornell in protest after the takeover, and the fact that I had since distanced myself from the kind of militancy that had led us to the occupation. The reporter also quoted me speaking about my hope to open a school for New York City boys "in need of surrogate parenting," and ended with the point that gave the article its title: "Mr. Jones will soon be able to shape Cornell policy again. In the latest of ironies, he is to become a trustee of his alma mater this summer."

I was surprised by the attention the article attracted. Clearly, every person at TIAA-CREF, and very many outside the company, had read it. By email, phone, and mail, congratulatory messages poured in for me, especially from African Americans. Nonetheless, some members of the senior management ranks expressed concern that the story might cause damage to client relationships among our predominantly college and university clientele. At TIAA-CREF board meetings, I could see doubt in the eyes of some board members who had not been aware of my background before reading the article. I felt, for a moment, that I was back in 1969—vulnerable, a target of conservatives' hostility toward any career success I might have or attain. And it would probably be like this for the duration of my career, I felt. Never, I vowed, would I give Allan Bloom or Walter Berns or other right-wing conservatives the satisfaction of pressuring me into repudiating what we black students had done at Cornell in 1969. I determined to walk a fine line—never disavowing what I had done at Cornell, but also never explicitly endorsing the threat of violence. My most effective response and best defense would be the one I'd always turned to: a commitment to professional excellence.

One good thing that resulted from this *Wall Street Journal* article was that I was contacted by Laurel Senger, principal of St. Aloysius School in central Harlem. She wanted to tell me about her school. St. Aloysius enrolled 180 students, 96 percent African American and 4 percent Latino or Asian. She had created the "Gonzaga Program" for sixth-, seventh-, and eighth-grade boys, emphasizing leadership skills, development of personal relationships, and academic achievement. Gonzaga instilled responsibility and accountability through small class size, regular group dynamics sessions, and individual counseling. The school's all-male faculty offered a challenging curriculum to prepare students for admission into competitive high schools. Classical literature, African American history, oratory contests, and museum visits were elements of the cultural enrichment program. Most of her middle school graduates succeeded in gaining admission to competitive-exam high schools, most of them graduated on schedule from high school, and most attended college.

Ms. Senger invited me to visit St. Aloysius, and I was so impressed with what I'd heard about the school that I accepted the invitation. After giving me a tour, she asked if I was serious about trying to help low-income inner-city schoolchildren. I told her I was. And so instead of trying to start something brand-new, I took the opportunity to work with her instead.

St. Aloysius students were confident. I could see it in the way they walked down the hallways and in the way they spoke in class, deeply engaged with the material, sure of their ability to discuss topics at a high level, to ask questions. I saw in the students the self-confidence and self-esteem that are critical for personal success. And I saw respect for others and positive social interactions, which are critical for social success. They were proud of their school, too. I was impressed with them and with Ms. Senger's educational track record.

As an adviser and donor to the school, I initiated a program called Courage to Succeed, which entailed three components: (1) TIAA-CREF donations of desktop computers to St. Aloysius and tutoring sessions by TIAA-CREF information systems specialists to teach computing skills; (2) fund-raising leadership by TIAA-CREF, which sponsored an annual awards and recognition dinner that raised several hundred thousand dollars each year to support scholarships for students who could not pay the tuition; and (3) classroom visits by successful minority executives whom I recruited to discuss their journeys to success in order to help Gonzaga boys visualize paths that were not part of their life experiences, and to encourage them to think that they could do the same things. I chose the title Courage to Succeed to reflect the need to confront ghetto peer group pathology, which often mocks and belittles academic high-achievers (another version of "not black enough" psychological intimidation).

In 1995 Laurel Senger sent us a short personal note:

Dear Tom and Addie,

I thank you both from the bottom on my heart for your generous personal gift. Your encouragement and consistent support have enabled us to thrive, and have attracted many other gifts. . . . but I wanted you to know, more personally, how much your support means to me. God bless you both,

Laurel

In 2003 Addie and I were the honorees at the St. Aloysius School's eleventh annual scholarship benefit cabaret. The invitation read "This year's scholarship dinner will honor Thomas and Adelaide Jones for their enduring commitment to the education of inner city children." It was a heartwarming event where we got to reflect, with the school and the students and many graduates, on all that the Courage to Succeed program had made possible in so many young men's lives.

My primary responsibility as president and chief operating officer at TIAA-CREF was to conduct the quarterly reviews focused on performance against financial and qualitative objectives for business units, investment units, and staff accountability areas. A second responsibility was to chair the Service Council, a newly created group charged with coordinating customer service improvements across business units and staff accountability areas. My third major responsibility was participation in the various investment committees that formulated and oversaw implementation of TIAA-CREF investment policies. These included the CREF Investment Committee for our publicly traded stocks in U.S. and international markets, the TIAA Mortgage and Real Estate Committee for our commercial mortgage and real estate investments, and the TIAA Finance Committee for our publicly traded and private placement bonds. In addition, I also continued to lead the annual financial strength review processes with the external ratings agencies.

CEO John Biggs and I were an effective team, and TIAA-CREF did well under our leadership. Biggs and I had a good personal relationship, and we regularly played tennis and golf together. Our only significant difference of opinion about company policies arose in 1996, when Biggs began to push his ideas to introduce a family of low-cost indexed mutual funds to attract non-pension personal savings of our individual clients, and to move TIAA-CREF back-office operations out of New York to reduce operating and compensation expenses. Biggs was an ardent admirer of John Bogle and the Vanguard Funds' low-cost index investment philosophy, and this greatly influenced his thinking. I agreed with the core objectives of Biggs's ideas, but I differed with him on some aspects of implementation. For example, I thought we should invest resources to market the new mutual funds to our clients in order to build sufficient scale more quickly. Second, I thought we should take another page from the Vanguard playbook and use TIAA-CREF's distribution power to attract talented boutique investment teams for sub-advisory management contracts for actively managed investment funds. My goal was to deepen our customer value proposition by offering customers a way to access unique investment talent that TIAA-CREF might not be able to hire as employees. Third, I was skeptical that we could sustain the most important elements of our unique company culture under a geographic configuration in which most employees were in remote locations away from New York, while senior management and the investment organization remained in Manhattan.

The June 1994 issue of *Black Enterprise* contained an in-depth profile of me written by Caroline Clarke Graves titled "#2 at the World's Largest Retirement Fund," which quoted Mark Wright, one of my colleagues at TIAA-CREF:

> Despite a penchant for numbers, being effective, Jones insists, is not about being the smartest person, or always having the right or best answer. "It's about getting the best out of other people, creating harmony, cooperativeness and a sense of purpose." Mark Wright, second vice president, pension and annuity services, and Washington, D.C., branch office manager, says Jones does just that. "I've been around here for 15 years and have reason to be jaded, but I've sat in meetings with him and I feel uplifted. I see it in other people's faces—the pride, the good feelings, the belief that what TIAA-CREF is doing is not just right, it's good. The bottom line for motivating people is getting that kind of buy-in. He gets it.

Teamwork, getting the best out of people, and infusing our employees at TIAA-CREF with a sense of purpose and pride about our company were my areas of focus as I led the company's customer service improvement initiatives. Biggs and I created a new Service Council early in 1993, shortly after we'd risen to our new leadership roles, and I chaired its first meeting in March. Not only did I bring in the executive vice presidents from each of our customer-facing divisions of the business, but also I made it a point to include managers with responsibility for front-line service. If these were the men and women wrestling with day-to-day service issues, I wanted their insight and ideas at the table. One of the council's main goals was to reshape the service infrastructure at TIAA-CREF, which entailed benchmarking our service performance against that of our peers in the industry and introducing non-trivial reforms that had a large impact on the company's way of doing things and levels of success. The October 1996 issue of *Topics*, TIAA-CREF's employee magazine, included the following it its cover story on our council and its achievements:

> Indeed, since the Council has been in existence, productivity is up, with a greater number of transactions processed in less time. For example, total telephone call volume into TIAA-CREF counseling centers and the ATS (Automated Telephone Service) is running at a five million call rate in 1996, compared to 2.9 million in 1993, but abandoned or blocked calls are now 2 to 3 percent versus double-digit percentages in 1993. In addition, while the number of allocation changes participants made between accounts increased from 140,000 in 1993 to 250,000 annual rate in 1996, the on-time record of completing the transaction within three business days is currently 100 percent, compared to seven business days in 1993. Likewise, transfers between accounts increased from 177,000 in 1993 to an annual rate of 500,000 in 1996, but 100 percent are currently completed within three business days, compared to 93 percent in seven days in 1993. While the number of transactions has grown at a phenomenal rate, the service quality scores—as measured by customer satisfaction surveys and transaction turnaround times—have significantly improved, with TIAA-CREF receiving the highest ratings from customers. For instance, a recent survey showed that 96 percent of premium-paying participants and 93 percent of paid-up participants are satisfied with the organization's overall performance.

While our customer transactions had been growing in excess of 15 percent annually between 1992 and 1996, the staff responsible for handling those transactions had grown only between 2 and 4 percent per year, and yet they were able to do the work well (in fact, better than before) because of the new efficiencies we'd put into place.

As the largest private pension system in the United States, TIAA-CREF enjoyed enormous credibility and an outstanding reputation with regard to the sound management of pension issues. My success at TIAA-CREF brought me to the attention of the Clinton administration, and I accepted President Bill Clinton's invitation to serve as a public member of the 1994 Social Security Advisory Council (SSAC). At that time, a provision of the Social Security Act required an advisory council every four years to review the status of the Social Security trust funds and their relationship to the program's long-term commitments. The 1994 council, which worked until 1996, focused on three subjects:

1. Social Security financing, including the long-range financial status of the Old-Age, Survivors and Disability Insurance (OASDI) programs.
2. Adequacy and equity of Social Security benefits paid to persons of various income levels, family situations, and age groups.
3. The relative roles of the public and private sectors in providing retirement income, and how policies in both sectors affect the retirement decisions and economic well-being of individual workers.

There was a strong push by conservatives in the late 1980s and early 1990s to allow employees to divert some or all of their individual Social Security payroll taxes into "private accounts" owned individually, and invested in an array of investment options similar to defined contribution 401(k) pensions or individual retirement annuity (IRA) accounts. The theory was that the current system places payroll taxes into the Social Security trust fund, but that since the fund is merely a government accounting fiction—because no "trust fund" with underlying invested assets actually exists—these balances are simply unsecured general obligation liabilities of the U.S. government, equivalent to government treasury bond debt. If an investment account holding underlying assets were actually owned by each individual, then the individual would in theory have the opportunity to earn a higher investment return than the treasury bond rate currently credited on Social Security trust fund balances, and the individual accounts could become part of an individual's estate. This "private account" approach, known as "Social Security privatization," was first suggested during Ronald Reagan's presidency in the 1980s. In 1995 I was invited to discuss these issues with Congressman Charles Rangel, chairman of the House Ways and Means Committee, a Democrat representing New York and one of the longest-serving members of Congress, and Senator Charles Grassley, chairman of the Senate Finance Committee, a Republican from Iowa. Rangel and Grassley were both interested primarily in probing me with questions to help improve their understanding of the pros and cons of individual accounts, in other words, Social Security privatization. I visited them in their Capitol Hill offices, and each meeting lasted approximately forty-five minutes.

Initially, in the earliest weeks of the advisory council's work, I was inclined to support one of the individual account alternatives. After all, TIAA-CREF was proof of the effectiveness of a private pension system with individual accounts. But during my first year on the council, it dawned on me that Social Security problems weren't so much a set of technical pension management questions at all. Instead, when one asked the more fundamental questions—what is the purpose of Social Security and what is the purpose of reform?—it became clear that Social Security plays a very different role in society. The advisory board, over the course of a year, formed three distinct factions. The *Washington Post* described this in a January 19, 1997, article by Brett Fromson titled "Wall Street's Social Security Maverick: To TIAA-CREF's Tom Jones, a Social Safety Net in Private Hands Isn't in America's Interest":

> One group, led by former Social Security Commissioner Robert M. Ball, championed the view that the overriding priority was to guarantee an adequate retirement income to those in the bottom half of the income distribution. A second faction—led by Sylvester J. Schieber, a vice president at Watson Wyatt Worldwide Co., a pension benefit consulting company, and Carolyn L. Weaver, a researcher at the American Enterprise Institute, a conservative think tank—emphasized privatizing Social Security through "personal security accounts." Under that approach, what someone received in retirement income would depend on the investment returns in their account. A third faction, led by advisory council Chairman Ned Gramlich, emphasized the role that Social Security could play in fostering national savings. They proposed increasing the payroll tax and mandating that money be put into individual accounts for all workers.

Through a process of elimination, I came to side with the first faction. If the size of poor people's retirement nest egg was going to be dependent on individual savings and how well they invested individual accounts in the stock market, many would be left with insufficient retirement funds, in part because their accounts would be small regardless of investment performance. And if we followed the third faction's vision, it was likely the government would still have to provide for those who selected investment strategies that performed poorly. Ultimately, Social Security had an overriding obligation to be a safety net for the nation's poor.

In January 1997 I testified on Social Security solvency and privatization issues at hearings convened in the Park Avenue headquarters of the

Council on Foreign Relations by the Senate Finance Committee and the Senate Budget Committee. The January 19 *Washington Post* article covered the event.

Jones was there as a member of the presidential Advisory Council on Social Security, and people may have assumed he would endorse the panel's proposal for putting the nation's retirement savings into the stock market via individual accounts. Jones, however, was not about to go along with the Wall Street line. He told the audience that this form of privatization was a bad idea that might hurt the ordinary Americans who depend on Social Security. "I said they were overstating the extent of Social Security's problems, waging a campaign to scare the public and then arguing that we need to privatize the system because young people don't think Social Security will be there when they retire," Jones recalled. "That strikes me as a bit disingenuous."

Jones, vice chairman and president of TIAA-CREF, is that rare maverick on Wall Street—an executive who is prepared to speak out boldly against a proposal that would enrich his firm and industry, but that he believes would harm the country. Wall Street stands to rake in hundreds of billions of dollars in fees if Social Security is privatized, according to both opponents and supporters of the idea. TIAA-CREF, which has large money management and pension consulting operations, would prosper "hugely," according to Jones, if Washington allowed the establishment of individual stock accounts. To fix the looming financial crisis of the system, Jones favors less radical steps than replacing the existing defined-benefit plan with one that would leave investment decisions up to individual recipients. He proposes modest reductions in benefits, small tax increases, and a gradual move to invest as much as 40 percent of the system's money in stocks under a giant pooled account.

Under law, Social Security "invests" the system's funds in low-risk Treasury securities that historically have not equaled the gain in stocks. Stock investing can be done by the government as part of the existing Social Security defined-benefit system, Jones argued. Jones says that he is agnostic on the actual returns to be obtained from stocks. They may match TIAA-CREF's internal forecast of a 10 percent average annual return, or the rosier 11.28 percent implicitly assumed by the advisory council. "Whatever the number is, I know based on my experience at TIAA-CREF that we can achieve higher returns for most people through a central investment fund rather than individual accounts because the costs would be lower and the discipline of professional investment managers would prevent people from mistakenly selling at market lows and buying at the tops," he said. In response to worries that politicians might use Social Security's stake in our biggest companies to push a social agenda, Jones argues that the system can be insulated from such pressure. "Social Security should divide the pool of stock investments among 10 to 20 investment managers who invest passively with an eye to getting the market rate of return rather than making bets on particular companies or industries," he said.

It is no accident that Tom Jones is both a member of the financial establishment and part of the loyal opposition. "Tom is a man of great passion," said Spencer M. Rice, the former rector of Trinity Church in Boston and a long-time counselor to Jones.

Fellow advisory council member Edith H. Fierst, partner at the Washington law firm Fierst + Moss, said . . . "I think his main interest was to make sure poor people were taken care of."

Now with some twenty-five years' hindsight, I stand by the policy positions I adopted with the 1994 Social Security Advisory Council. Most Americans who had defined-benefit pension plans replaced by 401(k) or similar defined contribution pension plans are approaching retirement with severely inadequate retirement savings. The shortfalls are driven primarily by high fees and expenses, and by poorly timed investment purchase and sale activity. Very few individuals can manage stock market investments successfully through periods of severe market turmoil such as the dot-com boom and bust in 1999–2001 or the financial crisis in 2008. The retirement income floor provided by Social Security as a defined-benefit system is even more critical to basic income adequacy for older Americans today than it was twenty-five years ago.

Outside of TIAA-CREF I began to take on additional board responsibilities. In 1992 I became a director of Thomas & Betts Corporation, a public company industrial parts manufacturer, and I also joined the Cornell University Medical College Board of Overseers and the Brookings Institution

Figure 15 / *Tom and Addie dressed for black-tie event,*
April 1995

board of trustees. In 1993 I was invited to join the Cornell University board of trustees, and served on the presidential search committee in 1994. In 1996 I was invited to hold a "public member" seat on the board of directors of the Federal Reserve Bank of New York, and was appointed vice chairman in 1997. I also joined the Public Broadcasting Corporation (WNET Channel Thirteen) board of trustees. In 1997 I joined the public company boards of Travelers Group and Freddie Mac (Federal Home Loan Mortgage Corporation). These experiences enhanced my skills by helping me develop deeper insights into different CEO leadership styles and board governance practices.

I first met Sanford Weill, CEO of Travelers Group, on the Cornell Medical College Board of Overseers, and we began to interact more frequently after I joined the Cornell University board of trustees because Sandy was on both of those boards and we often worked on the same committees. In September 1996 Sandy invited me to breakfast and asked me to join the Travelers Group board of directors, which I did in January 1997. In July Sandy invited me to lunch, and then invited Addie and me to join him and his wife, Joan, for dinner at their home later that month. Sandy and I had dinner again one week later and he asked me to become CEO of asset management at Smith Barney, the brokerage firm subsidiary of Travelers Group.

This was a very difficult decision for me. On the "no" side, I was content and satisfied with my job at TIAA-CREF, and I wasn't looking for new opportunities. I had a good relationship with John Biggs, and we were an effective team. TIAA-CREF was doing very well under our leadership, and I had formed a strong emotional bond with many TIAA-CREF employees. In the "yes" column, by contrast, one consideration was the fact that I was impressed with Sandy Weill's energy and track record, and his stated ambition of building a dominant global financial services company. Here was a man who might very well become a pioneer in his impact on the financial services industry, and the idea appealed to me to experience working with someone of that vision and stature. I've always been attracted to big personalities—people with big dreams and vision and energy and achievement.

The fall of the Berlin Wall a few years earlier and the emergence of China and the dynamic Asia Pacific economies suggested the possibility that the world might be in the early stages of a major wave of economic globalization, and here was a chance to work in global finance. While TIAA-CREF was a major global stock investor, all of its customers and business operations were in the United States, as was all of my prior professional experience at John Hancock and Arthur Young. Global business exposure and experience would strengthen my résumé.

As usual, I placed significant reliance on Addie's assessment of the situation and her recommendations.

"I love Joan," she told me. "And I think that Sandy really likes you and cares about your career." She had said the same thing about Clifton Wharton and his wife, Delores, but she was neutral in her assessment of John Biggs.

So I decided to leave TIAA-CREF and join Sandy Weill at Travelers Group. This continued a consistent pattern throughout my career: I gravitated to bosses with whom I formed an emotional bond. Perhaps this was because from the very first day of my business career, after the "black militant/guns at Cornell" branding, I was always looking over my shoulder and preparing for the worst while hoping for the best.

I went to Arthur Young to work for someone who already knew me and personally recruited me. I was also recruited to John Hancock by people who already knew me personally. I went to TIAA-CREF to work for Clifton Wharton, who personally reached out to recruit me, and who was well known for caring about the careers of his subordinates. You don't have to look far to find former subordinates who praise Dr. Wharton's positive impact on their careers and lives. But I had ended up working for John Biggs, who did not have a strong reputation in this regard. In August 1997, I went to work for Sandy Weill, who was surrounded by people whose lives had been transformed by being part of his team.

I sent a resignation memorandum to the TIAA-CREF employee community:

> I regret to inform you that I am resigning from TIAA-CREF effective August 15, 1997. Many of you have heard me speak of my desire for continual personal growth, and that is the primary factor in my resignation. I have accepted a unique opportunity to be Chairman and Chief Executive Officer of Smith Barney Asset Management, a new company being organized by the Travelers Group to consolidate their asset management business. I will also be Vice Chairman and a member of the board of directors of Travelers Group.
>
> I am especially heavy-hearted to leave you during this period of turmoil and uncertainty . . . It is important that you not misinterpret my resignation as a sign of lagging confidence in the company's future. TIAA-CREF is a great institution . . .
>
> I would like to think that you will perhaps remember me in the words of Lao Tzu, a fifth century Chinese philosopher:
>
> > *A leader is best when people barely know he exists*
> > *Not so good when people obey and acclaim him*
> > *Worse when they despise him*
> > *But of a good leader, who talks little*
> > *When his work is done, his aim fulfilled*
> > *They will say*
> > *We did it ourselves.*

I was not expecting or prepared for the emotional outpouring my resignation triggered from TIAA-CREF employees. I'm proud that the messages I received suggested that I had inspired many of my associates, and reflected the comments that Mark Wright had made about me to *Black Enterprise Magazine* several years earlier: "I've sat in on meetings with him and I feel uplifted. I see it in other people's faces—the pride, the good feelings, the belief that what TIAA-CREF is doing is not just right, it's good. The bottom line for motivating people is getting that kind of buy-in. He gets it." The emotional response made me doubt my decision. The more melancholy the letter, the more detailed in its recounting of our time together and the impact I'd made on that particular person, the more regret I felt. I gathered the many letters, printed out some of the hundreds of emails, and put them in a keepsake folder. I wondered if I would ultimately regret walking away from a unique and truly enjoyable business and life situation which I might not be able to replicate. Here are just a few of the sentiments expressed:

Mr. Jones,

Your announcement yesterday certainly took me by surprise because you had become such an integral part of TIAA-CREF, its mission, operations, and, I thought its future. While I'm saddened by your departure, I am also inspired by your personal example. Thank you for leaving behind a legacy of tremendous energy, clear thinking, and wisdom for me and others to follow. Best wishes for success and continued achievements in your new role and in your life.

Barbara Palmerino

Dear Tom,

I regret not having the opportunity to talk with you before you left TIAA. It so happens that when the announcement of your departure took place I was touring colleges with Michael (it's hard to believe that he's a senior).

I do want to take this opportunity to tell you what a privilege it's been knowing you and working for you. I've always had a deep sense of pride when I spoke to others of "our President," Tom Jones, but I've had an even greater respect for Tom Jones, the person.

I will cherish the fond memories of quiet discussions we've had on the meaning of life; the basketball games; the golf outings and the many laughs with Dick Gibbs.

Tom, I think you're the ultimate example that "good guys don't come in last." I wish you continued success, and to you, Addie, and the children I wish a life of happiness and fulfillment.

Respectfully,
Richard Adamski

Dear Mr. Jones,

It is with mixed emotions that I write you this letter. I was saddened to learn of your resignation from TIAA-CREF, yet elated to learn about your new endeavor with Smith Barney Asset Management. It is rare that people at my level are given the opportunity to work with the Vice Chairman, President and Chief Operating Officer. I am truly grateful to have been given that opportunity. What I have admired most about you is the respect and dignity that you showed your subordinates, and the genuine care that you have shown me regarding my success here at TIAA-CREF.

I will never forget your words of encouragement at the 1997 IICS Business conference on achieving maximum potential for leadership and growth. My favorite, and I quote: "only you know in your heart if you're being all that you can be. Give 100% for yourself because achieving your fullest potential is one of the greatest fulfillments possible in life."

Again, I appreciate your leadership and direction and wish you continued success in the days that lie ahead.

Sincerely,
Tonya Ramey

Dear Tom,

Although I'm happy for you, I'm sad for all of us. I always felt a great sense of reassurance knowing you were "on the case" on the 26th floor, and I already feel bereft that you are not going to be there anymore.

Deanne's voice broke several times when she announced you were leaving at this morning's marketing meeting, and I certainly shared her emotions, as did my colleagues. It's not often that the departure of a senior manager occasions such powerful feelings, and I hope you realize what an exceptional tribute they represent, not just to the job you've done but to the person you are.

All best wishes,
Bob Pilpel

Was I wise to leave TIAA-CREF? I think I'll never know. It probably would have been fairer for me to have given John Biggs the benefit of the doubt and served the entire term as his COO partner during his CEO tenure. In a prescient warning, one TIAA director, a Wall Street veteran who had advocated for me to become TIAA-CREF CEO in 1993, according to Wharton's biography, said to me as I was leaving, "Tom, I wish this wasn't happening but I also wish you well. You know, Sandy Weill attracts all kinds of people. Some of them are good and some are not so good. You should be careful."

Biggs did not step down as CEO until late 2002, which for him was one year after the normal retirement age of sixty-five, and only then in the context of newspaper reports that he was expecting to be nominated by the Securities and Exchange Commission to become the first head of the new Public Company Accounting Oversight Board (PCAOB). TIAA-CREF was left with no president in place and no obvious internal succession candidates, so the board went outside for a new CEO.

I was contacted by two members of the search committee and was encouraged to "put my hat in the ring" as a candidate for the CEO position. I responded that I would be very interested if the TIAA-CREF board wanted to offer me the position, but I declined to be one of several candidates in the search process. My reasoning was that there was a high risk for me that someone would "leak" the information regarding my candidacy and Sandy Weill would learn about it and be furious at what he would perceive as my disloyalty. I was not willing to risk losing my position at Citigroup before being assured of obtaining the CEO position at TIAA-CREF.

In late 2002 the TIAA-CREF board named Herbert Allison from Merrill Lynch as Biggs's successor. Less than one year into Allison's term, the expense-cutting ax began to fall at TIAA-CREF. The company laid off five hundred people, 8 percent of all employees. I blamed myself because I felt partly responsible. The cuts, I believe, almost certainly would not have happened if I had stayed at TIAA-CREF and become CEO. I'm certain that we would have developed growth strategies to offset expense pressures, and we would have preserved the TIAA-CREF "caring culture"—caring about customers and caring about employees.

Over the years I have stayed in touch with the TIAA-CREF alumni network in the New York metro area, and even today there's an overriding air of sadness among the alumni that TIAA-CREF took a wrong turn in the years following Biggs's tenure. Most significant was the destruction of the company culture and of TIAA's unique fixed-income investment capabilities in private placement bonds, commercial mortgages, and commercial real estate, which delivered superior investment returns and lent a critical competitive advantage. I suspect that the CEOs who followed Biggs didn't fully understand and appreciate the capabilities of the TIAA investment organization.

Sandy's Family

When I first set foot on Cornell's campus as a sixteen-year-old, my feelings were appreciation for something wonderful mixed with determination to make the most of it. When the elevator doors opened onto the lobby at Arthur Young in 1974, that same twin feeling of appreciation and ambition filled me. It happened again when I walked into the lobby of the soaring glass tower of the John Hancock Building in Boston, when I joined TIAA-CREF as chief financial officer, and when I arrived at Travelers Group as its CEO of Smith Barney Asset Management in 1997. This was the Big League of Wall Street. The *New York Times*, the *Wall Street Journal*, and *Business Week* all ran major stories covering me and my move from TIAA-CREF to Travelers. Press and pressure, and the great potential for success or failure, had the same effect on me as always: I resolved to do the best job I was capable of.

Among the resources at Travelers were many brilliant financial minds. In my first few weeks there, I was nearly always in one-on-one meetings with Smith Barney Asset Management's (SBAM) money managers and department heads—the people whose work I would oversee. On my second day, I called Joe Deane, one of the best fixed-income bond managers in the country, and asked if he was free to meet with me. Down on his floor, I introduced myself to the entire bond team, asked questions to get to know them, and then I sat with Joe. He ran the tax-exempt side of the fixed-income bond operation and was responsible for a series of long-term-bond mutual funds. A Staten Island native, he'd started with E. F. Hutton in 1972, which then merged with Shearson, which was later bought by Smith Barney. He graduated from college in New Rochelle in 1969, the same year I graduated from Cornell. To keep himself from being drafted and sent to Vietnam, he joined the Army Reserve and started working in finance right out of school.

Another particularly talented member of my team was Henry "Hersh" Cohen, senior stock portfolio manager. Hersh had come over to money management from an earlier career in neurobiology. He had a Ph.D., but during his postdoctoral work at Albert Einstein College of Medicine, he'd realized two things: he couldn't spend every day in a lab by himself, and he loved making money in the stock market. He'd invested small amounts of his university stipend on Kodak, RCA, and Exxon and done well. After leaving academia, Hersh joined a new asset management and brokerage firm in 1969, Hornblower & Weeks. By the time I met him, he was already a Wall Street legend for the good performance of his stock mutual funds. I liked his passion and single-mindedness, as well as his natural leadership with the other money managers on the team. Joe and Hersh were SBAM's investment leaders, in terms of both their investment performance and their personalities.

In my first weeks, I also had individual introductory meetings with my fellow business unit senior executives including Jamie Dimon, Mike Carpenter, Joe Plumieri, Bob Willumstad, Bob Lipp, and Marge Magner, all of whom I would be in close proximity to for longer periods of time than I might have anticipated thanks to Sandy Weill's management style.

The Travelers Planning Group meetings were held once a month at the company conference center in Armonk, New York, a wealthy town one hour from the city in Westchester County. The meetings started with cocktails and dinner on the first day, and continued for a full day through dinner on the second night. The entire top management team of approximately fifteen line and staff executives were mandatory attendees and stayed overnight at the conference center. Starting in the morning in the mountain lodge–style great room, we'd sit by the fireplace on comfortable lounge chairs and couches arranged in a circle, which Sandy intended to create a sense of teamwork and partnership. Each business unit head presented current performance against key financial, operations, and strategic metrics, and anyone from any other unit could comment on any aspect of a business unit's performance—a practice that had the potential to gather valuable input and foster a sense of camaraderie and engagement on major strategic initiatives. But it also allowed for political gamesmanship to abound and territorial tension to grow.

At my first Planning Group meeting, in September, Sandy disclosed to us that he was engaged in merger discussions with the investment bank Salomon Brothers, pioneer of the mortgage-backed security. This would represent a dramatic change in the company I had just joined. Sure enough, one week later, on September 24, Travelers Group announced the merger, a $9 billion deal to purchase Salomon. The October 6 *Business Week* cover story was headlined "Sandy's Triumph: By Buying Salomon, He Thrusts Travelers into Wall Street's Top Tier." We would now become, by Sandy's estimation, among the top three or four global investment banking firms in the world.

If there was one skill set Sandy had demonstrated in his career, it was extraordinary and disciplined cost cutting. He was good at buying companies in trouble and immediately taking cost out of them by reducing headcount, office space, and other overhead expenses. As the *Business Week* story put it, "His modus operandi has been to buy cheap and then cut deep." Because the lion's share of expense cuts is to personnel—including top management, whose salaries and benefits are considerable—the merger meant that some top people at Salomon suddenly didn't have the job security they'd enjoyed the day before. The question hung in the air: Who will survive the cuts? And the more significant question for the business's future was: How will the newly merged companies be managed? How will they work together?

It was time for me to take stock of my counterparts at Salomon and see just that: how we could work together. On September 24 I had dinner with Thomas Brock, CEO of Salomon Asset Management. My purpose was to forge a personal relationship, discuss the relative strengths and weaknesses of our two asset management businesses, and develop a roadmap of the synergies we would try to achieve. Even though I'd been around Wall Street for years, I was naïve. This was my first merger. What I didn't know was that mergers bring out Wall Street culture at its coarsest. In some respects it is life or death, a street fight. I had not been privy to that process before and wasn't even aware at first that a fight was under way. I did not fully understand that the only thing someone like Thomas Brock would be reaching out with now that he was heading a redundant department in a bought-out company was a knife. Two weeks later we met again. This time he'd brought with him his two top lieutenants–chief operating officer Michael Hyland and general counsel Gary Shapiro. Brock made it clear that he thought *he,* not I, should be the surviving CEO of asset management. I immediately shifted my focus to developing relationships with the three best-performing Salomon investment management teams, led by Peter Wilby, Ross Margolies, and Rick White. Brock met with Sandy Weill to press his case to be named CEO of asset management and then accepted a severance package when told that Weill wanted me to be CEO. Mike Hyland was also let go, along with most of Salomon Asset Management's administration and operations units. Most important, however, was that we were successful in retaining virtually all of Salomon's key investment managers and assets under management while eliminating significant operating costs.

Just as I had faced a media "baptism of fire" in 1993 when I was named president of TIAA-CREF, I now encountered a new round of media scrutiny. In November 1997 the *Wall Street Journal* ran a front-page article about my older brother Edward and me which carried the headline "All in the Family: The Jones Brothers Frame a 'Great Debate' over Success and Race. Can Blacks in Corporations Be True to Themselves? Ed Says No, Tom Says Yes. Vietnam Vet vs. '60s Radical." The story, which was written by Jonathan Kaufman and Anita Raghavan, was extraordinarily long; it filled the entire right-hand column on the front page plus a full page inside the first section of the paper. I had known the article was coming, of course, because I'd given interviews to the reporters, but that morning, when I first saw it on my desk at work, I was surprised that the most important business newspaper in America had given such prominence to this black family/human interest/ American racial-progress story, a story that revealed so much about my family dynamics. The fundamental fairness of the tone and content deepened my respect for the journalistic quality of the *Wall Street Journal,* at that time under Bancroft family ownership.

This story, which detailed my career, my brief stint as a campus radical, and my philosophy on race and achievement as contrasted to my brother Ed's career and philosophy, had an important unintended bonus of introducing my new colleagues at Travelers to me in a way that reinforced their perception of me as a successful and important figure. Their respect made it easier for me to be effective in doing my job. Also, I was pleasantly surprised by the numerous expressions of sympathy I received from people who perceived me as having to manage what struck many readers as a difficult brother's jealousy and ill will. It was comforting to realize that outsiders had come to the same conclusion I had—that my brother was too bitter to be proud of or happy about my success and that he'd ceased being my friend.

My brother Ed was unable to see that his ego was his biggest barrier to success, and he was unwilling to acknowledge that he had been treated very generously by corporate America. In the early 1970s, following his military service in Vietnam and in the early days of corporate affirmative action, Ed was a junior executive at New York Telephone Company, where he was designated "high potential" by the CEO and sent to Harvard Business School, all expenses paid. To Ed's credit, he did well at HBS and graduated with high honors as a Baker Scholar. But Ed got so cocky and full of himself that he became an ineffective leader because other highly talented people did not want to work for him. His career stalled and he grew embittered. In his own eyes he was more qualified than anyone else, but he never rose to the top. He chose to blame racism rather than blame himself.

In any event, I focused all my energies on my job. I concentrated on business performance. The key to growing asset management revenue and earnings was to increase our sales volume in the various Travelers Group distribution channels. To increase the market share of proprietary mutual funds and managed accounts, I maintained an intense pace of "due diligence meetings" with the sales organizations at the brokerage firm Smith Barney and the insurance company Primerica. My standard agenda was to discuss my commitment to excellence in the asset management business, highlight our best-performing investment products, and ask for their support in increasing sales of proprietary products so that we would have the financial resources to invest in building excellence. I asked them to give me the benefit of the doubt, to trust me to deliver on my promises. I would usually be accompanied by two or three of our top portfolio managers—Joe and Hersh, for instance—who would discuss the current investment climate and outlook for the stock and bond markets. I was also invited to make presentations at the Smith Barney and Primerica rewards and professional development meetings for top sales producers. My "road show" usually attracted one hundred to two hundred sales professionals to each due diligence meeting. In 1998 I presented at approximately twenty-five events in New York City, Atlanta, Boston, Chicago, Los Angeles, San Francisco, Minneapolis, Denver, Miami, Rochester, Rye, New Brunswick, Bermuda, Atlantic City, Dana Point, Lake Tahoe, Beaver Creek, and Boca Raton.

In January of 1998, Travelers and Salomon senior management was invited to a Planning Group dinner with our spouses at Armonk. It felt like the *Godfather* movies: food, wine, music, the mixing of business with family. I knew the idea stemmed from Sandy's genuine desire to inculcate teamwork and a family-like culture among his top management team. He wanted us to bond personally as well as professionally. Unfortunately, professional and personal animosities between "Travelers people" and "Salomon people" simmered just beneath the surface. Addie, an astute observer with a world-class poker face, noticed the tension but never for a second let on through word or gesture that these dinners were anything less than perfectly comfortable. She made conversation effortlessly. "Maybe you should have been a talk show host," I teased her one night after a company dinner. She would have made an excellent TV personality if she'd had any interest in that, because Addie is a person who always has her nose in a book or a magazine, knows about all the latest films and museum shows, and can speak with nearly anyone on any topic.

Just a few months into the Travelers-Salomon merger integration efforts, Sandy called all of us in his senior management team to attend an urgent dinner meeting at the Armonk Conference Center on Sunday, April 5, 1998. "I've come to an agreement with John Reed," he announced when he had us all gathered. "We're going to do a merger with Citibank. We'll announce the Travelers-Citibank merger agreement tomorrow, Monday morning." This news was stunning in its audacity. The combined entity would have approximately $700 billion total assets, $75 billion annual revenues, and $6 billion annual net income. In addition to being on this unprecedented scale, the proposed merger also broke new legal and regulatory ground by proposing to overcome the depression-era Glass-Steagall Act, which separated commercial banking and investment banking. As was his custom, Sandy once again pulled spouses into the fold by hosting a Travelers board and senior management dinner on April 22 at Carnegie Hall.

I was named CEO of the combined Travelers-Citibank-Salomon asset management businesses, contingent upon the merger receiving the requisite regulatory approvals. I had been confident that Sandy would be loyal to me, barring an overwhelming case favoring my Citibank or Salomon counterparts—and there was no such case.

As soon as my new position was announced, I reached out to the various parts of the Citibank and Salomon investment businesses around the world. I met with Peter Carman, my Citibank Asset Management counterpart on April 6. In May I visited the London offices of both Citibank Asset Management and Salomon Asset Management. In June I traveled to Frankfurt,

London, Melbourne, and Sydney. In July I visited Tokyo, Singapore, Hong Kong, and Beijing. I went to London again in September, and to Tokyo again in both September and November. My goal was to make the key people in these asset management business units feel that they were important to the future of the new combined business, and to let them know that they had a personal relationship with the asset management CEO. Asset management is a talent-driven business, and it was important to stabilize the organization. I knew that our most talented people were probably receiving calls from headhunters exploring their willingness to consider outside employment offers. I didn't want any of them to say, "It's been months since the merger announcement, and I haven't even met the guy who's supposed to be my boss."

The Travelers-Citibank merger received all required regulatory approvals and was completed on October 6, 1998. The *Wall Street Journal* ran an article on October 15 by Paul Beckett titled "Citigroup Is to Name Asset Managers and, Again, Most Are from Travelers." The article read in part:

> Citigroup Inc. is expected to announce today the new hierarchy in its $300 billion asset-management business and, again, managers from Travelers Group will take most of the top jobs.
>
> The three chief operating officers of the business lines within the global asset-management business are from Travelers. And they will report to Tom Jones, chief executive officer of the asset-management business. Mr. Jones, whose appointment was announced in the spring, was chairman of Travelers' Salomon Smith Barney Asset Management unit.

On October 21–25, 1998, the new Citigroup senior management team, plus spouses and significant others, met at the Greenbrier, an exuberantly decorated golf resort sprawling over a few hundred acres in a natural mineral spring town in West Virginia. Since its original founding in 1778, the Greenbrier has hosted twenty-seven U.S. presidents and many members of Congress. While Greenbrier County is virtually all white, much of the resort's staff is recruited from Jamaica, Asia, and eastern Europe, so one has the interesting experience of being waited on by West Virginia mountain people whose families have worked at the Greenbrier for generations, along with blacks, Cambodians, and Ukrainians. We rented out the entire resort and had the wide hallways—which were covered in carpets printed with over-the-top floral patterns in bright colors (clashing wildly with the wall-papered walls)—and dining room and ballroom to ourselves.

It seemed to me that intimacy and teamwork were values Sandy pretended to himself we already had, but we didn't. We on his team usually didn't follow those practices with one other. We were running separate businesses, and in the end, everybody knew you'd better get your numbers done.

That weekend there was a significant undercurrent of tension and uncertainty. Regarding the strategic roadmap for combining the businesses, almost none of the important decisions had been made. For one thing, both the Travelers and Citibank management teams had been in limbo while awaiting regulatory approvals since the merger announcement in April. And there had been little detailed merger integration planning or collaboration during the intervening six months because Travelers and Citibank were still legally competitors. Since the proposed merger might not receive the required approvals, the two companies could not legally work together yet on business strategies, lest it be deemed collusion. A second major source of underlying anxiety was the yet to be completed "work in process" merger integration between Smith Barney and Salomon, which was now overlaid with integrating the Citibank corporate client businesses too.

The merger was what one *Business Week* reporter would later call "a vast, audacious project." Indeed, a global company that was selling insurance, credit cards, corporate banking services, investment banking services, and mutual funds hadn't yet ironed out who was in charge or what processes and business rules would be followed.

On Saturday evening after dinner, Addie and I swayed to the music on a dance floor crowded with my colleagues and their wives. We heard loud talking, and suddenly it got even louder and angrier. It was coming from only a few feet away, near the center of the dance floor. Jamie Dimon and former Salomon Brothers CEO Deryck Maughan had been shouting at each other, and now they were actually pushing each other back and forth, like boys on a schoolyard. I glanced at Addie and her expression was carefully neutral, but I knew from living with her for so many years that she was thinking something along the lines of an unimpressed "Are they serious?" Jamie's lieutenant Steve Black had apparently asked Deryck's wife, Va, to dance, and Deryck hadn't reciprocated with the expected gallantry by asking Debbie Black to dance. Steve Black's intended goodwill gesture had morphed into insult and anger at the perceived slight. Jamie intervened to confront Deryck over the insult to Steve, and angry words and shoves commenced.

I'd noticed Steve dancing with Va and thought in passing, "That's nice," although I myself wasn't going around asking other men's wives to dance. Sure, maybe to Steve's mind he was making a nice gesture. But how could he be so certain Deryck had understood? Maybe Deryck had been too engrossed in conversation even to notice! For all I knew, Deryck, when confronted about not asking Steve's wife to dance, might have replied, "What the fuck are you talking about?" It wasn't obvious to anybody outside that little group what was happening. All we knew was that our spouses had been there to see and hear it unfold, and that it was embarrassing.

This confrontation had the effect of ending the first Citigroup senior management retreat on a sour note. Jamie had been evincing significant frustration with the Salomon situation for several months and clearly believed Sandy had overpaid for the Salomon acquisition. He had voiced comments along those lines in several Planning Group meetings, to such an extent that I had taken it upon myself to suggest that he try a more circumspect approach. "Be careful," I told Jamie. "You might be close to creating an untenable confrontation with Sandy. Don't force his hand."

Jamie was frustrated by the difficult merger integration challenges facing his business unit, Corporate and Investment Banking. It was what was called a client coverage business model, in which bankers sought to forge advisory relationships with senior executives—especially CEOs—at client companies. If both Travelers and Salomon investment bankers had such relationships at a particular company, it was likely that the company would find it time-consuming and confusing to have both bankers continue calling to present the combined Travelers-Salomon platform. While it was necessary to rationalize the client coverage model, it was by no means assured that the combined Travelers-Salomon unit would retain all the business that a client had awarded previously to the separate firms. It was not uncommon to encounter negative merger synergies, that is, when one plus one equaled . . . one (as opposed to positive synergy, in which the sum of one and one can equal three). It was possible that the acquiring company in the merger was paying for business revenue and earnings that would evaporate post-merger.

This unresolved challenge facing Jamie was compounded by the Citibank merger, because Citibank had its own client coverage model for many of the same corporate clients. While I sympathized with Jamie's frustration, I thought it was unwise and undisciplined for him to be as vocal as he was. It was clear to me that Sandy was interpreting Jamie's complaints as personal criticism.

I liked Jamie and thought he was very talented, and I appreciated that he and his wife, Judy, had graciously invited Addie and me to dinner twice in the prior year to help make us feel welcome in the company. But Jamie's frustration continued boiling over. The unfortunate outcome was that Sandy Weill and John Reed requested Jamie's resignation in early November, presumably to send a message to the senior management team that interpersonal conflicts would not be tolerated.

Michael Carpenter from Travelers and Victor Menezes from Citibank were named co–chief executive officers of the Global Corporate and Investment Bank, as successors to Dimon. The Global Consumer business unit also had co-heads, with Robert Lipp from Travelers and William Campbell from Citibank as co–chief executive officers. So the two largest business units were led by co-heads, mirroring Sandy Weill's and John Reed's titles as Citigroup co-chairman and co–chief executive officer. I was the exception, as sole CEO of Citigroup Asset Management, but I was hearing rumors that Peter Carman from Citibank was agitating behind the scenes to be elevated to co-head status as well. This unwieldy management structure generally slowed decision making throughout the company, as all significant issues in the two largest business units required agreement between co-heads.

I made good progress with the asset management merger integration, and we retained almost all our significant client accounts and talented managers. I was pleased when the Citigroup 1998 annual report called out some of our unit's accomplishments:

> Asset Management's assets under management grew 25% over the prior year with strong growth in all major asset categories. Contributing to the year over year increase was . . . cross-selling efforts throughout the organization resulting in $10 billion of long-term mutual fund sales (up 67% from 1997), strong growth in institutional and private client separately managed account assets, and the overall positive impact of market performance on all asset management products.
>
> Asset Management business income of $273 million in 1998 was up $30 million or 12% from 1997 . . . Revenues, net of interest expense, rose 18% to $1,244 million in 1998 . . . This increase is predominantly in advisory fee revenues and reflects the broad growth in assets under management.

Sandy continued trying very hard to bring the senior management team together in a "family" culture. He would talk about family and the importance of knowing one another and knowing the other executives' spouses, for all of this, he explained, creates a team. I think he saw himself as the father, the Godfather figure, of a team that was close-knit. Of course, the people who were cut every time a new company was acquired—they weren't part of the family. We were getting rid of the mess, cleaning up the inefficiencies. But now, after that cleanup, whoever was left was supposedly "part of the family." I understood, however, that only his very loyal inner circle was really part of the family.

In January 1999, we held a five-day retreat with spouses at Saranac Lake in the Adirondacks, where Sandy and Joan had a lodge and camp. In March, we had a dinner with spouses to celebrate Sandy's birthday. In April, Sandy took a group of his senior executives to Augusta National Golf Club for a weekend of golf shortly after the Masters Tournament. And in September, Sandy and Joan hosted a family apple-picking picnic at their estate in Greenwich, Connecticut. We were all familiar with one another's complete wardrobes by now—from formal wear to apple-picking jeans to golf shorts. We had danced together, eaten together, swum together, and chatted with one another's spouses. Despite it all, Wall Street generally perceived Citigroup to be struggling with management and culture conflicts. At one of the Planning Group meetings, following tense discussions on business unit strategies and performance, Citigroup general counsel Charles Prince asked an ironic rhetorical question: "If we held a reunion twenty-five years from now, I wonder how many of us like each other enough that we would attend?"

The June 7, 1999, *Business Week* cover story was titled "Citigroup: Is This Marriage Working?" illustrated by photographs of both John Reed and Sandy Weill. The story hinted at tension between Sandy and John and pointed to their stark differences in leadership style. Sandy was a cost cutter who "lives for the next acquisition," the writer pointed out, whereas John Reed was a long-term visionary who believed that good business processes and smart spending were the way to go.

I liked John Reed. He was a tightly contained man who looked like a marathon runner. At the Godfather meetings, he avoided the buffets and seemed impatient for the wining and dining to end and the work to start. He had a reputation for being coldly analytical, but I respected his rationality and his focus on results. In the 1980s, he'd been the whiz kid responsible for the development of the Citibank ATM network, and his success at pulling that off had propelled him to the top. Being on his team was not about being his friend. In fact, historically the people below him who seemed to be likely successors somehow had a habit of disappearing. He was not magnanimously grooming his own replacement.

The one thing I knew John particularly prided himself on was his technique for running a global organization. It was a technique that had led to Citibank earning a wonderful reputation over the years before its merger with us for attracting and developing the very best young talent out of each country—India, Latin America, Asia, and throughout Europe. Early in their careers, people with special potential would join Citibank's international services organization. Like diplomats in the Foreign Service, they would go through a series of postings, gaining experience in different countries and different businesses and, over the years, becoming a cadre of elite global citizens who could see the big picture, beyond the perspective of any particular country or business unit. Not only that, but also they developed a deep loyalty to Citibank, and an affinity for the Citibank business processes. In this way, John Reed had built a global corporation that adhered, no matter where in the world it was operating, to a common set of business standards and procedures.

The bedrock of Citibank's business process was something called the "six-quarter roll." These were quarterly business reviews that required each business to come to the New York headquarters for two-to-three-day meetings a couple of weeks before quarterly earnings were released. The six-quarter roll meant that they would present financial statements and other key metrics for the two most recent past quarters, the current quarter, and three quarters going forward, for a total of six quarters. In effect: Here's what we looked like two quarters back. Here's what we look like now. Here's what we're predicting we'll look like next quarter and two more quarters beyond that. John developed this practice so he could really see the businesses—really get a picture—and all the pictures had to be painted with the same-size brushes, on the same canvas, following the same rules. The six-quarter roll addressed the problem of having multiple businesses spread across every corner of the globe, letting senior management look at each unit's key variables, risks, and financial characteristics.

But the Travelers people hated the six-quarter roll. They grumbled that it was too much bureaucracy. "This is all just b.s.," many thought. They resented the control that is imposed by that kind of process—the control of transparency. Of course, under Travelers' old method, they also had to talk about what the future earnings results were going to be, as with the six-quarter roll, but they could more or less choose which aspects of the future other than earnings they were making projections about. But under Citibank, those aspects were strictly defined by corporate. This can be a really binding system when you're talking about risk dimensions. What exactly are going to be the risk characteristics of your loan portfolio, your credit loss experience, the precise characteristics of your borrowers, their credit scores? The Citibank method required business heads to have transparent command of their business at a granular level, which appealed to me. It seemed to me that transparency and accountability were the path to a world-class operation.

While I was concerned with the lack of cohesion between Sandy and John, I was pleased that asset management was making good progress. I maintained my focus on trying to drive revenue growth momentum through sales growth in affiliated channels and through retaining and growing our institutional client assets and trying to build a sense of connection and teamwork with key leaders around the world in our global business. My 1999 travel schedule was intense and demanding, including twenty Smith Barney financial consultant and branch manager "due diligence" meetings across the United States. My international travels included many institutional client meetings to reassure clients that our existing investment teams were stable, and to build momentum for winning new business. My itineraries included three trips to Europe, two to Asia, two to Australia, and one trip to South America.

One day, on the corporate jet on a flight from New York to California, Joe Deane and I were sitting opposite each other, reading our newspapers. I glanced over at him and suddenly wondered what he thought about my involvement with the takeover of Willard Straight Hall at Cornell. Joe and I spent hundreds of hours in close proximity to each other every month, played golf occasionally, worked as a team looking at new investment issues, talking about bonds in the secondary market, pitching institutional salespeople all over the country and the world, but I didn't know how he'd reconciled my Cornell history with what he knew of me in the present, as his boss.

"Joe," I said. He looked up from his paper and lowered it to his lap. "Yeah?" he asked.

"Do you have a problem with what went on at Cornell?"

Joe was quiet for a beat. Then he said, "Yes, I do. You knew you were going to probably get arrested, right?"

"Yes," I said.

"And you must have known you'd be photographed. Then what were you doing wearing those red high-top Converse sneakers? After you bought your pair, they gave the rest to charity they were so ugly."

So, he'd studied the famous photograph of us leaving the Straight with our weapons, followed by the university officials. We laughed and both turned back to reading our papers.

In August I was rewarded for my hard work and team-building efforts by having Citigroup's private banking unit moved under my leadership. This would represent a doubling of assets under my unit's management. A *Wall Street Journal* article by Paul Beckett headlined "Citigroup Merges Asset-Management, Private-Banking Units in Boost to Jones" detailed the move and speculated on my chances of eventually becoming Citigroup's CEO, "though neither of the current co-chief executives, Sanford I. Weill and John S. Reed, are expected to leave soon."

The Citigroup 1999 annual report showed my new business, Global Investment Management and Private Banking Group (GIMPBG), with revenues that year of $2.7 billion and net income of $604 million. The text read in part:

> Global Investment Management and Private Banking core income in 1999 of $604 million, up $95 million or 19% from 1998, reflecting improving revenue momentum, which outpaced moderate increases in expenses and the provision for credit losses. Revenue growth was primed by the continued growth in managed assets in most sectors, while expense increases were driven by investments in technology, and sales and marketing capabilities . . . Aggregate assets under management totaled $364 billion as of December 31, 1999, up 11% from $327 billion in 1998 . . . Approximately $269 billion is managed in the United States, $58 billion in Europe, $23 billion in Japan, $8 billion in Latin America, $5 billion in Australia, and $1 billion in Asia Pacific. Cross-selling efforts helped fuel a 12% increase in institutional client assets to $155 billion, with the Corporate Bank channel generating $8 billion in sales. Sales of proprietary mutual funds represented 34% of Salomon Smith Barney's retail channel mutual fund sales for the year versus 31% in 1998. Sales of Smith Barney Private Client separately managed accounts were up 117% from the prior year. Citi Asset Management Group sold $3.0 billion of mutual and money funds through the Citibank consumer bank in Europe in 1999. In Japan, 1999 sales through both the Citibank consumer bank and nonproprietary channels generated $2.9 billion in mutual and money funds.

There was a Citigroup Management Committee retreat at the Boulders resort in Scottsdale, Arizona, February 9–13, 2000. Each business unit and corporate function reported progress against key strategic and financial objectives and three-year-forward plans. We had multiple meals together, and time for recreation. There was nothing unusual or remarkable about this retreat until the last afternoon session on the next-to-last day, when Sandy insisted on going around the room and having everyone say what was uppermost on our minds. Bob Lipp, co-head of Global Consumer, was the second or third person to speak. He said that the co-CEO situation with Sandy and John was creating a heavy burden for their direct reports, who often received conflicting directions and signals. This management confusion was making it difficult for business units to make crisp decisions and react quickly to marketplace dynamics. He said furthermore that in his opinion, the co-CEO structure should be ended and resolved in favor of one or the other—John or Sandy—and that the same consolidation of power should happen in every business unit that was now burdened with dual leadership.

My ears perked up immediately. This was highly unusual. A supposedly unscripted challenge to the prevailing management structure thrown down in an open discussion forum? I didn't buy that it was coincidental or spontaneous. My suspicions were reinforced when Sandy immediately pounced on Lipp's comment and said he would like to hear what everyone else in the room thought. One by one we spoke, with every former Travelers executive and most former Citibank executives saying they agreed with Lipp. I suspected that this might have been planned by Sandy and Lipp. When my turn came, my maverick personality wouldn't let me just quietly go with the flow. Not only did I disagree with Lipp's analysis, but also I didn't like the idea of being bullied into compliance by mob action.

"You know, I think the current managerial stalemate is okay," I said. "At this stage in our evolving merger, it's probably best for the company to tolerate stalemate a bit longer, to allow enough time for employees to discern and absorb the best elements of each company culture." Sandy was watching me hard. The others were very still. "For instance," I went on, "Travelers is probably better at managing businesses and achieving superior business execution, while Citibank is probably better at attracting talent from diverse cultures around the world, training them to a common and consistent set of operational processes and corporate values, and implementing oversight and control processes that allow decentralized decision making twenty-four hours a day around the globe. If we end this co-CEO stalemate too early, it might appear that one culture has won and the other culture's lost, which would hurt our ability to retain the best elements of the losing culture." The room was momentarily silent after I spoke, then it was the turn of the next person in the circle to weigh in.

My comment almost got me fired. On the way to dinner that evening I encountered Sandy in the hallway. He looked at me angrily and said, "So stalemate is okay, huh?" and kept on walking. Back in New York three days later, I was summoned early in the morning to go see Sandy. His assistant told my assistant that I was to report to Sandy's office "immediately." I had just arrived at work, and my diary says it was 7:15 am.

Sandy was sitting behind his desk, and his eyes were very cold as he looked at me. He didn't invite me to sit down. Without preamble, he said again with a chill in his voice, "So you think stalemate between me and John is okay?" It suddenly flashed through my mind: He's going to fire me! All these years later, I'm still sure that my hunch was correct. I steeled myself to speak slowly and quietly. I said, "Sandy, you're surrounded by people who tell you what they think you want to hear. I don't do that. I tell you honestly what I think. I may or may not be right in my opinions, but I'm honestly trying to help you. And I think you're better off having someone like me around you. But if you think that firing me is going to make things better, then so be it. It won't be the end of my life. I'll survive." There was a long silence, with Sandy staring intently at my eyes and face. I met his gaze and my eyes didn't waver. I was not afraid. I felt both calm and alert. It seemed as if the silence lasted for at least two or three minutes. Finally, Sandy said, "You're right, I'm better off with you than without you." Then he half-smiled and waved me away. Our meeting was over.

Sandy got his way in the end. John Reed was out. He announced his retirement in February. For two years he'd hung on as co-chairman, but in January, Bob Lipp, who headed the largest part of the business (global consumer banking), threatened to leave Citigroup if the dual leadership situation wasn't resolved. An emergency board meeting was called, and John proposed that both he and Sandy step down simultaneously. But Sandy had been working behind the scenes, I suspect, to line up his own support on the board, and the board decided that since John had been willing to leave, albeit along with Sandy, he should be willing to take a demotion. A front-page *Wall Street*

Journal story on April 14, 2000, titled "Alone at the Top: How John Reed Lost the Reins of Citigroup to His Co-Chairman" by Charles Gasparino and Paul Beckett described those final moments of the board meeting:

> As the hours stretched on and Mr. Reed waited, he became increasingly fed up. He thought, "I'm not going to stick around to save the world," according to the account he later gave an associate. Eventually, Mr. Franklin Thomas emerged from the boardroom with a proposal: Mr. Reed could stay on as nonexecutive chairman, while Mr. Weill became the sole chief executive (the two had been co-CEOs as well as co-chairmen). Mr. Reed declined. "It wouldn't be good for the company," he told Mr. Thomas, according to an associate of Mr. Reed. Mr. Thomas returned to the boardroom, and shortly thereafter the board made its unanimous decision: Mr. Reed would retire. Mr. Weill had won.

In the same month, I attended both Sandy's sixty-seventh birthday party and John Reed's retirement party. Sandy's party was uproarious, celebratory. He wore a fake white beard, to go along with the biblical theme he'd decided on, and Charles Prince as master of ceremonies and narrator recited these lines, obviously alluding to the co-chairmen situation we'd just exited: "We have been lost now for two years, wandering in the desert. Now Moses saves us and brings us to the Promised Land!" *The Wall Street Journal* noted that Prince later that night added an aside: "You know, Sandy, Moses never made it to the Promised Land."

John Reed's retirement cocktail party had a much different vibe and theme. It was smaller and more somber, held in a conference room in the iconic Citibank building on Lexington Avenue. There were drinks and hors d'oeuvres, but no music. The only speeches were made by veteran Citibank executives, none from the Travelers side of the family, and very few Travelers people were even in attendance.

Paul Collins, John's longtime vice chairman at Citicorp, praised him by saying that his legacy was fourfold, consisting of: (1) a great global consumer business; (2) a culture of intellectual rigor, high standards of excellence, and absolute integrity; (3) the Five Point Plan in 1990–1992 to rebuild Citibank from the brink of insolvency; and (4) the Citigroup merger, which had potentially created the dominant global financial services company. I felt that Paul's remarks were thoughtful and gave a fair assessment of John's career; it was clear they were appreciated by John. And although I didn't know it at the time, Chuck Prince's humor was ironically accurate. In some respects Sandy never did enter the Promised Land with Citigroup, because regulatory investigations soon began to engulf the company.

Arguably, the year 2000 was the pinnacle of Citigroup's overall success. The Citigroup 2000 annual report was titled *Lead. By Example.* The "Financial Highlights" page showed Citigroup's net revenue of $77.7 billion and a core income of $14.1 billion, up 14 percent and 25 percent, respectively, over 1999. Sandy Weill's letter to shareholders read, in part:

Dear Fellow shareholder:

In a short amount of time, Citigroup has emerged as the most exciting financial services company in the world, a place where clients want to do business and employees want to build their futures. Our intense focus on our clients and employees has resulted in record performance for our shareholders.

Just two years after Citicorp reported income of $3.5 billion and Travelers reported $2.9 billion, the combined company has more than quadrupled each of these figures. Clearly, Citigroup is not a larger version of Travelers or Citicorp but a new company altogether, with more exciting growth possibilities than either predecessor had alone.

Our achievements are the result of the energy and commitment of 230,000 people working in more than 100 countries. I am very proud of their efforts to make Citigroup the great company we have built today, and the even greater company we will build tomorrow.

Our record core income of $14.14 billion made us one of the most profitable companies in the world, with all of our businesses contributing to those results. Our total equity topped $71 billion, giving us a superior capital position among financial services providers. This solid capital base provides us the means to be both strategic and opportunistic, as well as endure and prosper, during turbulent economic times.

Our return on common equity reached 24 percent. Importantly, your stock closed the year at $51.06, up 22 percent—which was

28.4 percent better than the performance of the Dow Jones Industrial Average. What's more, we have delivered to our shareholders
a 110 percent total return on their investment over the last eight
quarters.

The new model of financial services we are building rests on
three pillars that, put together, give us significant advantage. First,
we have created more distribution channels—both physical and
virtual—than any other company in financial services, serving customer segments across the entire wealth spectrum. Second, we have
created an unparalleled global footprint, being locally embedded
in more than 100 countries and the leading nondomestic player
in most. Third, the breadth of our products and services creates
cross-service opportunities through our global distribution channels that are unavailable to any other company in the industry. This
unique combination of competencies gives us enormous strategic
flexibility for growth.

The final paragraphs of Sandy's letter recognized senior managers and directors who retired in 2000, including Paul Collins, Edgar Woolard, Keith
Hughes, and Bob Lipp. It did not say a word about John Reed.

The 2000 annual report showed my business, GIMPBG, with $3.3 bil-
lion total revenues, up 22 percent from 1999; a net income of $674 million,
up 12.5 percent from 1999; and assets under management of $401 billion,
up 6 percent from 1999 in a difficult stock market environment. The report
also emphasized the success of GIMPBG cross-marketing initiatives. "Sales
of proprietary mutual funds and managed accounts rose 30% to $21 billion
in the Salomon Smith Barney (SSB) brokerage channel and represented
41% of SSB's total retail channel sales for the year. Sales of mutual funds
through Global Consumer Bank were $13 billion, representing 56% of
total channel sales. Primerica sold $1.8 billion of proprietary mutual funds
in 2000, a 10% increase from 1999 and comprising 50% of total channel
sales."

I was proud to be part of Sandy's top team at Citigroup and appreciated
his feedback that he was pleased with my performance. The opportunities
and challenges of global financial services businesses were as interesting
and intellectually engaging as I had anticipated when I left TIAA-CREF
to join him.

Addie and I were enjoying the best of New York's cultural and social life. Our family, which didn't see a whole lot of one another during the work week, was making up for it by taking exciting vacations together, including regular ski trips to Vail and Steamboat, winter vacations at Club Med resorts in the Caribbean, Christmas holidays in Maui in 1998, and a South African safari in 1999.

Our older daughter, Evonne, graduated from King Low Heywood Thomas School (known as King), a co-ed private day school in North Stamford, near our home in New Canaan, Connecticut, and enrolled at Georgetown University in September 2000. Our two youngest children, Michael and Victoria, were also doing well at King, where Addie was president of the board of trustees, presiding over a successful capital campaign to fund a new middle school building. We personally contributed $500,000 to that project, and the school named an atrium in our honor.

When Nigel graduated from Harvard in 1991, he was drawn to service in the marines. He wanted to do something where success depended entirely on character and determination, and not on family background or economic class or social status. He asked me what I thought. I replied that it's very honorable to serve in the marines, but that he should think carefully about the responsibilities of marine officers. I asked him to consider the possibility that he and his men could be trapped in a war zone or so-called police action like Grenada, knowing the fight they were facing meant little in the span of history. Most of his "men" would be teenagers who enlisted seeking economic and educational opportunity, and they would be scared. It would be his job as their officer to rally these young men to fight like marines, to fight for each other, and to face death with honor. I told Nigel that if he had the stomach for that, then he should go ahead. But if not, he should leave it alone.

Nigel did a four-year tour in the Marine Corps, and became a captain in the Force Reconnaissance Company, the marine equivalent of the Navy SEALs. After graduating from Stanford's business school with an MBA in 1997 and working at Goldman Sachs for several years, Nigel joined the Carlyle Group in 2000 to work in private equity investing.

Addie was actively involved with the Alvin Ailey American Dance Theater, the modern dance company founded in 1958 by the famous African American dancer and choreographer. We gave $500,000 there as well, to support their $50 million capital campaign, led by Joan Weill. The successful fund-raising resulted in construction of the Joan Weill Center for Dance at the corner of Ninth Avenue and West 55th Street in Manhattan, in Hell's

Figure 16 / *Vicky, Tom, Nigel, Michael, Evonne, and Addie (left to right) at Nigel's graduation from Harvard, June 1991*

Figure 17 / *Nigel, Nigel's mother Stephanie, and Tom's mother (left to right) at Nigel's graduation from Marine Corps Officer Candidate School, August 1991*

Figure 18 / *Nigel, Addie, Vicky, Evonne, Michael, and Tom (left to right)*
at home in New Canaan, December 1993

Kitchen, a once gritty neighborhood that was becoming more vibrant and attractive by the year. The new rehearsal studios, with large windows looking out onto the busy southbound traffic on Ninth Avenue, allowed dancers to see the city, and pedestrians and people in passing busses and cars to see the beautifully athletic and graceful dancers—many of them black or brown—as they leapt, stretched at the barre, and danced. One of those rehearsal studios was named for Addie and me. Joan and Sandy's leadership of this important philanthropic initiative for the leading African American dance company illustrated a primary reason why Addie and I liked them so much. Joan and Sandy were generous, and their vision of America was inclusive.

Ground Zero

To witness the collapse of the World Trade Center was to confront not only our vulnerability as a nation in spite of our power, but also the personal vulnerability of each of us to events and circumstances that overtake us.

—FRANK T. GRISWOLD, *presiding bishop of the Episcopal Church from 1998 to 2006*

If it had been a Monday morning, I would have been at 399 Park Avenue for the Management Committee meeting that Sandy convened every Monday at 8:00 am. But it was a Tuesday, so I was at my Citigroup Asset Management (CAM) office at Seven World Trade Center. I was working at my desk, and the view through my windows was of the Hudson River and New Jersey to the west, midtown Manhattan and the river to the north. The day had dawned particularly clear and beautiful. There really is nothing else quite like late summer in New York—bright blue skies, a mildness in the air, the thousands of glass and stone and metal buildings rising to the sky, millions of people, the trees still green but just about to turn russet and gold. Suddenly, from overhead but very close, a stupendous roar of aircraft jet engines filled my office, followed by the loudest noise I had ever heard in my life—an ear-shattering explosion behind me.

My office was on the forty-fifth floor, the top floor, of the northwest corner at Seven World Trade Center. The plane flew right over my head, with approximately three hundred feet clearance above our building, to smash into the eightieth floor of the building across the street behind me. Had Seven World Trade Center been a few stories taller or the plane dipped a little lower, I most likely would have died that morning.

Hersh Cohen was three floors lower, on the forty-second floor. He later told me what he saw and heard at that same moment. Visitors from a Cleveland real estate company were in his office. "I thought it was a sonic boom," he recalled, "and I remarked, 'It's a bit early for that!' but one of the Cleveland guys said, 'That wasn't a sonic boom, it was a seven-forty-seven and it just missed us.'"

Up on the forty-fifth floor, I jumped up from my desk and crossed the hallway to the empty conference room, where I stood and looked up across the street. There was a gaping hole in the north side of One World Trade Center, roughly thirty stories above me. Metal and glass were falling from the building façade around the hole and down into the street. As I watched, huge flames spewed out of the gaping hole. Then, small figures that were people appeared at the edges of the hole. Some crawled out and dangled from the bottom edges of the hole before falling to the plaza eighty floors down. Others looked over their shoulder a few times into the fiery inferno before jumping out toward the street in what looked to me like slow-motion free fall until their bodies smashed against the pavement far below. I saw dozens of people leap or fall and die on the ground. The heat from the flames must be so overwhelming, I thought, that people are choosing to take their chances on jumping from so high. It was a terrifying spectacle. I felt calm. Things seemed to be happening very slowly.

I walked back to my office and turned on the television news to try to get information about what was going on. CAM senior staffers came to my office. "Some people are rushing the elevators and stairs to leave the building," they told me. "Should we issue an evacuation order?" Several CAM employees had been working in the World Trade Center during the 1993 terrorist bombing in the buildings' underground garage, and now they assumed immediately that something similarly horrible and intentional was transpiring. "It doesn't look like it's safe to leave right now," I said, gesturing to the steadily falling debris raining down from One World Trade Center. I wasn't inclined to order an evacuation without more information on what was happening. "People who want to leave should be allowed to leave the building on their own decision," I said. "But ask security to find a safer exit route through the rear." Within a few minutes, building security informed us that it was safe to evacuate through the kitchen on the ground floor, north onto Greenwich Street. They had stationed officers in our building lobby to direct people who wanted to leave to exit by the rear route. A few minutes later, I was still watching television, hoping for information, when a plane flew into the side of Two World Trade Center. I immediately thought, "This isn't an accident or a coincidence," so I ordered immediate mandatory evacuation of all CAM employees at Seven World Trade Center. Seconds after my order was relayed, the alarm and flashing lights came on, along with an announcement through the PA system from Brad Thomas, CAM head of human resources. Brad and Evan Merberg, CAM chief administrative officer, walked the floors to ensure that all CAM employees were leaving the building. Around 9:30 a.m., twenty-seven minutes after the second plane struck, they reported to me that all CAM floors had been evacuated, and together we left Seven World Trade Center through the kitchen exit onto Greenwich Street.

I was unable to contact my driver, Ritchie Reyes, since there was virtually no operative landline or cellular telephone service, so I started walking north on Greenwich Street with Evan Merberg and Joe Deane. Joe had been on a call with people in Michigan when the first plane struck. He'd heard a tremendous roar and then a *poof.* He'd jumped over the credenza in front of his window, looked down, and seen that there wasn't a speck of dust on the street, but then, after a pause, large objects started falling out of the sky—chunks of insulation, a chair. His immediate thought had been "This is a terrorist attack," and he'd cleared the forty-first floor. After the basement bombing of One World Trade Center in 1993, where Joe had worked at the time, he and others had huddled on the rooftop for hours and then evacuated down the pitch-black stairwell. This time, the stairwell was well lit when he walked down.

Joe and Evan and I weren't two blocks away from Seven World Trade Center when several women who were looking back toward the destruction started crying and pointing. We turned to see what they were pointing at. The smoke rising from the hole in the North Tower had gathered into a massive black cloud just above the building, and the cloud was in the iconic shape of the devil with horns and a pointy beard. "This is a scene of pure evil, triumphant," I thought. Joe, a devout Catholic, said, "God always answers that." And indeed, the next day we saw God's answer in the newspaper: photographs of the World Trade Center wreckage where fallen steel girders formed the sign of the cross. In my office today I have a small rough-surfaced steel cross, approximately nine inches tall and six inches wide, which was carved from one of the collapsed steel girders at World Trade Center ground zero which formed that cross. A photographer for *Time* magazine captured that moment when the smoke formed the image of the devil above the ruined tower, but the photographic definition when it was printed in the magazine wasn't sharp enough for most viewers to see Satan's image as clearly as it had actually appeared.

As we walked north alongside hundreds of strangers, it gradually became clear that we would probably have to walk all the way to Citigroup's headquarters at Park Avenue and 53rd Street. Subway service had been halted. The few northbound public buses passing us were packed, with no possibility of room for additional passengers. Every taxi was full. Sirens screamed. There was a steady parade of emergency vehicles, wailing and flashing, heading south toward the World Trade Center. We were walking on West Broadway just below Canal Street when Evan looked back and said, "I wonder if those buildings could collapse?" We stopped to look, and as if on cue, the North Tower began pancaking down, crumbling from the top. A giant cloud of dust and debris came billowing through the canyons formed by the streets and buildings. People around us started running and screaming. We turned east off West Broadway and worked our way west-to-east and south-to-north via smaller side streets to avoid the funnel effect of the large north-south thoroughfares, which were being hit with the worst of the debris cloud and panicked crowds of frightened people. One World Trade Center collapsed at 9:50 am, just twenty minutes after we left Seven World Trade Center.

As we walked I thought, "This is a bad dream." A perfectly beautiful September day with sunny, cloudless skies and mild temperatures had become a terrifying nightmare. Lower Manhattan looked like a war zone with refugees on foot streaming away from a battle. I tried repeatedly to call home and to reach my Citigroup office at midtown to let people know I was okay and making my way uptown, but I couldn't get cellphone service. We continued walking east and north, and were on Park Avenue at East 23rd Street near Madison Square Park when Two World Trade Center collapsed at 10:29 am. Lower Manhattan was completely enveloped in dust, smoke, and ash.

Just after 11:00 am, we arrived at Citigroup headquarters. I went to Sandy Weill's office to report on what had happened and what I had seen. The mood was very somber as we realized there was a high probability of Citigroup employee casualties in the World Trade Center collapse, and it was still very difficult to establish telephone communications with Citigroup offices around Manhattan. Evan Merberg activated the CAM disaster recovery plan, and Brad Thomas began the process of trying to account for all CAM employees.

Around an hour after I arrived, Citigroup CFO Todd Thomson came to my office to say Addie had called him and said she had been trying to reach me to find out if I was all right and had been unable to get through to my cellphone or my downtown office. She wanted to know if Todd knew anything about my whereabouts. I tried repeatedly to call my house in New

Canaan, and eventually got a dial tone and my call went through. Addie sounded surprised to hear my voice and was very emotional. It seemed as if she might have been mentally bracing for bad news.

That afternoon I was able to get through on the telephone to my daughter Evonne at Georgetown University in Washington, and as we spoke she described the smoke she could see in the distance rising from the Pentagon. Later in the day I learned that Seven World Trade Center was on fire, apparently because fuel storage tanks in the building had exploded after being pierced by debris from the collapsed North Tower. At 5:25 that afternoon, Seven World Trade Center collapsed. All of my personal mementos there were gone, of course—family photographs, photographs of events with colleagues over the years, photographs of the apartment buildings we rehabbed in Boston, reprints of newspaper stories dating back to Cornell '69, various awards and honors, daily diaries and business records.

All roads, bridges, and tunnels into and out of Manhattan were closed for security reasons. But I would not have been able to drive to Connecticut anyway because my driver had had to abandon my car in the chaos near the World Trade Center. We learned later that it was destroyed when the buildings collapsed. I stayed at my Park Avenue office until around 7:00 pm and then took the once-hourly Metro North emergency service outbound train from Grand Central Terminal. All trains ran as locals that day, making all stops, and each train station along the route was packed with crowds of people waiting and looking for loved ones, some of whom were never going to arrive.

The next day CAM commenced a schedule of twice-daily disaster recovery team conference calls to keep the entire management team informed and to facilitate immediate decisions as issues and problems arose. CAM had a designated block of seats at Citigroup's primary disaster recovery facility in Rutherford, New Jersey. Unfortunately, much of Citigroup's corporate disaster planning in the metro New York region was based on the premise of losing a single building for one reason or another. Now, all of Citigroup's facilities in downtown Manhattan had been destroyed or closed, and sixteen thousand employees were displaced, including 2,500 CAM employees from Seven World Trade Center. As a result, CAM's allocation of seats in the Rutherford disaster recovery facility was reduced significantly, and our teams scrambled to set up alternate recovery operations in temporary facilities at West 34th Street and at Broad Street in Manhattan, and at several buildings in Stamford, Connecticut. Our technology and facilities teams worked eighteen-hour days to prepare over three hundred workstation seats and telecommunications infrastructure by Thursday, September 13, when U.S. bond market trading reopened. Then they prepared an additional one hundred workstation seats and telecommunications infrastructure over the weekend of September 15–16 to be ready for Monday, September 17, when U.S. stock market trading reopened.

CAM portfolio managers, led by Hersh Cohen for equities and Joe Deane for fixed income, initiated portfolio manager conference calls for clients on Thursday, September 13. The goal was to reassure clients and calm their fears. Investment decisions made when emotions and fear are running high are rarely good decisions. Our portfolio managers conducted twice-daily client conference calls each day for two weeks, and over thirteen thousand clients dialed in. I believe our efforts, and other efforts like ours, helped to mitigate the potential for panic in U.S. financial markets.

Two months later, in November 2001, I commissioned a video that featured a montage of CAM employees' faces and voices discussing the events we had experienced starting on September 11. My thinking was that we had lived through a historic experience together, and it should be commemorated in a form that employees could keep forever and share with their families. I wanted CAM employees and their families to have a tribute to their courage and dedication, as expressed by their colleagues. Each CAM employee received a copy of the video. My cover letter read:

Dear Colleague:

The events of September 11, 2001, will forever be etched in our memories. We are all filled with profound sadness for the victims of these unspeakable attacks. Yet, great calamity often gives birth to great strength, courage, and compassion.

This video is the story of Citigroup Asset Management in the hours and days following the attacks on the World Trade Center and the loss of our headquarters building at Seven World Trade Center. In the words of your colleagues, it tells the story of that day and of our incredible recovery.

I fervently hope that, in some small way, this video does justice to your unsurpassed courage and your herculean efforts in putting Citigroup Asset Management back on its feet so quickly after a disaster of truly historic proportions.

I hope that you will treasure this video as a keepsake in the years ahead. And that you will never forget your resolve during this time of national crisis. I am proud to be associated with you.

Warmest regards,
Thomas W. Jones

The video was set to the heroic and majestic music of Aaron Copland's *Fanfare for the Common Man* and the theme from *Chariots of Fire* and was filled with heartfelt statements from employees, such as "We won't let terrorists shut us down," and "Commutes are now three hours each way, which is totally exhausting, but in life you get judged by how you act in a crisis," and "We're stronger, we're closer, and that spirit will stay with us." In my introductory remarks on the video, I said:

This videotape is the story of Citigroup Asset Management during and after the events of September 11, 2001. It is your story as told by you and your colleagues. All I would add is to say thank you. Thank you for the courage and calmness you showed in achieving a safe evacuation of Seven World Trade Center without casualties. Thank you for your courage and compassion in assisting your colleagues who had physical difficulties evacuating and moving north away from Seven World Trade Center. Thank you for your commitment and dedication in turning immediately to implement our disaster recovery plan. Thank you for having our business back in operation two days later on September 13 when the fixed income markets reopened for trading, and on September 17 when the equity markets resumed trading. And thank you for your continuing willingness to suffer through difficult working conditions and difficult commutes for what will be an extended number of months until we can permanently relocate our business. I am proud to be associated with you, and I believe that through this experience we are going to learn that we can trust each other and rely on each other, and that together we can build a great asset management business. Thank you.

The CAM video was well received and was especially appreciated, I think, because it created a vehicle for our employees to share their experience with others. CAM was fortunate in having no employee casualties, while other

Citigroup business units suffered six casualties. But directly across the street from CAM headquarters, there were over three thousand casualties at ground zero, One World Trade Center. If the first hijacked airplane had targeted the closest World Trade Center building in its flight path, or lost just a few hundred feet of altitude before impact, it would have been a direct hit on my office and probably resulted in hundreds or even thousands of CAM casualties. I probably would have perished instantly, without knowing what was happening. I occasionally think about that, and it reminds me of the fragility of life and prompts me to tell my wife and children more frequently that I love them. It is one of the reasons why I pray for God's grace when I wake every morning, and when I retire every evening. I know that no person is guaranteed a safe return home on any given day.

I had a golfing friend, Michael Berkeley, who died that day in the North Tower. Ironically, it was his thirty-eighth birthday. I had seen him just two days earlier on Sunday, September 9, at the U.S. Open tennis finals. Michael had a lovely wife and two young sons ages seven and five. The image of his wife and boys at the funeral has stayed with me for years. It made me wonder how the lives of Addie and my children would have changed if I hadn't made it out of Seven World Trade Center that morning.

Addie and I owned a condo in Tribeca at the corner of Duane and Hudson streets, approximately eight blocks from the World Trade Center. We used it primarily as a pied-à-terre for when I worked late at my downtown office, or when we had late evening or weekend charity events or other social commitments in Manhattan. One week after 9/11, when some lower Manhattan streets were opened to allow access for residents, I went to the condo, and the smell of death hung in the air. The odor of burning flesh permeated everywhere below Canal Street, a constant reminder that unimaginable evil had occurred in that place. I stopped using the Tribeca apartment in part because, no matter how late the hour, I preferred to go home to Connecticut every evening to be with my family.

Caught in Freddie Mac's Perfect Storm

Mr. Biggs says any concerns about Mr. Jones—who he says has a "very high sense of rectitude"—would be "a good example of the death of common sense."

—JON E. HILSENRATH AND JOANN S. LUBLIN,
Wall Street Journal, June 25, 2003

Corporate boards are a world unto themselves. And they are often about personal relationships—friendship, intersecting careers, social circles—connecting a company's top executives to the people serving on the board. A recurring tension in American capitalism flows from this intersection: Just how effective is the board in influencing and overseeing what the company's management does? There's a natural tendency for top management to want board members they feel will be sympathetic toward them, and for board members to operate with a Golden Rule mentality: "I will treat management the same way I would like to be treated at my corporation, by my own board."

In 1997 I joined the board of directors of Freddie Mac, also known as the Federal Home Loan Mortgage Corporation, the second-largest financier of mortgages in America. It was an extracurricular activity, outside my duties at Citigroup, and it paid a couple of hundred thousand dollars annually and entailed eight two-day meetings per year, and the requisite preparation work for those meetings. My primary interest in service on the board of directors was that it afforded me additional insight into mortgage risk analytics. Top executives tend to serve on corporate boards for several reasons—the prestige of advising and shepherding an important company, networking, the pay, and the chance to acquire skills and knowledge that might be called upon in their own career. But their main duty is to put their expertise and guidance into service for the company's shareholders.

Freddie Mac was led by a South Dakotan named Leland Brendsel, its CEO, who had been with the company since 1982. He had a Ph.D. in economics and had served first as Freddie Mac's chief financial officer before becoming CEO in 1985 and chairman of the board in 1989, when it went public. He'd overseen the organization's growth from a small player in the mortgage market to an entity that had a major role in improving access to mortgages and financing homes for some 30 million Americans. Freddie Mac's president was David Glenn, a Mormon from the Midwest who'd joined the company as chief financial officer in 1987 and been named president in 1990. The chief financial officer was Vaughn Clarke. There were eight independent outside directors on the board, and we each served as well on two or three of five board committees.

Beginning in 2001, Wall Street and large swaths of corporate America were overcome by wave after wave of financial scandal. Scandal became the drumbeat of the financial news, and as the stories accumulated, they created a widespread public impression of pervasive corporate malfeasance. Increasingly, the financial press and the SEC alike were becoming exuberantly prosecutorial. (To give a sense of the prevailing atmosphere, this book's appendix lists two hundred *Wall Street Journal* articles regarding fraud and illegality at major American corporations between February 2001 and December 2004.) Just as the scandals were building steam, I was appointed chairman of the audit committee of Freddie Mac's board of directors in 2001.

Then, in 2002, Enron collapsed. In March, the U.S. Justice Department charged Enron's auditor, the Arthur Andersen accounting firm, with obstruction of justice over the destruction of documents related to its Enron audit. Arthur Andersen just happened to be Freddie Mac's auditor as well. An article in the *New York Times* on March 14, 2002, "Audit Firms Await Fallout and Windfall," by Jonathan D. Glater, was prescient in some of its observations on the possible consequences of an Andersen collapse:

> If Arthur Andersen cannot find a savior, some of America's biggest companies will be thrust into a period of uncertainty as they scramble to find someone else to bless their books . . . If Andersen's efforts to find a merger partner fail, and that seems likely, more client defections are expected . . . For companies, switching auditors is neither simple nor cheap, accountants said, and where problems arise, it is usually soon after such a change is made. Filings with the Securities and Exchange Commission could run late, depressing share prices. In

addition, accountants said, companies may find that a new auditor has a different approach to handling certain transactions . . . complicating matters, accountants said, is the scarcity of expertise within firms. The partners with the most experience may already be taken, and accountants who are less familiar with the client's industry are more likely to make mistakes. That could have an effect on financial disclosures.

A core component of corporate finance is based on one simple idea: borrow money at one rate and lend or invest that same money at a higher rate to make a profit. When the scale of that simple idea is expanded, and when questions of timing, uncertainty, and regulations make things more complex, the opportunities for great profit, and great risk, grow. One of the most important but high-risk audit areas at Freddie Mac was the "retained portfolio" of mortgage-backed securities, which were held on Freddie Mac's balance sheet instead of being sold into the secondary market to third-party investors such as pension funds and insurance companies. In essence, Freddie Mac issued corporate bonds to raise funds and used the funds to purchase consumer and commercial mortgages originated by commercial banks, savings and loan banks, and mortgage companies. Freddie Mac's core business was to charge a "guarantee fee" for guaranteeing the purchased mortgages against default, bundle the mortgages into new "mortgage-backed securities" (MBS), and sell those to investors such as pension funds, insurance companies, and fixed-income-bond mutual funds. But Freddie Mac's retained portfolio was an increasingly important source of profits because Freddie could borrow at very low interest rates because of its implied backing by the U.S. government, and capture the "interest rate spread" if it used those borrowed funds to purchase and retain mortgages paying higher interest rates than the bonds issued by Freddie Mac. This maneuver required sophisticated management of the underlying "interest rate risk" to maintain targeted spreads between Freddie Mac's cost of borrowed funds versus the interest rate yield on the purchased mortgages, and the "duration risk" resulting from the possibility that borrowers could prepay the underlying mortgages (by selling or refinancing the mortgaged property). If the underlying mortgages were prepaid prior to maturity, it created a mismatch between the maturities and associated interest expense of debt securities issued by Freddie Mac versus the maturities and associated interest income of the purchased mortgages—which went away if the mortgages were prepaid.

While straightforward in concept, this "interest rate and duration risk management" was enormously complex when implemented at Freddie Mac's scale of several hundred billion dollars in retained portfolio comprising millions of specific, unique mortgages and MBS securities and hundreds of billions of dollars in outstanding Freddie Mac bond obligations spread across thousands of unique specific debt offerings. In practice, Freddie Mac executed "portfolio-hedging" strategies to achieve and maintain targeted retained portfolio interest rate and maturity/duration risk characteristics. The Freddie Mac team that managed this process was led by senior vice president Greg Parseghian, and was regarded highly on Wall Street and among sophisticated investors as one of the best in U.S. capital markets.

An extraordinarily complex new accounting standard, FAS 133 Accounting for Derivative Securities, went into effect on January 1, 2001. At several hundred pages in length, it governed accounting for derivative securities and prescribed rules governing portfolio-hedging activities. Freddie Mac's implementation of FAS 133 in 2001 was advised by Arthur Andersen, and the related 2001 quarterly accounting and financial statement reviews and 2001 annual audit were also conducted by Arthur Andersen. We on the audit committee were assured by Andersen that the company had done a good job implementing FAS 133.

But by early 2002, after the 2001 audit had been completed, we could see that Arthur Andersen might not survive the Enron scandal. For Freddie Mac to wait and monitor Andersen's situation would be highly risky, because we might become trapped later in 2002 with a last-minute need to replace Andersen for the 2002 audit. In that scenario, our choice of audit firms might be severely curtailed; the best firms might not have the manpower to undertake a major new client so late in the 2002 accounting period. With those considerations in mind, we triggered a search for a new independent auditor and retained PricewaterhouseCoopers (PwC) for the 2002 audit. When Andersen collapsed shortly after being convicted on one felony count in June 2002, our decision to switch to PwC was proved correct, while at the same time the switch in auditors led, almost inevitably, to differing accounting interpretations between the two firms. Further complicating the situation was that Arthur Andersen had been Freddie Mac's only independent auditor since 1970, the year Freddie Mac was founded. Freddie Mac's accounting department had zero experience in audit firm transitions.

We didn't have to wait long for the first problem to arise. In the third quarter of 2002, PwC representatives informed the audit committee that they had serious concerns regarding our FAS 133 implementation. According to PwC, Freddie Mac had continued to use some overall portfolio-hedging techniques and had failed to adequately link each derivative security intended for hedging to a specific underlying retained portfolio security, which was the object of hedging. If PwC's concerns were correct, it meant that our retained portfolio might not qualify for "hedged portfolio accounting" and would have to be classified as "marked to market" and reported in Freddie Mac's quarterly financial statements at current market values. Since the retained portfolio market values would fluctuate with interest rate movements and changes in credit market conditions, this would introduce into Freddie Mac's financial statements enormous volatility from quarter to quarter on net income and shareholders' equity.

The second problem developed in December 2002, a day after our board meeting. Someone inside the company had sent two anonymous whistle-blower letters to the SEC and the Office of Federal Housing Enterprise Oversight (OFHEO), Freddie Mac's federal regulator, alleging that management had engaged in improper earnings management transactions and committed accounting errors in 1999 and 2000. Leland Brendsel phoned to tell me. I called an emergency audit committee meeting, at which we accepted management's recommendation to engage the law firm of Baker Botts LLP to conduct an independent investigation, led by partner James Doty, who had served as a general counsel to the SEC from 1990 to 1992 and therefore had firsthand knowledge of the point of view from the other side of the table. In reports dated May 1, July 22, and November 13, 2003, Baker Botts reported its findings: the allegations in the anonymous letters were false in most material respects, but, during its investigation, the firm had identified additional accounting transactions that raised questions and required further inquiry. PwC and Baker Botts eventually named eight specific transactions or accounting policies that might go beyond issues of simple accounting error.

These events caused PwC to insist on a re-audit of Freddie Mac's 2001 and 2000 financial statements rather than relying on the Arthur Andersen audits of those years. This in turn meant that Freddie Mac could not issue 2002 financial statements until the re-audit was completed, because a baseline of audited 2000 and 2001 financials was necessary for the multiyear 2000–2002 comparative financial statements. In January 2003, Freddie Mac announced publicly that it was conducting a re-audit of 2000 and 2001 financial statements, that it would be restating results to reflect higher earnings from derivatives that should have been recognized in prior years, and that the re-audit and restatement were expected to be completed by the end of the second quarter 2003. Freddie Mac, a major publicly traded corporation and one of the largest debt securities issuers in the global capital markets, was now crippled by being unable to issue timely current financial statements.

I knew that these developments might place Freddie Mac's audit committee in the regulatory bull's-eye. Outside legal counsel warned us it was likely that the SEC was looking for opportunities to prosecute a public company audit committee to make an example for independent director accountability and culpability. As audit committee chairman, I knew this meant that I was probably going to be the Freddie Mac director most directly targeted by the regulators.

The core underlying problem, it seemed to me, was that Freddie Mac's senior management for many years had focused primarily on hiring top-tier executive talent in those business areas that were regarded as mission critical to the company's success—interest rate and duration risk management, credit risk management, single-family mortgage origination, and multifamily mortgage origination. Unfortunately, senior management hadn't devoted a complementary focus to recruiting top talent in "back office" functions such as accounting, internal controls, and financial reporting—maybe because Freddie Mac had historically been technically exempt from SEC registration, and because the company had operated on a much simpler business model for most of its history. When Freddie Mac adopted a more complex business model in the mid-1990s by beginning to grow the retained mortgage portfolio aggressively, the complexity of the related accounting and financial reporting increased dramatically.

In addition, FAS 133 in 2001 had triggered a geometric increase in the complexity of accounting and controls and financial reporting, for which the company was not well prepared. For several years, Freddie Mac's audit committee had been pushing senior management to strengthen the company's capabilities in these functions, and under my leadership the audit committee insisted on tying 25 percent of senior management bonuses to successful execution of a Financial Reporting Controls Improvement Plan. But I knew we would likely receive little sympathy from the regulators.

In April 2003 Baker Botts reported to the audit committee that six of the eight questionable transactions or accounting policies involved the "unintentional misapplication of generally accepted accounting principles (GAAP) based at least in part on the advice and concurrence of Arthur Andersen." One of the issues involved a known departure from GAAP, which management and Arthur Andersen deemed immaterial. And one transaction involved a deliberate effort to smooth "operating earnings," a non-GAAP metric, which had little practical effect on the company's GAAP earnings.

Also, by April 2003 it was apparent that the time and management talent required to fix the accounting and reporting problems and complete a restatement was going to be much greater than management's estimates. I was surprised when Leland Brendsel asked to visit me at my office in New York to discuss his plans and personal commitment to fix the problems. He sat across from me at my desk. "I'm sorry this stuff is happening, Tom," he said. "I promise I'll get this fixed."

I told him, "I'm glad you're sorry, Leland, but with all due respect, I'm not sure you're the guy to fix the problem. The audit committee has been warning you for years and you haven't fixed it, and now we're in this mess. In my view, it's unpardonable for a company of Freddie Mac's stature not to have audited financial statements that investors can rely on. You had your chance, but in this league, you don't get second chances."

He looked surprised at the candor and severity of my assessment. He said, "I am the right person to fix it."

I shrugged. "Fine, but I'm just being honest with you. I've lost confidence in your leadership and you won't get my vote."

Leland said that he couldn't accept my assessment of the situation, that I was wrong. I told him that I understood his point of view. "I think we should simply agree to disagree," I said.

In June 2003, when Baker Botts was nearly finished with its investigation, the law firm discovered that the president of Freddie Mac, David Glenn, had altered his personal diary to obscure his role in approving some of the questionable transactions. I was shocked by this new evidence of evasion and concealment. You never know, I thought, how a person is going to react in the face of immense pressure. I could almost imagine how the scenario had unfolded. Someone was being questioned about the implementation of various accounting transactions and was asked for a specific date on which the topic had been discussed in a meeting. That person may have mentioned, offhandedly, that David Glenn was in the habit of keeping careful notes at meetings, that he kept a business diary: "I can't remember exactly what day it was, but you should check David's diary. He would know." The note in question might not have revealed any obvious misdeed at all, but in a panic, or perhaps from an impulse to be less than completely candid with the investigators, the president had torn it from the diary.

His decision should have been, of course, to go to the investigator, Doty, at the outset, give him the diary, and say, "I don't know if this will come to your attention or not, but I was in various meetings and I've got some entries here which can help explain my thoughts." His decision should have been to control the story and get out in front of it. In that way, you're saying, in effect, "I want to help the investigation and I have nothing to hide." He didn't make that decision.

The board understood that the removal of the diary pages could be construed as an intentional effort to impede a board investigation. It required a strong response. The board decided to terminate Glenn and requested the resignations of Brendsel and Vaughn Clarke, the CFO, too, on the basis of developments in the burgeoning accounting scandal.

We also promoted Greg Parseghian to president and chief executive officer, and elected Shaun O'Malley (retired chairman of PwC) as nonexecutive chairman. Our rationale was that Parseghian's exceptional understanding of the risk characteristics of mortgage-backed securities portfolios, and his strong reputation in capital markets, would keep investors confident in the business side of Freddie Mac, while O'Malley would focus on managing the accounting and regulatory storm. It was a smart decision which unfortunately was undermined when OFHEO, the company's federal regulator, ordered Freddie Mac to replace Parseghian on August 22, 2003, claiming that his investment group had been involved in some of the questionable accounting transactions. We on the board felt that Parseghian's team had constructed transactions at the direction of the company's president and was not responsible for the accounting or financial reporting of those transactions.

I had taken Greg Parseghian aside at the board dinner the evening before we promoted him to CEO and implored him to think carefully before letting us go down that path. I told him, "Greg, you're the only one who knows in your heart the extent of your involvement in these questionable transactions, but it is certain to be discovered and brought into the light. If you've done anything questionable you will not survive as CEO, so it's better to face that now and not let the board take you there. You don't have to answer me now. You should think about this overnight and let me know tomorrow morning before the board meeting."

"Sure, I'll think about it overnight, but I'm okay," he said. He hadn't to his knowledge done anything inappropriate, he told me, or that could impugn his credibility or impair his effectiveness as CEO. He said that, after all, he'd always relied on the directions of the president and the CEO, and on the accounting personnel and Arthur Andersen for vetting the accounting treatment of transactions. The next morning Greg told me that he was comfortable moving forward, and I was a strong advocate for electing him CEO.

Freddie Mac finally completed the PwC re-audit and in November 2003 issued its audited financial statements for 2000, 2001, and 2002. The board recruited an outsider, Richard Syron, former head of the American Stock Exchange, to be Parseghian's successor as CEO in December 2003.

Baker Botts's final report to Freddie Mac's board summarized the problem not as an abuse of authority for personal gain but instead "serious failures by senior management to discharge responsibilities entrusted to and placed upon them by the Board."

On June 25, 2003, the *Wall Street Journal* ran a story headlined "Freddie Mac Board Played Key Role in Executive's Ouster" that raised questions regarding my independence as a Freddie Mac director, since Freddie was a large client of Citigroup, while at the same time pointing out that most major financial institutions in the country also had dealings with Freddie Mac and that our vote to fire the company's three top managers showed an independence and toughness unusual in corporate governance. I was gratified to read statements about me that were included in the article, among them this: "David Palombi, spokesman for Freddie Mac, noted that Mr. Jones' role as audit committee chairman isn't in violation of any current rules of the NYSE, adding that the board was aware of the proposed rules and would address them at an appropriate time. Mr. Palombi added, 'Anybody who knows Tom Jones knows his independence, integrity and judgment are beyond question.'"

I was subpoenaed to testify by both the SEC and OFHEO. The interrogators at both depositions focused on my personal role in setting audit committee agendas and in linking senior management incentive compensation to effective execution of the Financial Reporting Controls Improvement Plan. They also wanted to probe my knowledge of the accounting issues at stake and the board's role in overseeing or advising management. Both depositions also sought to learn how much I understood about the relevant accounting standards, and the board of directors' role and responsibilities in ensuring that those standards were implemented correctly.

My OFHEO deposition was on August 12, 2003, at the OFHEO offices in Washington, D.C., starting at 10:00 in the morning. Hostile and accusatory, the questioning made it clear to me that regulators were "scalp hunting," looking for an opportunity to bring charges against prominent business executives.

I testified that the audit committee was the driving force behind creating the Financial Reporting Controls Improvement Plan in late 2001 after the company encountered a problem reconciling guaranteed mortgage securities accounts. I further testified that the audit committee was the driving force insisting on rigorous definition and controls with regard to calculating and reporting Freddie Mac's new non-GAAP financial reporting metric, called "operating earnings." I described the role and functions of internal audit and the duties and responsibilities of board members and audit committee members, and the role of the audit committee with regard to financial statement disclosures. I described my understanding of the breakdowns that led to the restatement and re-audit of Freddie Mac's 2000 and 2001 financial statements. I described the economic purposes of debt repurchase transactions and explained why they did not constitute earnings management. I described my understanding of the GAAP standard for loan loss reserves, and why Freddie Mac's reserves were positioned appropriately at the conservative end of the allowable range of loss estimates. And I discussed various conversations I'd had with former CEO Leland Brendsel and CEO-designate Greg Parseghian.

It was clear to me that the OFHEO and SEC interrogators did not like · me, and there was significant tension in the room throughout both depositions. The regulators were probably accustomed to investigatory targets who were deferential, conciliatory, and anxious to avoid conflict—but I exhibited none of those characteristics. I refused to yield any ground on any question that implied wrongdoing by Freddie Mac's board or audit committee.

What follows is an excerpt from my OFHEO testimony. I am being grilled about various accounting transactions and estimates and financial statement disclosures. You will see from the nature of the questioning that the government investigators are focused on finding malfeasance at the board level. I was able to provide a clear and detailed explanation of the board's actions.

OFHEO: Have you heard the term "earnings management"?

JONES: Yes, I have.

OFHEO: In what context have you heard that term?

JONES: Lots of newspaper articles and SEC pronouncements. It's been an issue in the Doty investigation. It was implied within the whistle blower letter.

OFHEO: Mr. Jones, the court reporter has handed you Exhibit 9. It's another presentation. It bears the name John Gibbons, Board of Directors Meeting, June 4, 1999. It is entitled "Financial Review and Outlook." If you could look at the second page entitled "Overview," and if you look at the second diamond on that page it's entitled "Financial Prospects." Look at the second indentation there which reads "NII [net interest income] is surging and we are undertaking transactions to smooth the time pattern of 1999–2000." Do you see that statement?

JONES: Yes, I do.

OFHEO: Did that statement give you any concern in or around 1999?

JONES: Not especially, because the question is what's the nature of the transactions that were planned to undertake, and how appropriate are they and are they in accordance with GAAP.

OFHEO: Do you recall questions of that nature being asked of Mr. Gibbons who apparently made this presentation?

JONES: Of course. I remember items like this being discussed, and the typical technique that was used was debt repurchases because you usually record an accounting loss on the repurchase of the debt. That takes down the current year income, and it's made up as increased earnings emerge over time due to lower interest expense within the reduced debt portfolio. That was never a type of transaction that was ever suggested or identified as being inappropriate. It was fully disclosed in the financial statements, and usually discussed within the earnings press release itself. There was nothing hidden or misleading.

OFHEO: What's the economic reason behind a debt repurchase as you understand it? What's the business purpose, as opposed to the accounting impact coming from the debt repurchase. It has some effect, if I understood your answer, on undertaking transactions to smooth the time pattern of NII over 1999–2000. What is the economic purpose behind the transaction besides the accounting purpose?

JONES: When you run a large portfolio of securities, you do purchase and sale transactions all of the time in terms of whether there are advantageous pricing opportunities in the market. Prices go up and down on a daily basis, and so the economic advantage is within being able to get attractive pricing on the securities purchases or sales. Sometimes a company will buy and sell its own securities just to make sure there's an active market in those securities. There can be an economic purpose to a company that there's a certain level of trading volume, because it's a more attractive investment instrument to other investors when they see significant trading volumes which imply efficient pricing. It all depends on the company's particular economic situation, its strategy, trading volumes in the securities, and how efficiently the securities are priced. There can be many economic implications.

OFHEO: Do you know whether that particular one that you just referenced was engaged in by Freddie Mac?

JONES: Which particular one? I mentioned several.

OFHEO: Engaging in transactions of buying and selling its own stock?

JONES: We're not talking about stock. We're talking about debt securities.

OFHEO: Sorry, debt securities.

JONES: Yes, Freddie Mac does a lot of buying and selling its own debt securities.

OFHEO: In order to create a market or activity in the market, which I thought was what you said the purpose was?

JONES: When this crisis broke and our agency debt securities spreads started to widen against Treasuries, management came to the board and said we should step into the market and show support for our own securities so the pricing doesn't collapse. So yes, we agreed to step up and support our own debt securities. That's not earnings manipulation. That's trying to support the efficiency of the pricing of our securities in the market, and trying to ensure that there was sufficient liquidity for other investors to sell without driving prices down to fire sale levels. There is nothing inappropriate about that at all.

OFHEO: Now one of the things that I heard you say earlier, Mr. Jones, was that the company formed a task force to prepare itself for the implementation of FAS 133. Is that correct?

JONES: Yes.

OFHEO: One of the things that was considered, was it not, was reporting not only GAAP earnings but also generating a new type of reporting metric, isn't that right, called operating earnings?

JONES: Yes.

OFHEO: Who was responsible for that idea, if you know?

JONES: My impression was that the primary champion was [president] David Glenn. I don't know who he assigned to the working team to actually come up with the calculations and the design, but in board meetings the most outspoken proponent of that being one of the strategies was David Glenn.

OFHEO: Do you recall what he said as to why he advocated reporting on this basis as well as GAAP reporting, this basis being operating earnings reporting?

JONES: Primarily that the volatility of the financial statements was inevitably going to be greater under FAS 133, and not reflective of the underlying economics of the company, as I described to you earlier regarding marking to market on derivative hedges in different time frames than the realization of values on underlying hedged securities. So to make sure that investors could understand what the company thought its underlying economics really were we needed to create a measuring technique to communicate the economics.

OFHEO: And that was in contemplation that the measuring technique of marked to market for these derivatives required by FAS 133 would not present a true picture?

JONES: That is correct. It would be a distortion.

OFHEO: When Mr. Glenn advocated for presenting this other presentation of the company's financials, this operating earnings, do you remember how the board reacted?

JONES: We thought it sounded reasonable. After all, the GAAP financials were still there and it's not uncommon to see companies in different industries develop a non-GAAP measure because of what they feel are the unique characteristics of the particular company or the particular industry. That's not an uncommon phenomenon.

OFHEO: Is it correct to say—I think I got your answer with respect to the board's reaction. Was your reaction the same, that this would be an appropriate technique to employ, this use of operating earnings?

JONES: Yes, it sounded reasonable to me.

OFHEO: Sometime later, if I understood your earlier answer, you developed some concerns about the use of this non-GAAP metric to report the company's financials. Is that right?

JONES: That is correct.

OFHEO: How did those concerns surface with you over time, from the time you first heard about using this technique as opposed to the time when you had these concerns?

JONES: I believe the company first started using operating earnings at the beginning of 2001, and then as that year evolved I thought I was hearing slightly different nuances in terms of how management was describing operating earnings. I thought I was hearing slightly different nuances, and it made me feel that we needed to pin this down. We needed to make sure that we were reporting something that is defined rigorously, and calculated consistently, and reported consistently. The fact that it's an alternative reporting metric doesn't mean that you can just do whatever you want to do with it.

OFHEO: It keeps changing along the way, is what I'm hearing.

JONES: I wasn't sure what I was hearing, and so I started asking questions, asking for a written definition of operating earnings. Then I made it an issue that I thought PwC ought to opine on operating earnings as they did on GAAP. PwC said they could not opine on a non-GAAP measure, but they could perhaps do some agreed procedures. But to do agreed procedures, PwC required an appropriate audit trail regarding the definition, the calculations and measurements, and controls regarding data accuracy.

OFHEO: This was in 2002 that you were having these discussions with PwC, is that right?

JONES: Yes, that's correct. As we started to prepare for the 2002 audit with PwC there was discussion of having some audit procedures to give the audit committee some assurance regarding operating earnings. That's when PwC's feedback was there had to be documentation of the definition, and documentation of the calculation, and control processes in terms of the data that was being fed into the calculations. It reached a stage where I think it was third or fourth quarter of 2002, the audit committee said that we would not agree to disclosure of operating earnings in the quarterly earnings press release if there was not a definition and calculation and data verification satisfactory to PwC. A lot of that wasn't in place.

OFHEO: With respect to reserves, you talked about reserves earlier. Do you understand what the GAAP standard is for the creation of reserves?

JONES: I think it's changed over time. I would paraphrase it as saying that it's an event that is probable of occurring and reasonably estimable. That is the general standard behind creating a reserve— the degree of probability of loss occurrence, and the degree of reasonability of the loss estimation.

OFHEO: So probable of occurring and reasonable of estimating? Did I understand those to be the two elements?

JONES: Yes. That's my understanding of the key elements.

OFHEO: With respect to the maintenance of reserves at the company, and here I'm talking about the loan loss reserve, wasn't it brought to the board's attention that it instead made its loan loss reserves on a much more conservative basis, if that's the right terminology. Instead of most probable or probable of occurring, that they took the most adverse consequence and used that as a measure for probability of occurring?

JONES: Yes. At least I clearly understood that.

OFHEO: What was your reaction with your understanding of what the basis is for reserve, probable or most probable of occurring as opposed to the most adverse circumstances, as to why the company was permitted to engage in that?

JONES: My personal view is that strong financial companies want to maintain conservative reserve levels, and this was a company that had a not too distant history of not having adequate loan loss reserves.

OFHEO: When was that?

JONES: In the early nineties, I believe 1990 or 1991. An extra charge in excess of $100 million was taken through the P&L [profit and loss statement] because of inadequate reserves in the S&L [savings & loan] crisis. I personally had the experience in my earlier career at TIAA-CREF, which was one of the largest mortgage lenders in the country, of seeing a real estate implosion which caused the bankruptcy of many S&L's, and I had seen the "Texas loss scenario" firsthand in terms of how adverse mortgage and real estate loss experience can be. I had seen triple-A rated financial institutions downgraded to junk status because they underestimated the severity of mortgage and real estate loss cycles, and so to me first class financial institutions appropriately want to be at the very conservative end of the reserve spectrum. The fact that Freddie Mac had gone through a number of years without its reserves being really stressed was to me reflective of nothing other than the fact that we hadn't had an economic recession recently. We were in a prolonged period of economic growth, so what does that prove? The fact that the reserves aren't stressed when the economy is strong doesn't tell you what's going to happen when the next recession comes. So, my personal view was to stay on the conservative end of the spectrum and see how the reserves behaved when they were stressed in the next recession, and then be in position to make a better judgment. Let's see how the reserves behave through a full economic cycle. Let's not just watch what they're doing during the economic growth phase. Let's see the reserve levels through a full cycle of growth and recession, and then we can make an informed judgment with regard to whether we're in the right position.

OFHEO: Was it your understanding then based on your understanding of what GAAP required with respect to the maintenance of a reserve and the amount of that reserve, that using the most adverse consequences was appropriate under GAAP?

JONES: Rob Arnall [the Arthur Andersen engagement partner] was there in the audit committee meetings when this was discussed. Clearly, he was opining to us that the financial statements were in accordance with GAAP. The loan loss reserve was the largest reserve on the balance sheet. Every quarter when we had the sensitive estimates and judgments report, the loan loss reserve was the biggest number in the report and Rob Arnall was sitting right there. It was clear to us that we were on the conservative end of the spectrum. Never was it indicated that we were not in compliance with GAAP.

OFHEO: In connection with concerns expressed by the SEC about earnings management and use of cookie jar reserves, did the intersection of maintaining reserves at such a conservative level, even with Mr. Arnall's blessing, did the board ever discuss maintaining reserves at that level in connection with the SEC's concerns about cookie jar reserves?

JONES: It was a non sequitur because it's not like we were taking the reserve level up and down in order to either reduce earnings or increase earnings. They were maintained at a high level, period. Flat, at the peak, through the period. So it wasn't like the reserve level was being manipulated in order to achieve a P&L impact. The reserves were kept at a high level purely for the balance sheet protection.

The OFHEO and the SEC did ultimately bring civil fraud charges against Freddie Mac's chief executive officer, president, chief financial officer, and several other executives, but no charges were filed against any Freddie Mac board member. My deposition testimony made it clear that the audit committee had very credible rationales for all its decisions and actions. In that context, I think my testimony was successful. I believe that my stout defense of the audit committee in both depositions was a key element in this outcome.

On September 7, 2007, the SEC issued a press release titled "Freddie Mac, Four Former Executives Settle SEC Action Relating to Multi-Billion Dollar Accounting Fraud." It read in part:

> The Securities and Exchange Commission today charged the Federal Home Loan Mortgage Corporation (Freddie Mac) with securities fraud in connection with improper earnings management beginning as early as 1998 and lasting into 2002. To settle the SEC charges, Freddie Mac agreed to pay a $50 million penalty, which is expected to be distributed to injured investors through a Fair Fund.
>
> The SEC's complaint alleges that Freddie Mac engaged in a fraudulent scheme that deceived investors about its true performance, profitability, and growth trends. According to the complaint, Freddie Mac misreported its net income in 2000, 2001, and 2002 by 30.5 percent, 23.9 percent, and 42.9 percent, respectively. Furthermore, Freddie Mac's senior management exerted consistent pressure to have the company report smooth and dependable earnings growth in order to present investors with the image of a company that would continue to generate predictable and growing earnings.
>
> The charged former Freddie Mac executives are David W. Glenn (president, chief operating officer, and vice chairman of the board);

Vaughn A. Clarke (chief financial officer); and former senior vice presidents Robert C. Dean and Nazir G. Dossani.

According to the Commission's complaint, Freddie Mac's violations were a direct result of a corporate culture that placed great emphasis on steady earnings, and a senior management that fostered a corporate image that was touted as "Steady Freddie" to the marketplace. Among the violations alleged in the complaint is the use of certain transactions to nullify the transitional effects of the company's implementation of accounting standard SFAS 133 (which relates to accounting for derivative instruments and hedging activities); the improper change in valuing the company's "swaptions" portfolio at year-end 2000; the improper use of derivatives to shift earnings between periods; the improper use of a reserve in connection with the company's application of SFAS 91 (which relates to accounting for loan origination costs); the use of certain transactions to nullify the effects of an accounting pronouncement known as Emerging Issues Task Force Issue 99–20; and the maintenance and reporting of a reserve for losses on loans materially in excess of probable losses. A similar settlement was announced on November 7, 2007, with regard to the civil fraud charges OFHEO brought against Freddie Mac CEO Leland Brendsel, who agreed to pay $16.4 million.

For me, the primary impact of this Freddie Mac saga was as an enormous drain of time for special board meetings, meetings with Freddie Mac legal counsel, and meetings with my personal legal counsel to prepare for the OFHEO and SEC depositions. It was a distraction from my responsibilities at Citigroup. There were also newly proposed New York Stock Exchange and SEC rules on director independence which, if implemented, might create an appearance of conflict with Citigroup's ongoing business relationships with companies whose boards I served on. The risks and potential negatives of my Freddie Mac board membership had tilted to the point where they outweighed the positives, so I resigned in 2004.

Ironically, in 2008 Freddie Mac had inadequate mortgage loan loss reserves to weather that year's global financial crisis. It was consequently taken into receivership by the U.S. government. Just four years earlier, the SEC and the OFHEO had charged Freddie Mac with civil fraud and fined it for "maintenance and reporting of a reserve for losses on loans materially in excess of probable losses."

It was also ironic that Greg Parseghian's exceptional understanding of mortgage-backed securities, and his exceptional skills in managing MBS portfolio risk characteristics, were precisely what Freddie Mac most needed when the U.S. mortgage crisis exploded in 2008. Freddie Mac was more vulnerable to the mortgage crisis because its most talented mortgage portfolio management executives had been driven out of the company by the OFHEO and the SEC.

8

Hung Out to Dry

"A lot of the people I liked and respected are gone," Mr. Weill
told a friend.

—WALL STREET JOURNAL, *November 9, 2007*

By 2003, Citigroup was indisputably the world's largest financial conglomerate. Yes, its reputation had suffered some setbacks—SEC investigations into Citigroup's dealings with Enron and WorldCom, Inc., and an embarrassing settlement with regulators that had barred Sandy, as the *New York Times* reported, from "communicating with his firm's stock analysts about the companies they cover unless a lawyer was present." Back in the fall of 2002, under government scrutiny of the Enron and WorldCom dealings of our Salomon unit, Citigroup had reassigned Michael Carpenter, head of Citigroup's corporate and investment bank, and later that same September, Citigroup had paid $215 million to settle allegations of deceptive lending against its First Capital subsidiary. In March, when Sandy was nominated to the board of the New York Stock Exchange, New York State attorney general Eliot Spitzer called it "an outrage," and within days Sandy had withdrawn his name.

Sandy was seventy years old and he had no succession plan in place. The world waited and speculated about his next move. As head of a major business unit in the organization, and one that was performing above expectations, I felt secure. I might very well be at or near the top of Sandy's yet to be revealed list of possible successors, as far as I knew. I was fifty-four years old.

Then, on July 16, 2003, Sandy announced that he was relinquishing his CEO position at the end of the year and naming Citigroup general counsel Charles Prince as his successor. I was caught off guard by the choice. We all were. The timing of Sandy's departure, and the selection of Prince as his successor, flummoxed both the broader Wall Street community and those of us closest to the situation, members of his senior management team. Chuck was not a proven effective senior business manager. He wasn't a leader. So why choose him? Maybe, the whispered speculation went, Attorney General Spitzer or the Securities and Exchange Commission was close to bringing charges against Sandy, and he had offered to step down as part of a deal to avoid such charges. Or, alternatively, maybe Sandy trusted Chuck more than anyone else in senior management to use company resources to protect and defend him from possible charges by Spitzer or the SEC, and to refuse any negotiated settlements that might imply or acknowledge any wrongdoing by Sandy. Chuck Prince, popular opinion concluded, would simply be a figurehead to placate regulators while Sandy continued running the company behind the scenes.

Sandy's motive for naming Chuck might be explained in retrospect by a *New York Times* article regarding Hank Greenberg, CEO of American International Group, who was also under pressure from Spitzer at about the same time. The article, by Danny Hakim, headlined "Wall Street Titan Takes Aim at the Law That Sidelined Him" and dated April 16, 2018, read in part:

> At 92, Maurice R. Greenberg is not done fighting. Mr. Greenberg, known as Hank, is a revered figure on Wall Street who built the American International Group into an insurance giant, only to lose it in 2005 amid a securities fraud investigation . . . Mr. Greenberg has taken aim at the Martin Act, the sweeping state securities law that was used against him . . . The Martin Act, a 1921 New York securities law that predates the creation of the Federal Securities and Exchange Commission, grants sweeping powers exceeding even those of Washington. In addition to bringing the case against Mr. Greenberg, the former New York attorney general Eliot Spitzer used the act to force investment banks to curb abuses related to how investment analysts overhyped stocks . . . Mr. Greenberg has disputed much about the case. "Eliot Spitzer decided he wanted to take me down," he said. "He was successful, destroying a company that had a $180 billion market cap."

I viewed Chuck Prince as Sandy's *consigliere*. He was both the right-hand man who protected the boss's back and also the court jester who organized and presided at Sandy's unfailingly humorous birthday celebrations year after year. "Sandy will still be in charge," I thought, "unofficially." But that presented me with a quandary: I did not *want* to work for Prince, and I was mindful that a key ingredient in my career success had been that I had always avoided working for people with whom I was unlikely to form a strong personal bond. I thought hard about putting feelers out now for a position at another company. But I hesitated. I knew it would be difficult to secure external opportunities as interesting and stimulating as my position running one of Citigroup's global businesses.

Adding to my inertia was the fact that Sandy and Chuck went to great lengths to convince us in senior management, especially Citigroup president Bob Willumstad himself, that Chuck and Bob would operate as a team. Three-quarters of the operations would report to Bob, they pointed out. Their reassurances were significant, because the senior business leaders, including myself, would report to Bob, who was universally held in high regard by the senior management organization. "I'll give this new arrangement a year," I decided. Maybe it would turn out to be positive. But my decision to stick around ultimately proved to be the biggest mistake of my career.

At the end of July 2003, Citigroup and J. P. Morgan Chase & Co. announced a $305 million settlement with the SEC and the Manhattan district attorney related to loans and trades made with Enron and Dynegy that were allegedly central to the frauds perpetrated by those companies. In September 2003 it was announced that Citigroup's succession plan would be accelerated, and Chuck Prince would take over as CEO on October 1. Then in May 2004, Citigroup announced a $2.65 billion settlement with World-Com investors, which the *New York Times* termed "the second-largest ever in a securities class-action case."

The *Times* followed up on May 16, 2004, with a feature article by Gretchen Morgenson and Timothy O'Brien, "When Citigroup Met World-Com," detailing the numerous intricate relationships between Citigroup, WorldCom, and WorldCom CEO Bernard Ebbers's personal finances. It also discussed the involvement of Sandy Weill, his son Marc Weill, CEO of corporate and investment banking Michael Carpenter, head of investment banking Eduardo Maestre, and Tom King, the head of telecommunications investment banking. "Besides [telecommunications analyst Jack B.] Grubman, Eduardo Maestre, Citigroup's head of investment banking, pursued WorldCom ardently," concluded the article, as did Mr. Maestre's chief telecom banker, Thomas King. To keep Mr. Grubman from bolting to a rival firm, Mr. Weill paid him handsomely and closely monitored his involvement with the telecom industry . . . With WorldCom headed for bankruptcy, the reckoning had begun. Mr. Grubman left Citigroup in August 2002, paid a $15 million fine to regulators and was barred from the securities industry for life. Mr. Carpenter was reassigned. Mr. King and Mr. Maestre moved on to new duties at the bank. And, of course, there was the $2.65 billion the bank paid last week to settle the class-action suit. Mr. Weill stepped aside as chief executive on October 1, 2003.

Inside Citigroup, these events further fueled the speculation that Chuck Prince's appointment as CEO was motivated by Sandy's desire for protection from charges. I kept my head down and focused on working with Bob Willumstad and interacting very little with Prince. On the few occasions when we did interact, I was friendly and respectful but not especially deferential. I was operating on the theory that Chuck was a harmless figurehead.

Then I was hit with an unexpected tidal wave of regulatory problems in two of my business units. A whistleblower letter to the SEC alleged Citigroup Asset Management (CAM) regulatory violations in 1999 when First Data Corp, which was both a Citigroup investment banking client and a service provider, sought to renew its 1999 transfer agent contract with CAM's mutual funds business unit, using its banking client status to bring pressure within Citigroup for the contract to be renewed. I had insulated myself from that pressure by assigning CAM executive vice president Michael Yellin to conduct an objective business review of transfer agent alternatives, with a focus on quality and cost. I also had assigned global investment management and CAM general counsel Michael Rosenbaum to oversee vetting of legal issues, assisted by an experienced CAM assistant general counsel, Christine Sydor, who had worked with the mutual fund boards for many years. I had adopted a "tied score goes to the home team" posture, meaning that CAM would support renewal of the First Data contract only if it was objectively better or equal to the best alternatives available to the mutual funds business unit.

Prior to my arrival at Travelers Group in 1997, the asset management business had operated as a division within Smith Barney's brokerage and investment banking business unit. Many asset management decisions had been subordinated to the priorities of the brokerage and investment banking businesses, which is why asset management had been placed in a mediocre contract in the first place with a second-tier transfer agent like First Data Corp. To create breathing room for my asset management team to exit or restructure the First Data contract, I had required this careful review of the contract and competitors, all without sparking open conflict with Smith Barney's brokerage and investment banking senior executives.

Mike Yellin's team had recommended, in the end, that we internalize the transfer agent function, using First Data on a subcontracting basis only, for certain transfer agent functions. The new contract documents had been vetted by CAM attorneys Rosenbaum and Sydor. It is noteworthy that the supervision and reporting for legal and compliance teams in all Citigroup business units were what we called "matrixed," with one line of reporting to the business unit and a second line of reporting to the Citigroup corporate general counsel or chief compliance officer. This structure was intended to ensure independent and objective legal and compliance advice to the business units and visibility of important legal and compliance issues to the corporate general counsel or chief compliance officer. Rosenbaum and Sydor reported to me, and they also reported to Chuck Prince, who was corporate general counsel when the new transfer agency contract was executed in 1999.

The proposed transfer agency arrangements had been coordinated with the various mutual fund boards by Heath McLendon, a highly experienced and respected thirty-year veteran of working with the mutual fund boards, as well as by Lew Daidone, an experienced financial executive, and attorney Sydor. I was responsible for the transfer agent internalization decision, but I did not participate in the preparation or presentation of materials for the mutual fund boards, and I did not attend the mutual fund board meetings. The presentation materials were prepared by Mike Yellin's team, including Lew Daidone, reviewed by Sydor and Rosenbaum, and presented by Yellin's team with legal counsel Sydor present at each mutual fund board meeting.

Five years later, a staff person who had been terminated by CAM wrote a whistleblower letter to the SEC claiming that proper disclosures hadn't been made to the mutual fund boards. When notified by the SEC, Citigroup's general counsel initiated an investigation and determined that $17 million should be repaid to the mutual funds, which we reported to the SEC. In July of 2004, the SEC let us know that it was considering an investigation and enforcement action against Citigroup over the handling of this renegotiated contract. The *Wall Street Journal* ran a story, "Citigroup Inc.: SEC May Recommend Action Tied to In-House Disclosure," which summarized a Citigroup regulatory filing:

> Citigroup Inc. was notified that the staff of the Securities and Exchange Commission may recommend an enforcement action in connection with the previously announced probe at the company's Smith Barney mutual-fund family. In November, Citigroup said that it had informed regulators about a problem with transfer-agent agreements related to its mutual-fund business.
>
> Citigroup said the agreements, related to the creation of an internal transfer-agent unit, weren't properly disclosed to its in-house mutual funds. In response, it said it was paying those funds about $17 million that its asset-management arm received under the arrangement. In a regulatory filing yesterday, Citigroup said it received notification, known as a Wells notice, that the SEC staff is considering recommending a "civil injunctive action and/or an administrative proceeding against certain advisory and transfer agent entities." It said the SEC staff hadn't made a formal recommendation, and that Citigroup was trying to resolve the matter in discussions with the SEC.

While the announcement of this regulatory probe was embarrassing for my business unit, I did not feel any sense of personal vulnerability because I was confident that I had handled the situation properly. The alleged failure to disclose the transfer agent economics to the mutual fund boards was primarily a mistake in the board materials review comments from the CAM legal team to the business team. No information regarding the deal with First Data had been withheld from the legal team. There were no red flags raised by the CAM legal team to alert the business team that the board materials had inadequate disclosures, and there were no red flags raised by the CAM legal team to the Citigroup corporate general counsel regarding issues or concerns with the board disclosures. I think the CAM business and legal teams reasoned that since the mutual funds were going to pay lower costs in the proposed new arrangement than they had under the previous First Data contract, and since the total fees paid by the funds were clearly and accurately disclosed, the mutual funds had objectively benefited from the new contract and the mutual fund boards were receiving adequate disclosures. Under this line of reasoning, it wasn't necessary to disclose the details of the revenue split between the new CAM internal transfer agent function and the new First Data subcontract to CAM. I believe that in a normal regulatory environment and with strong corporate support, this issue probably would have been settled with the SEC as a minor oversight which had not harmed the mutual funds. But in the overheated regulatory environment surrounding Citigroup in 2004, the alleged errors were magnified and distorted into yet another example of Citigroup's "need to reform its corporate culture," as the *Wall Street Journal* put it.

In September of 2004, the second regulatory storm hit. The Japanese banking authorities ordered us to close all Citigroup private banking operations in Japan. As the *Wall Street Journal* reported in an article titled "Japan Orders Citibank to Halt Private Banking," by Andrew Morse and Mitchell Pacelle, it was the "harshest banking penalty in Japan since a Credit Suisse Group had its license pulled in 1999." The article continued:

> In nine pages of strongly worded charges, regulators said Citibank employees failed to prevent transactions that may have been linked to money laundering, extended loans to manipulate publicly traded stocks, routinely misled customers about the risk involved in financial products and tied loans to the purchase of specific investments. The FSA [Financial Services Authority] also said Citibank officials tried to obstruct its investigation, and it criticized the efficacy of the unit's internal controls. The severity of the punishment and the nature of the complaints are likely to further damage Citigroup's already tarnished reputation. Questions over its controversial work for Enron Corp. and WorldCom Inc. have brought regulatory inquiries, shareholder lawsuits and costly settlements. Citigroup also was engulfed in a scandal over the honesty of its stock research.
>
> Charles O. Prince, Citigroup's chief executive, has been working to convince investors, customers and regulators that Citigroup has reformed its corporate culture. Yet in the 11 months since Mr. Prince took over day-to-day management from Chairman Sanford I. Weill, Citigroup has been bedeviled by a series of embarrassments. Questions have been raised about its involvement with collapsed Italian dairy giant Parmalat SPA. In May, it disclosed that the Securities and Exchange Commission had opened an investigation into its accounting treatment of investments, business activities and loan losses in Argentina. In some cases, Citigroup quickly has acknowledged mistakes. Last week it told employees in an internal memo that

it "regretted" having undertaken a controversial trading strategy that roiled European-government-bond markets in August.

Douglas Peterson, who has been Citigroup's CEO of Japan since May, issued an internal memo outlining steps the company has taken to address the FSA's concerns and admonishing employees to follow all compliance and regulatory obligations. "Let me state clearly that this bank does not condone, and it will not tolerate, behavior that violates the trust of our clients or the regulations under which we operate," Mr. Peterson wrote. How quickly Mr. Peterson will be able to restore confidence in Citigroup's Japan operations remains to be seen. The FSA investigation portrayed a culture that tolerated lax practices and suspicious transactions linked to possible criminal activity by clients as long as aggressive business targets were met. FSA officials said Citibank salespeople took advantage of Japanese customers, suggesting unrealistic returns on investments, encouraging them to purchase complicated derivative products they didn't understand and overcharging them.

The FSA officials said details of the investigation had been passed on to a unit within the agency responsible for investigating money laundering. That unit will determine whether the case merits further investigation.

I was stunned by the severity of the Japanese regulatory sanctions. Several months earlier, Chuck Prince had retained Promontory Financial Group to conduct an independent review of the looming Japanese regulatory fiasco. I had argued to both Promontory and the internal Citigroup working group that was addressing the Japanese regulatory problem that many of the issues raised by the FSA were in areas where regulations were ambiguous, and the charges themselves were vague. "Failure to prevent transactions that may have been linked to money laundering" is very different from a factual finding that those transactions actually were linked to money laundering. "Routinely misled customers about the risk involved in financial products" is a charge that must be evaluated in terms of specific facts and circumstances, because it is not uncommon for customers who are unhappy with the outcomes of their investment decisions to claim that they were misled about the risk. "Tied loans to the purchase of specific investments" also has to be evaluated with regard to specific facts and circumstances, because many bank loans are intended to support customer purchases of new investments.

Most important, I argued that the record showed that I had been diligent in my management oversight. I had visited Japan three or four times each year since 1998, and my visits always included a half-day "business review" with each of my business units, including the private bank. Every private bank business review agenda included presentation and discussion of the most recent audit and compliance reports. The Japan private bank audit and compliance reports from Citigroup corporate internal audit had been "clean opinions" for the past several years, I pointed out, and had even recommended reducing the frequency of Japan private bank compliance audits. The matrixed reporting lines of the private bank compliance team to the Citigroup corporate head of compliance and the Citigroup corporate head of internal audit had not raised any red flags to alert either private bank management or me as sector business head to any issues in private bank compliance. It was inconsistent and ironic, I suggested, that Doug Peterson, the former head of Citigroup corporate internal audit, who issued the recent laudatory reports on Japan private bank compliance and controls and recommended reduced frequency of compliance audits, was the person whom Chuck Prince named as Citigroup Japan CEO in May 2004. The email records also showed clearly that my efforts to engage proactively with Japanese regulators in April 2004 regarding a corrective action plan had been blocked by the Citigroup country manager in Japan.

I also opined privately to Bob Willumstad during the independent review that he should consider the possibility that Japanese regulators were using ambiguous rules to punish the private bank for its rapid growth and success compared to its Japanese rivals. Citigroup's private bank was the fastest-growing and most successful private bank in Japan, which had probably made it a target of complaints to the regulators from jealous and disgruntled Japanese competitors. And I also told Willumstad that he should consider the possibility that Japanese regulators were scapegoating a relatively small business unit—the private bank—as punishment for perceived regulatory abuses in Citigroup's huge consumer finance business, which was being criticized in Japanese media for charging 29 percent annual interest rates in Japan; or punishment for Citigroup's corporate and investment banking business, which was at the center of a securities-trading scandal in Japan; or punishment for Citigroup's consumer bank, which had stirred Japanese regulatory ire by losing confidential Japanese customer records from a truck in Singapore; or punishment for an incident at Citigroup's consumer bank in which a Japanese branch manager embezzled customer funds.

I suggested that Japanese regulators might be applying unusually harsh sanctions to a small business like the private bank in order to deliver a warning to Citigroup about its overall business operations in Japan while diplomatically avoiding direct attacks on the larger Citigroup businesses, which generated over $1 billion in earnings in Japan each year. My arguments were dismissed as alibis and rationalizations, which was highly frustrating. I believed that my business unit's compliance practices were at least as strong as, if not stronger than, those at any other Citigroup business unit in Japan.

It was clear to me that Promontory Financial and its CEO Eugene Ludwig were planning to issue a harsh report. I surmised that they would issue the report they thought their client wanted, and it was clear that their client was Chuck Prince. And so I was pleasantly surprised when I was allowed to read the draft report the day before Citigroup's October 2004 board meeting and did not find any severe criticism directed at me. In fact, the only mention of my name was in two footnotes which said that I had not followed up on my promise to Japanese regulators to deliver a corrective action plan addressing their draft regulatory findings. "To be fair, the Promontory report should also say that my efforts to deliver said corrective action plan were blocked by Citigroup's country manager in Japan," I pointed out to Willumstad. One thing I will never know is whether the Promontory report's references to me were changed after I read the draft and made more pointed in the report to Citigroup's board. It's also possible, or even likely, that few or none of Citigroup's board members actually read the Promontory report but instead simply accepted Chuck Prince's characterization of its findings.

The Citigroup board met at corporate headquarters, at 399 Park Avenue, on October 19, 2004. I made a presentation to the board in the morning and attended an audit committee lunch meeting. I was waiting to present to a board committee at approximately 2:30 that afternoon when I was summoned to go to Chuck Prince's office immediately. I was directed to the adjacent sitting room, where Prince and Bob Willumstad were waiting in easy chairs. I took a seat across from them, and Prince said, "We feel we've got to make some difficult decisions. We feel the best thing to do is separate the management responsible for this situation. The board has decided that you and Deryck Maughan and Peter Scaturro are being terminated. The announcement will be made at five pm today. I'm telling you now so that you will have an opportunity to speak to your people before the announcement. Michael Schlein [in Human Resources] will be available to inform you of the separation arrangements when you're ready." I was quiet for about thirty seconds, studying their faces and calming my emotions. Bob Willumstad was looking down and away, as if he was embarrassed and did not want to look me in the eye. Chuck Prince, by contrast, was looking directly at me. His face was very somber, but I thought I could see a glint of enjoyment in his eyes. I spoke quietly and calmly and said, "Chuck, how is this a fair thing to do?" He replied dismissively, "I'm not interested in getting into degrees of culpability."

"Does Sandy know about this?" I asked.

"Sandy was part of the decision," he said. Again, I breathed slowly and gathered myself. I looked at Prince and said quietly, "Why do you feel the need to do this? You're probably ending my career. All you had to do was tell me that you are the new CEO and prefer to have your own team, and tell me I have six months to transition out of the company. There's no need to conduct a public execution."

"I'm doing it this way," he replied coldly, "because I prefer to do it this way." Bob glanced up at me briefly and then returned to looking down at the floor. I summoned all my willpower and self-control to remain calm. I did not want to give Prince the satisfaction of seeing the pain and anguish I was feeling. I said, "Okay. I need to call my wife and talk to my people," and I returned to my office.

Once there, I called Addie. "There's going be a press release at five pm announcing that I've been fired by Citigroup," I told her. "I wanted you to hear it first from me." She gasped and then was quiet for a moment. Then she said, obviously shocked, "What happened?"

"I'm going to meet briefly with my senior staff prior to the announcement," I said, "and I'll probably leave the office around five pm to come home. I'll explain what's happening when I get home."

My senior direct reports had been asked to assemble in the conference room near my office. I told them, "I've been terminated from the company, and there will be a public announcement at five pm today. I want you to know that I've really enjoyed working with you and I'm proud of what we've accomplished together." The staff reaction was stunned disbelief followed by an emotional outpouring. It took longer than I had expected to shake hands with everyone and say good-bye, and then I returned to my office to pack my personal items into cardboard banker boxes.

At 6:39 pm I sent the following email message to my senior staff around the world, had two boxes of papers, family photographs, and memorabilia sent down to my car, and left the Citigroup office:

Tuesday October 19, 2004, 6:39 pm
FROM: Jones, Thomas W.
RE: Good-bye and Best Wishes

By now you have been informed that I have been asked to leave Citigroup, along with Deryck Maughan and Peter Scaturro. I want you to know that I have always held myself to the highest ethical and moral standards, and I have not knowingly violated my fiduciary duties to our clients or my moral obligations to you my colleagues. I wish you well and I will miss our professional partnership. I have every hope and expectation that we will continue our friendships.

My driver was waiting in the usual location on 54th Street just east of Park Avenue. The traffic was heavy so the drive took longer than usual. I didn't want to talk. My mind was racing: "This isn't a dream, this is real. You were just fired and your career is over. What a fool you are. You thought you were important. Big job. Big title. But you were nothing—they threw you out like an old dishrag. What are you going to say to Addie? How are you going to explain this to your family?" My mind raced in circles, around and around and around.

Three days later, on October 23, 2004, another shoe dropped. I received, via a registered letter delivered to my house, a Wells notice—a warning letter from the SEC informing me that I could expect to face an imminent civil complaint from the commission. That same day, the *New York Times* ran a story by Thomas Landon Jr. about me headlined "S.E.C. Warns It May Act on Ex-Officer of Citigroup," which read in part:

On the surface, the S.E.C. investigation would seem to pale in comparison to the other regulatory run-ins that Citigroup has encountered over the last three years. All the same, it raises some uncomfortable questions with regard to the quality of executive decision making at the top tier of Citigroup's business units. Between 1997 and 1999, Mr. Jones decided to bring in house the bank's transfer agency operations, a business that documents the ownership of securities within the firm's mutual funds.

The initiative was aimed at reducing fund fees, a goal Citigroup executives say was met. Subsequently, Mr. Jones and other executives within the unit decided to pass on a portion of the agency business to an outside vendor, the First Data Corporation. The agreement with First Data included a revenue guarantee of $16 million that was paid to Citigroup Asset Management but that was not passed on to its mutual funds as it should have been. Nor were the payments ever disclosed. Citigroup is repaying the amount to its funds with interest although it has offered no explanation as to why it received such a revenue guarantee. While Citigroup itself received a notice in July, securities lawyers said yesterday that the payment and the nondisclosure were at the heart of the S.E.C. investigation.

In the days following my departure from the office, I called three senior Citigroup board members to request that they conduct an independent board investigation, to ensure that the board understood all of the facts before locking in final decisions. I called Reuben Mark, CEO of Colgate Palmolive; Richard Parsons, CEO of AOL–Time Warner; and Frank Thomas, retired president of the Ford Foundation. Each of them took my call, but all three told me they supported the actions taken by CEO Chuck Prince. None of them seemed to want to hear what I had to say, and none of them wanted to conduct a board investigation. Finally, I called Sandy Weill. He said that he was sorry, but it was Chuck's decision, and he, Sandy, had had nothing to do with it.

Citigroup allowed me to access my work email for several days after I was terminated, and I received a steady stream of messages. I was proud, again, that many of the messages echoed those I had received when I left TIAA-CREF and suggested, again, that many of the people who worked with me had been lifted by our interactions. I offer a few of those messages as examples of how my people expressed their feelings.

October 19, 2004, 6:47 pm
From: Alan Blake
Re: Goodbye and Best Wishes

Thank you for everything you have done to help build asset management. I have nothing but the highest regard for you and have felt that you provided great business and moral leadership. This is a sad day for me.

Alan

October 19, 2004, 7:00 pm
FROM: Farzan Riza
RE: Goodbye and Best Wishes

Tom, I am hurt, sad and shocked to hear this news. I have the highest regard for you and believe that you showed tremendous leadership and courage in leading GIM/CAM. You always have and will continue to exemplify in my mind the highest ethical and moral standards. I have learnt a lot from you and will miss you. I hope to continue our friendship.

Best, Farzan

October 19, 2004, 9:15 pm
FROM: Joseph Lohrer
RE: Goodbye and Best Wishes

Tom, I am unable to express the full degree of my appreciation, gratitude, and unwavering loyalty to you for all you have done for me and for the organization, in the form of an email. You have influenced me both professionally and personally in a significantly positive fashion for which I will always feel indebted. As a demonstration of true leadership, your contributions not only lifted an organization, but the people within it, to levels never believed achievable. I hope to have an opportunity to acknowledge your impact in person. Thanks for all you have done!!!!!

Your partner and friend,
Joe Lohrer

October 20, 2004, 6:50 am
FROM: Cyrus Taraporevala
RE: Goodbye and Best Wishes

Tom, I am still stunned by the announcement . . . Of all the people I have met at Citigroup, you have been the one who has most impressed me by your high moral standards, and your dictum to always "do the right thing" for clients. You have been wonderful to me every step of the way. THANK YOU for the opportunities you have provided me since I got to Citi only 4 months ago. I am forever in your debt.

Cyrus

October 20, 2004, 9:29 am
FROM: Joseph Deane
RE: Goodbye and Best Wishes

Dear Tom,

In my mind and heart you're the best I've ever worked for and with. Even your golf game was starting to come around as we witnessed at the Valley. Sometime in the next week I'd love to come up to Connecticut and take you out to lunch and just chat. Hersh and I look like two kids who were just told there is no Santa Claus, doubly hard on Hersh, cause he's Jewish and never had one to begin with. As you get older in your career you can really appreciate a mentor who can deflect some heat and allow you to do what you do best. You're a wonderful human being and nothing will ever change that opinion for me, not to mention you're pretty funny (for a corporate titan). All the best to the best!

Joe

October 20, 2004, 4:33 pm
FROM: Juliet Willetts
RE: Thanks

It is hard to put into words the tremendous loss I feel as a result of the recent developments, you will be and are greatly missed. Your leadership and integrity as a business head have been examples and motivation for me as a professional to continue to try harder to be the best that I can be. I truly believe the credit for the positive migration of our business, in making it a competitive force in the industry, lies with you as a result of your steadfast commitment and business savvy. At CAM, you harnessed great resources, glued it together, directed it and gave it a brand, one that I have been proud to be a part of under your leadership. That feeling is borne out by the numerous calls that I have received today from FCs [financial consultants] and BOMs [branch office managers] alike, all echoing astonishment and loss. Thank you for the many years that I truly believed that I worked for the greatest company in the world and giving us the "urgency to be excellent."

Respectfully,
Juliet Willetts

October 20, 2004, 6:07 pm
From: Gordon Bell
Re: CAM

Dear Tom,

I am deeply saddened by the news of your departure. While your enormous contributions to CAM and Citigroup are a matter of public record, also know that your listening, encouragement, and support have contributed greatly to me. Tom, your brilliance and integrity are a shining example to all, and my loyalty remains with you.

Regards,
Gordon

October 21, 2004, 1:06 am
From: Hirohisa Tajima
Re: please check

Tom,

I am very sorry to have an announcement of your resignation. You are a great leader and the best boss I have ever worked with in the industry in nearly 30 years. We, all CAMco staff will miss you. Our clients you met had been impressed on your presence as a leader in CAM. You are a gentleman and earnestness. I learned tons of things from you whenever you visit Japan as a professional businessman. You showed us that top management should be like this. My appreciation of your help in establishing of asset management business in Japan is beyond my description. Your strong support and vision on our business makes the foundation of CAM's retail business in Japan. Kane-san, your friend and President of Mitsubishi Securities, would be grateful if he can meet with you to say Hello during his stay in New York in the period of Nov. 18th to Nov. 23rd. Tom, please visit Japan with your family for your refreshment. I will show you wonderful places in Japan.

October 22, 2004, 11:51 am
FROM: Harry Cohen
RE: Goodbye and Best Wishes

just a note to say we are thinking of you . . . hope you are ok . . . know that you are loved by so many here.

Also, a few days later, I received a small package from Thomas Pulling, one of my senior executives in CAM. It was a framed quotation from Theodore Roosevelt, which read:

It is not the critic who counts, not the man who points out how the strong man stumbled, or where the doer of deeds could have done them better. The credit belongs to the man who is actually in the arena; whose face is marred by dust and sweat and blood; who strives valiantly; who errs and comes short again and again; who knows the great enthusiasms; the great devotions; and spends himself in a worthy cause; who, at the best, knows in the end the triumph of high achievement; and who, at the worst, if he fails, at least fails while daring greatly, so that his place shall never be with those cold and timid souls who know neither victory nor defeat.

I appreciated this gesture from Tom and have kept this framed quotation in my office to this day.

At home there was that first strange Wednesday, October 20, with nowhere to go. I could have left the house, of course. I still had dozens of friends, hundreds of business associates, after all. Emails and notes of support and affection were still pouring in for me. But I was essentially alone—more alone than I'd ever felt before. I woke up at my normal time, 5:30 in the morning. (My usual routine had me up at 5:30, picked up by my driver at 6:30, and at my Citigroup office on Park Avenue by 7:30.) In my closet, my dark suits and white shirts hung in a long row. I reached instead for something more casual, the kind of thing I usually saved for the weekends, chinos and a blue oxford shirt. Addie, who normally slept through my early morning routine, was awake in our bed, propped up a little on her pillows, watching me in the dim room. In her yellow silk nightgown, with her slim arms resting at her sides, she looked as beautiful as I'd ever seen her, but more worried, too. "I'm going downstairs to my office," I said to her.

I tried to think how to soothe the pain my family was suffering. How could the brutal events that were unfolding occur in the elite corporate business world, they must have wondered? As long as they could remember, I had been the master of my own fate, it seemed, always excelling, always calm, always prepared. My constant watchword to the children was self-discipline, and mastery of the self had seemed to be enough to reach any height, achieve any dream. I knew they were probably embarrassed and humiliated by the constant stream of negative news stories and the questions from their friends and acquaintances. I knew they were probably apprehensive about what might happen to me, and how all our lives might be affected. I suspected that they wondered, but would not ask, whether perhaps I had indeed done something unethical.

I reassured Addie and our close relatives and the kids as best I could that I hadn't done anything improper, let alone illegal, and everything would eventually work out, but it would take some time to get through this. "I need," I told them, "quiet time to meditate and pray and think."

Addie was afraid. She couldn't conceive how a decision like this could be made at Citigroup without Sandy's blessing. And if the decision did have his blessing, it meant that Sandy must have thought I'd done something terribly wrong. I must be facing potentially severe legal and financial punishments by the SEC, Addie concluded.

To their credit, Sandy Weill's wife, Joan, and Bob Willumstad's wife, Carol, were among the Citigroup spouses who called Addie to express their horror at what had been done to me. The messages from company insiders that I was not deserving of the treatment I received were somewhat reassuring to Addie.

Most important, I turned to my faith for comfort. Despite how alone I felt those first few hours and days, in fact I knew I was never alone; none of us ever is. God was with me. One of my daily prayers, which stood me in good stead during this period, said in part, "I affirm my belief, my Father, that all things work together for good to those who love Thee . . . And I will not walk in fear because I know that Thou hast not given me the spirit of fear, but rather the spirit of power and of love and of sound mind."

I spent the next two weeks meditating and praying, trying to understand what good could possibly come from being suddenly and summarily fired from a job I had loved and done well in, in the context of my prayer affirming my faith that "all things work together for good to those who love Thee." It was difficult to fathom how any good could possibly come from such a calamity. Everything that I was as a man—a success, a proven manager, an excellent provider for my family, a Wall Street leader, a straight shooter with the highest ethical standards for myself and those around me, competent, careful, diligent, principled—all those things seemed to have been thrown in the mud, spat upon. Nothing like this combination of being fired and simultaneously abandoned to face SEC charges alone, without company protection, had ever happened before to another Citigroup senior executive, but now it was happening to me. Why? I prayed for healing for my family's pain, and for my own pain. And I prayed for the strength to pick myself up and move forward.

In the months following my firing in October 2004, Citigroup's public relations machinery tried to bury me in negative publicity while attributing noble motivations to Chuck Prince for his actions. It started with Citigroup providing the *Wall Street Journal* with selected portions of the confidential Promontory report, which led to a major article by Mitchell Pacelle, Martin Fackler, and Andrew Morse on December 22, 2004, headlined "Mission Control: For Citigroup, Scandal in Japan Shows Dangers of Global Sprawl; Obsession with Bottom Line and Bickering Executives Created a 'Perfect Storm'; A Scathing Internal Report," which cast the Japan unit fiasco as a result of ethics failings. "Mr. Prince has declined repeatedly to comment on the dismissals," read the article on the topic of my firing, "but he has been vocal about steps he is taking to prevent another disaster. Compliance officers, for example, no longer answer to business heads . . . but report up an independent chain of command directly to the head risk officer in New York. Mr. Prince says he plans to revamp employee training to focus on ethics."

Two articles, one in the *New York Times* and one in the *Wall Street Journal,* made it clear that Citigroup intended to settle the SEC charges and exclude me from the settlement. Citigroup provided information for the *New York Times* story on January 22, 2005, headlined "Citigroup Warns of S.E.C. Action." It read in part:

> Citigroup said yesterday that regulators of the Securities and Exchange Commission were considering recommending a civil injunction, administrative proceedings or both against two of its units and four current or former employees. The S.E.C. may take action against Citigroup Asset Management; Citicorp Trust Bank; Thomas W. Jones, the former chief executive of the asset management unit; and three other people, one of whom is still with the unit. Citigroup said the commission took issue with actions related to its creation and operation of an internal transfer agent unit serving more than 20 closed-end funds that the company managed. The company said it was cooperating with the commission and was seeking to reach a settlement.

Citigroup began negotiating to settle the SEC investigation with regard to possible charges against Citigroup but did not include my attorneys in the settlement negotiations, an unusual omission. Citigroup's settlement, which included no admission or denial of guilt, was announced on June 5, 2005: the company would pay $208 million. The *Wall Street Journal* article noted that "the settlement relates to [Citigroup's] 1999 decision to set up an internal transfer agent to service its Smith Barney family of mutual funds," and that the SEC claimed Citigroup had "reaped nearly $100 million in profit at the funds' expense." The article also announced to the world that I, personally, was still under a cloud of suspicion (and probable threat of SEC charges): "Citigroup disclosed last fall that its asset-management arm; its former chief, Thomas W. Jones; two other former employees; and an unnamed current employee, had received so-called Wells notices from the SEC, indicating possible enforcement actions against them. In announcing yesterday's settlement, the SEC said its investigation was continuing with respect to the individuals involved."

When I read about Citigroup's settlement, I suspected immediately that someone had set me up. Someone must have instructed Citigroup's legal counsel to initiate settlement discussions with the SEC on the transfer agency investigation, but to omit the usual and customary condition in all previous Citigroup regulatory settlements that any corporate settlement would also extend to and include all the senior executives who were potential targets of the investigation. If my suspicions were correct, if someone had indeed instructed counsel to omit that usual provision, it would have immediately stood out to the SEC, which probably would have interpreted it as signaling that Citigroup had conducted an internal investigation of the transfer agency allegations and concluded that I was at fault and therefore not deserving of company protection. This scenario would parallel the recent disclosure by Citigroup that Promontory had been retained to conduct an "independent investigation" of the Japan private bank situation and had concluded that I was one of those at fault, even though the Promontory report I was shown didn't say that at all. If my suspicions were correct, it meant that someone was essentially painting a target on my back for the SEC.

During the entire ongoing firestorm of Citigroup's corporate ethics scandals, which had begun with Enron and WorldCom in 2000 and swirled around Citigroup every year since, this was the first and only time that Citigroup entered into a regulatory settlement without including and protecting the senior executives of the affected business unit in the terms of the settlement. In every other case, Citigroup had crafted settlements, paid fines, and agreed to the usual and customary language of "neither admitted nor denied wrongdoing," with the terms of settlement applying to both the company and the senior executives of the business unit under investigation. This was the only time that a Citigroup business unit head who had reported directly to Sandy Weill was excluded from the protections of a company regulatory settlement.

The Citigroup public relations machinery had been touting new CEO Chuck Prince's determination to "clean up" company culture and "hold senior executives responsible for bad behavior." I apparently had been selected to be Exhibit A in Chuck Prince's culture cleanup. But the irony of making an example of me was that roughly 90 percent of Citigroup's regulatory problems originated in the Global Corporate and Investment Banking business unit, roughly 9 percent originated in the Global Consumer Banking business unit, and perhaps 1 percent had originated in my Global Investment Management business unit.

My suspicions were corroborated by a *Wall Street Journal* article on August 9, 2005, which was headlined "Citigroup Ex-Officials Face Charges:

SEC Civil Fraud Complaint Says Two Former Executives Mishandled Fund Discounts." I focused on the two paragraphs:

> The Securities and Exchange Commission accused Thomas W. Jones, a former top Citigroup Inc. executive, of fraud yesterday in connection with fees collected by Citigroup from the mutual funds he once supervised. According to a civil complaint filed in Manhattan federal court, Mr. Jones and a second former executive, Lewis E. Daidone, were principally responsible for a fraud related to Citigroup's creation of an affiliated transfer agent to serve its Smith Barney family of mutual funds at discounted rates. Rather than passing on the discounts to the funds themselves, Citigroup reaped most of the benefit, which amounted to tens of millions of dollars, the complaint said.
>
> In late May, Citigroup agreed to pay $208 million to settle SEC fraud charges related to the matter. But Mr. Jones, 56 years old, former chief executive of Citigroup's global asset-management arm, had resisted agreeing to any settlement that suggested he acted improperly . . . In a prepared statement, a lawyer for Mr. Jones vowed to fight the charges in federal court. "Mr. Jones did not aid and abet any fraudulent activity during his watch at Citigroup Asset Management," said James R. Doty of Baker Botts LLP. "Mr. Jones is a victim of this situation, not a perpetrator of wrongdoing."

This statement that I "resisted agreeing to any settlement that suggested [I] acted improperly" is essentially a declaration that Citigroup did not stand with me and insist on including me in its settlement without implication of wrongdoing. I was not given the option of participating in Citigroup's SEC settlement on the same terms as Citigroup, "neither admitting nor denying wrongdoing," and consistent with the treatment extended to Sandy Weill's direct report business unit heads in all prior Citigroup regulatory settlements.

To put this in perspective, regulatory skirmishes related to other business units from that period cost Citigroup over $4 billion in fines and class action lawsuit settlements. This included a payment of $214 million for deceptive and abusive lending at Associates First Capital, a $150 million fine for improper vetting of Enron and Dynegy loans and trades, a $1 billion settlement of biased stock research charges, a $2.5 billion settlement with WorldCom investors, and major investigations of Citigroup's dealings in Europe and Argentina, leading to millions more in fines and settlement fees paid. In none of these cases was the affected business unit head excluded from Citigroup's settlement terms, or required to admit any wrongdoing, or subjected to charges by the SEC.

Chuck Prince had become Citigroup CEO in late 2003, and he was the only executive with the authority to approve a regulatory settlement agreement that excluded the affected business unit head. I wondered how Sandy Weill rationalized the treatment I was receiving at the hands of his protégé. Had Sandy or anyone else pointed out to the Citigroup board the massive discrepancy between my treatment and that of all other Citigroup business unit heads? I wondered if the three black directors on Citigroup's board thought about the raw deal the most senior black executive at Citigroup was getting on their watch. Would Mike Armstrong, who belonged to the Blind Brook Club, which was also my golf club, be able to look me in the eye the next time I saw him there? How could the Citigroup directors and their spouses, with whom Addie and I had interacted socially on many occasions, seemingly not care about what Citigroup was doing to me? The Citigroup board at that time included Michael Armstrong, retired chairman and CEO of AT&T; Alain Belda, chairman and CEO of Alcoa; George David, chairman and CEO of United Technologies; Ken Derr, retired chairman and CEO of Chevron; John Deutch, Institute Professor at Massachusetts Institute of Technology; Ann Jordan, wife of civil rights leader and investment banker Vernon Jordan; Reuben Mark, chairman and CEO of Colgate Palmolive; Anne Mulcahey, chairman and CEO of Xerox; Richard Parsons, chairman and CEO of AOL– Time Warner; Judith Rodin, president of the Rockefeller Foundation; Robert Rubin, former treasury secretary and chairman of Citigroup's executive committee; Frank Thomas, former president of the Ford Foundation; and Sandy Weill, who was still the chairman of Citigroup's board. These directors were all highly regarded and thought of themselves as good people. But I wondered if they gave any thought at all to the pain they were inflicting on me, and on my wife, and on my children.

They were parties to a level of brutality toward me that would previously have been unthinkable in any elite Wall Street firm, and had never been experienced by any of my white senior management peers at Citigroup. Somehow they must have rationalized that it was acceptable to inflict this fight for reputation, career, and solvency on me. I must have become invisible to them, I realized. I and my family just did not matter to them.

I thought the entire Citigroup board should be ashamed of themselves for their role in approving this betrayal, but most especially Sandy and the three black directors: Richard Parsons, Franklin Thomas, and Ann Dibble Jordan. Their participation lent legitimacy to what Chuck Prince was doing, and possibly even helped the other Citigroup directors rationalize that "it must be okay if Sandy and Ann and Frank and Dick aren't objecting."

Evil things happen in this world in part because those who think of themselves as good people are willing to stand by and let them happen. They may rationalize what is happening, or they may avert their eyes and pretend it isn't really happening, or they may change the subject to avoid talking about it. ("Let's get focused on the important issues that are facing this company and let's move forward.") Chuck Prince just might be the only person in the Citigroup power elite who took time to think carefully about what was transpiring.

Chuck Prince had for many years negotiated the details of every Citigroup or Travelers Group regulatory settlement agreement in his capacity as *consigliere*/general counsel for Sandy Weill. It is extremely unlikely, and thus inconceivable to me, that anybody other than Prince had exercised final executive decision authority for Citigroup in settling the Smith Barney transfer agency case with the SEC. If the Citigroup board members chose not to learn the details of the settlement, they were nonetheless implicit collaborators in the treatment I received. I also believe that Chuck did it because it was in the nature of his personality to enjoy this type of exercise of power directed against someone whom he did not like.

There's an important lesson here for aspiring minority executives, public company boards of directors, and the broader business community. It is to understand that these kinds of immoral and cynical events can occur even at the highest levels of the largest and most respected companies in America.

9

Beating the SEC

And I will not walk in fear because I know that Thou has not
given me the spirit of fear but rather the spirit of power and of
love and of sound mind.

—*2 Timothy 1:7*

My spirit wasn't broken. Daily prayers and meditation enabled me
to gather my strength, pick myself up, and prepare to fight. My
first important decision: I would *not* settle any SEC charges against
me. This was a point of honor and a statement of faith and allegiance to my
family and all those colleagues who had worked with me and believed in me
that they had not been mistaken and put their trust in an unworthy person.
I simply could not concede any wrongdoing on my part, and I would not
accept any regulatory sanction, no matter how minor, if it implied that I was
in some degree guilty of civil fraud as charged by the SEC.

I knew enough about the law to understand that the SEC would probably
have extreme difficulty obtaining evidence to substantiate "scienter" on my
part. "Scienter" is a legal term meaning "knowledge of and intent to commit
wrongdoing." This is a requisite element to obtain conviction for civil or
criminal fraud in the U.S. judicial system, and it is one of the most important
protections for defendants. In my case, it meant that my efforts to involve
Citigroup Asset Management attorneys in all aspects of the transfer agency
contract, coupled with the failure of those attorneys to signal any concerns
or misgivings of any sort, would provide protection from a legal conclusion
that I knew something was wrong and knowingly intended to commit that
wrong.

My decision to challenge the SEC led me to a second important decision,
because I understood that I would probably be unemployable in the regulated

financial services industry while fighting the charges. Since it was unrealistic to hope that any SEC-regulated financial institution would want to employ a senior executive who was embroiled in an antagonistic legal battle with the SEC, I needed to be self-employed for however many years the fight would require. I started thinking about a strategy to accomplish this.

My third important decision was to fight back against Citigroup as well. I did this by retaining a "junkyard dog" litigator to bring suit against Citigroup, Chuck Prince, and Promontory Financial Group and its CEO Eugene Ludwig for wrongful termination. I knew that Chuck Prince was unlikely to be willing to subject himself to document discovery, deposition under oath, and cross-examination by my attorneys regarding the role of Citigroup's legal department in approving the transfer agency contract while he was company general counsel, and CAM's attorneys who vetted and approved the contract reported to Prince. And I knew that Prince and Ludwig were unlikely to be comfortable with being subjected to document discovery, sworn depositions, and cross-examination under oath regarding Prince's role in shaping the Promontory report and questions about whether the report given to Citigroup's board was changed after I was shown a draft containing only minimal and peripheral criticism directed at me.

I retained Stanley Arkin, a Californian and Harvard Law graduate who had founded the New York law firm Arkin Kaplan LLC. Arkin had famously and successfully tried many complicated Wall Street cases, including the very first prosecution for insider trading, and I knew he had a reputation for toughness, even nastiness, and for winning. He would represent me against Citigroup, Promontory Financial Group, Prince, and Ludwig.

In addition to launching a public relations campaign in support of Chuck Prince and his purported efforts to improve Citigroup's business ethics and culture, Citigroup also moved quickly to sell two of my three former business units. Citigroup CFO Todd Thomson later told me that Prince's initial meetings with my former senior management team did not go well. "Your people are extremely loyal to you," Todd said to me. I was also hearing from others inside Citigroup that many of the senior leaders in my former business units just weren't buying Prince's storyline. They had firsthand knowledge and experience of my ethical standards. And I was told they were vocal in saying it was absurdly unfair that I had been fired at the first hint of regulatory problems in my business unit and was being charged by the SEC, following years of scandals in the corporate and investment banking business unit which had cost billions of dollars in fines and penalties and class action settlements, but with no business unit head being held accountable by separation from the company or SEC charges.

Citigroup provided background information for a December 3, 2004, *New York Times* story reporting that Citigroup was considering a shift in strategy by selling the asset management business. Then Citigroup provided background information for a *Wall Street Journal* story on January 31, 2005, noting that Citigroup was close to selling the Travelers Life & Annuity business unit. Both these transactions came to fruition in short order. On June 27, 2005, Citigroup announced an asset swap in which its asset management business was transferred to the investment management firm Legg Mason in exchange for Legg Mason's brokerage business. And on July 5, 2005, Citigroup announced the sale of Travelers Life & Annuity to Met Life.

After several months of negotiations with Citigroup attorneys, On March 5, 2005, my attorneys at Arkin Kaplan delivered a "nearly final draft complaint" to Citigroup legal counsel outlining the legal action we intended to file the following week in New York State Supreme Court against Citigroup, Chuck Prince, Promontory Financial Group, and Eugene Ludwig. The draft complaint was a thirty-four-page detailed recitation showing how the events in Japan had been manipulated and distorted by Prince and Ludwig to justify my termination from Citigroup. The complaint requested $100 million in damages for defamation and wrongful termination.

This action had its intended effect. In April 2005 we reached an out-of-court settlement with Citigroup. The terms included Citigroup's commitment to invest $50 million in a venture capital fund I was launching, and to pay all of my legal expenses related to any matters associated with my Citigroup employment tenure. These settlement terms were critical in insulating me from the two most common forms of SEC coercion.

First, the SEC often coerces settlements from individual defendants who are intimidated by the potential costs of a legal battle with the commission, which can run into tens of millions of dollars. This is a difficult fight for individuals to wage with only their personal financial resources, and it is an unfair fight because the legal costs of combating the SEC are usually non-recoverable even if the defendant wins. This means that those individual defendants who do win are nonetheless subjected to severe financial punishment. Consequently, many individuals make a rational economic decision to settle cases for small fines or other "slaps on the wrist."

Second, the SEC often coerces settlements from individual defendants because they face severe economic pressure to return to employment in the regulated financial services industry.

My settlement with Citigroup insulated me from both of these sources of coercion: it secured self-employment income from an investment fund which I controlled, and it secured virtually unlimited legal defense resources designated and controlled by me but paid by Citigroup.

My legal defense team against the SEC was headed by Irving Terrell, a senior litigator in the Houston office of Baker Botts LLP. I had come to know the firm during the SEC and OFHEO investigations of Freddie Mac in 2003–4, when Baker Botts was retained by the board of Freddie Mac to represent the independent directors; the lead attorney in that case was James Doty, a former SEC general counsel. I was impressed with Baker Botts's attention to detail and the success the firm achieved in avoiding charges against any Freddie Mac independent directors. I had a good basis for my assessment of Baker Botts's capabilities, as I arguably spent more time with its team than any other independent director of Freddie Mac, because my position as chairman of the audit committee had put me in the investigative bull's-eye. I felt comfortable turning to Jim Doty to represent me in fighting the SEC fraud allegations at Citigroup, and Doty brought in Baker Botts's top litigator—Irving Terrell. An additional important consideration in my selection of Baker Botts was that it was not a New York law firm with substantial economic ties to Citigroup, so I considered it a low probability that Chuck Prince would be able to directly or indirectly influence or manipulate the firm behind the scenes.

On August 8, 2005, the SEC filed civil fraud charges against me, and on the same day Baker Botts released this statement, issued by James Doty on my behalf. It was intended to put the SEC's lawyers on alert that they were in for a battle, and there would be no concessions of wrongdoing on my part:

We will contest the SEC charges against Mr. Jones in federal court as we believe they are unfounded and overreaching. Mr. Jones has not participated in, or aided and abetted, any fraudulent activity on his watch at Citigroup Asset Management. The record will show that Mr. Jones achieved substantial benefit for mutual fund shareholders by obtaining relief from a long-standing First Data transfer agency contract which had been in place for over ten years before Mr. Jones joined Citigroup, and which had been driven by investment banking interests in their client relationship with First Data. Mr. Jones conducted a rigorous management process in the Citigroup Transfer Agency matter, supported by both experienced internal staff and external consulting experts. Each step of the process and final decision-making was vetted by experienced legal counsel. At no time was a "red flag" brought to Mr. Jones' attention. Mr. Jones conducted this process despite significant opposition from Citigroup investment bankers. Unfortunately, the legal advice given to Mr. Jones by legal experts was fundamentally flawed. That legal error does not make Mr. Jones guilty of negligence or intent to defraud. Mr. Jones is a victim of this situation, not a perpetrator of wrongdoing, and he made all reasonable efforts to fulfill his fiduciary duty to mutual fund shareholders. We look forward to the opportunity to defend Mr. Jones before a jury of his peers.

My case was assigned to Judge Richard Casey in U.S. District Court for the Southern District of New York. Jim Doty and Irv Terrell told me that Casey's reputation was as a "tough, usually pro-government, but fair" judge. Eighteen months of discovery, depositions, and dueling legal motions then ensued. The SEC repeatedly extended feelers to my attorneys indicating that the case could be settled if I would accept a minor slap on the wrist, such as a small fine as low as $5,000. I refused any settlement short of exoneration and instructed my attorneys to tell the SEC's lawyers that they would get nothing from me unless they won it in court.

The SEC offered lenient plea bargains to my co-defendants in an effort to secure their testimony against me. CAM executive vice president Michael Yellin, a thirty-year Citigroup employee, accepted a plea bargain because he was emotionally exhausted by what Citigroup had done to us and was planning to retire from full-time employment. Mike just didn't have the energy to engage in a protracted battle with the SEC, so he agreed to a plea bargain that entailed a small monetary fine and regulatory censure. After negotiating the plea bargain with Yellin, the SEC was furious when Yellin's subsequent sworn deposition did not provide any incriminating testimony against me. The SEC staff went so far as to threaten to revoke Yellin's settlement, which in turn prompted a complaint from my attorneys protesting the commission's efforts to intimidate and coerce the witness. I suspected that the SEC's fury was caused in part by the dawning realization that it had been duped into bringing a case that wasn't warranted. The SEC was discovering that the CAM business team had relied on advice from Citigroup attorneys at every step of the transfer agency transaction. There was no evidence of fraud to be found.

On September 26, 2006, Baker Botts filed for summary judgment of our case: "After over nine months of discovery, Plaintiff is utterly without evidence to substantiate the key elements of its case against Defendant Thomas Jones. Although Plaintiff's Complaint accuses Jones of aiding and abetting CAM's alleged fraud of withholding pertinent information from the Fund's Boards of Directors, the record incontrovertibly establishes Jones' innocence." Baker Botts went on to argue that since total mutual fund fees were indisputably disclosed clearly and accurately to the mutual fund boards and shareholders, there could be no fraud or harm deriving from the underlying allocation of those fees between the First Data transfer agent and the CAM transfer agent. My attorneys also argued that all aspects of the transfer agency contract and mutual fund board disclosures had been reviewed and approved by Citigroup's legal department, so there was no "scienter" element of intent to commit fraud.

On February 26, 2007, just a few weeks before the trial was scheduled to commence, Judge Casey issued a "Memorandum & Order" in which he ruled, "Defendants' motion for summary judgment is GRANTED in its entirety." The case against both me and Smith Barney CFO Lewis Daidone was decided in our favor and dismissed "with prejudice," which meant the judge would not allow an appeal. We had beaten the SEC.

On February 27, 2007, the *Wall Street Journal* and the *New York Times* published stories reporting on Judge Casey's decision, but neither story included comments from Irv Terrell or me. And each story was afforded far less prominence than the headlines two years earlier that had announced the SEC enforcement action against me. The *Wall Street Journal* article, "Judge Discusses Suit over Transfer Agent: SEC Had Accused Two Ex-Citigroup Executives," read in part, "A federal judge dismissed a Securities and Exchange Commission lawsuit that accused two former Citigroup executives of cheating mutual-fund customers. . . . U.S. District Judge Richard C. Casey in Manhattan granted a summary judgment motion by Thomas W. Jones, the former chief executive of Citigroup Asset Management. . . . The SEC had requested civil penalties, a permanent injunction . . . and disgorgement."

Neither did the SEC issue a statement regarding Judge Casey's summary judgment decision. This contrasts with the press conference and major publicity efforts on August 8, 2005, when the SEC announced it was filing charges against me. Eventually, in 2008, even as its official website continued to trumpet the original August 2005 announcement of enforcement action against me, the SEC grudgingly posted a banner headline in red above the August 2005 announcement reading, "NOTE: On February 26, 2007, the United States District Court for the Southern District of New York granted motions for summary judgment filed by defendants Jones and Daidone, dismissing the case with prejudice." The SEC belatedly and grudgingly started posting these notices on its website following press criticism that the commission routinely tries to "bury" the cases it loses, without ever acknowledging that it has wrongfully charged innocent individuals or taking any remedial steps to alleviate the unjustified damage it has inflicted on the reputations of those individuals. An egregious and ongoing example of this abuse is that the SEC website continues to broadcast its original charges against me, despite the fact that those charges were dismissed in federal court.

My case is a good example of why it is unfortunate that the Dodd-Frank legislation passed after the 2008 financial crisis gave new powers to the SEC to bring charges through its "administrative judge" procedures. If my case had been tried under these rules, I am certain that the SEC would have worked very hard to force its weak case against me into the administrative judge process. Studies have shown that the SEC has a much higher probability of securing a guilty verdict from one of its administrative judges than in the federal courts. It is fundamentally unfair to deny any defendant the full protections of the United States judicial system in federal courts.

At Citigroup the attorneys responsible for the erroneous legal advice supporting the transfer agency contracts, Michael Rosenbaum and Christine Sydor, were quietly eased out of the company. I suspected that Citigroup did this to avoid drawing attention to the fact that its legal department bore significant responsibility for the transfer agency imbroglio while Chuck Prince was general counsel. Citigroup never acknowledged publicly that when the transfer agent contracts were signed and the mutual fund board presentations occurred, CAM attorneys Rosenbaum and Sydor had a direct functional reporting relationship to Prince in his capacity as company general counsel, as well as reporting to me as CAM business unit head. Under Citigroup's matrix organization structure, the company general counsel was co-equal to business unit heads with regard to legal staff performance evaluation and compensation decisions. Similarly, the SEC also chose to ignore the role the Citigroup legal department played in the CAM transfer agent contracts.

By the "accountability standard" that Citigroup applied in the Japan private bank regulatory problem, which was to hold the senior business unit executive and the senior functional executive jointly responsible for regulatory infractions, Chuck Prince should have been held equally accountable with me in the CAM transfer agency case. The documentary evidence and witness testimony established beyond any doubt that Citigroup attorneys had been consulted at all stages of the negotiations and had reviewed the contract prior to signing and raised no red flags to the CAM management team. The Citigroup legal staff simply gave bad advice to the business team. That's all there was to the transfer agency case. But the business team were the only ones charged by the SEC, and the only ones hung out to dry by Citigroup.

Over five years later, in August 2012, Judge William Pauley of the U.S. District Court, Southern District of New York, dismissed the class action civil fraud lawsuit filed against me as a piggyback to the SEC civil fraud litigation. On August 15, 2012, the Reuters news service issued a news release under the headline "Citigroup, Smith Barney Win End to Fund Fee Lawsuit." It read in part:

> A Manhattan federal judge dismissed nearly all of a long-running lawsuit accusing Citigroup Inc., its former Smith Barney brokerage unit and two executives of shortchanging mutual fund investors out of more than $100 million of fee discounts. U.S. District Court Judge William Pauley on Wednesday threw out all claims against Citigroup and the former Smith Barney Fund Management LLC, and Thomas Jones, formerly chief executive of Citigroup Asset Management. He also dismissed some claims against Lewis Daidone, a former Smith Barney senior vice president.

And so, after nearly eight years, stretching from October 2004 to August 2012, I was finally done with this chapter of my life. Unlike in 2004 and 2005, when headlines trumpeted the SEC charges filed against me, there were no headlines now trumpeting "Former Citigroup Executive Tom Jones Vindicated after Eight-Year Legal Ordeal." But that's okay, because I fought to defend my honor and my reputation. It was very personal right from the start.

Bob Willumstad left Citigroup in July 2005 as it became apparent that Chuck Prince did not regard him as a partner, and by late 2007 Prince had pushed out most of the business unit heads who had reported to Sandy Weill. It is not uncommon for CEOs who are insecure to surround themselves with subordinates who are adept at feeding the leader's ego, telling him what he wants to hear and not delivering bad news. This is the pattern that developed at Citigroup under Chuck Prince, and the company was on the verge of collapse by the end of 2007. Once again, Global Corporate and Investment Bank (GCIB) was at the center of the storm. GCIB was headed by Robert Druskin, who had been Sandy Weill's senior back office systems administrator for most of his career. Druskin had befriended Chuck Prince over the years and was arguably Prince's closest confidant at Citigroup. Druskin had no experience managing and controlling investment bankers and traders. It was like putting the inmates in charge of the asylum, and their insanity soon destroyed the company.

In October of 2007, Standard & Poor's downgraded mortgage-backed bonds, an area where Citigroup had enormous exposure and was largely unprotected against losses. Citigroup then suffered billions of dollars in new losses in its third quarter, and Chuck Prince, finally seeing his support from the board and from Sandy Weill dissolve, resigned.

Citigroup was operating a pipeline of purchased mortgages in the process of being repackaged into mortgage-backed securities and resold into the market to institutional investors—pension funds, endowments, sovereign wealth funds, and insurance companies. The pipeline was largely unhedged against price movements and was too large relative to Citigroup's equity capital. When mortgage bond prices collapsed, Citigroup was caught holding the bag on the unsold mortgages in its pipeline. The scale of the losses was so large that it essentially wiped out Citigroup's shareholder equity, and Citigroup became insolvent. Chuck Prince's approach to this business was reflected in his infamous line "You have to keep dancing as long as the music is playing." When the music stopped, Citigroup was unprepared. The disaster was, at its core, a management failure to implement basic operating discipline and control—with regard to both the size of the mortgage pipeline and bond portfolio, and the oversight of portfolio risk-hedging procedures and controls.

On November 9, 2007, shortly after the forced resignation of Merrill Lynch CEO Stanley O'Neal, the *Wall Street Journal* ran a story by Robin Sidel, Monica Langley, and David Enrich, headlined "Two Weeks That Shook the Titans of Wall Street: As O'Neal Tottered, Sandy Weill Turned on Protégé Prince," detailing Citigroup and Chuck Prince's disastrous decline:

On Monday, October 29, Mr. Prince met with Citigroup's lead independent director, Alcoa Inc. CEO Alain Belda, and handed him a resignation letter. "The magnitude of the losses incurred in our fixed-income business makes this the only honorable course for me to take as the chief executive officer of the company," the letter said . . .

On Sunday, Citigroup's board of directors met at the bank's Park Avenue headquarters and officially accepted Mr. Prince's resignation . . . The company issued a press release announcing the developments, and the new losses, shortly after 6 p.m. . . . .

Other investors expressed dismay over the big new losses on Monday, sending Citigroup's stock price to its lowest level since April 2003. Mr. Prince arrived at work on Monday as usual. Asked how he was doing as he exited an elevator on the executive floor, he responded, "couldn't be better." Shortly after 5 p.m. on Tuesday, a group of moving men wearing burgundy T-shirts arrived at Mr. Prince's office, pushing an empty cart and carrying rolls of bubble wrap.

One year later, in late November 2008, Citigroup had to be rescued by the federal government. The *Wall Street Journal* headline on November 24 read "U.S. Agrees to Rescue Struggling Citigroup: Plan Injects $20 Billion in Fresh Capital, Guarantees $306 Billion in Toxic Assets."

This was a total disaster for all of Citigroup's shareholders, but especially for tens of thousands of long-tenured Citigroup employees who for many years had benefited from Sandy Weill's compensation philosophy, which emphasized employee ownership through generous stock options and restricted stock compensation, but accompanied by stringent vesting requirements and onerous constraints on selling shares while employees were still working for the company. The Citigroup stock price plummeted to $3.77 per share on Friday November 20, 2008, compared to $47.14 per share on October 2, 2003, when Chuck Prince became CEO. The stock market valuation of Citigroup had plummeted as well from approximately $250 billion on the day Prince became CEO to less than $20 billion at the end of his tenure. This ranks as one of the greatest destructions of shareholder wealth by one short-tenured CEO in modern history.

Also from the vantage point of observing events ten years after Prince's resignation, there is vindication for my arguments regarding what happened in Japan with the private bank. At this writing, Citigroup has been unable to satisfy Japanese regulators, despite intense focus and attention from senior management over a ten-year period. My personal view is that this is a decade-long story of Japanese regulators using ambiguous regulations and subjective regulatory examinations to systematically drive Citigroup out of the retail consumer businesses in Japan. The private bank was just the first step. In fact, Japanese regulators have driven all of the American and European banks out of Japan's consumer banking and retail investments market.

The Sandy Weill era on Wall Street ended with the collapse of Citigroup and its subsequent rescue by the federal government. I don't feel any resentment toward Sandy, and I don't think he ever took any overt action that was intended to harm me. When I see him at social events we engage cordially, but I've never overcome the lingering disappointment that my friend Sandy failed to protect me when it mattered most. And I have been scarred by the fact that Citigroup's board of seemingly good people condoned the brutal treatment I received, which was unwarranted and unprecedented and has to this day never been done to anyone else at a senior level in the Citigroup corporate hierarchy.

An important lesson I gleaned from my Citigroup ordeal is that board diversity doesn't necessarily have a positive impact on corporate governance. In fact, board diversity may not matter at all unless those "diverse" directors are willing to be independent of the company's chief executive officer. Citigroup had three women and three black directors, none of whom chose to see that the only black business head at Citigroup was the only Citigroup business head summarily terminated and simultaneously left unprotected against SEC charges in a company regulatory settlement.

10

Life after Citigroup

I have fought the good fight. I have finished the race. I have kept
the faith.

—*2 Timothy 4:7*

N ow, from the vantage point of nearly fifteen years later, it is clear to
me that many good things did come out of the embarrassment and
betrayal of my ouster from Citigroup and the fight for my reputation
that followed. I had prayed to understand the good in my ordeal, and now I
found that I had been unexpectedly blessed in three ways.

One blessing is better physical health. I hadn't fully appreciated the toll
that was exacted by my work habits and the stress of the Citigroup environment. For over thirty years I had been working at a pace of 100 percent commitment to do my best every day. It wasn't until I slowed to a more normal
work routine that I realized the physical price I'd been paying.

A second blessing is better spiritual health. I have spiritual peace, and
I'm content with the life God has given me. I have grown closer to my wife
and children than ever before, in part because I'm able to spend more time
with them and focus more of my energy and attention on their needs and
well-being.

The third blessing is better financial health. In February 2005 I sold all
my Citigroup stock out of conviction that Chuck Prince would not succeed as
CEO. (My sale prices ranged from $45 to $48 per share, ten times the value
those same stocks had by the end of the Chuck Prince era.)

In April 2005 I launched my own investment business, TWJ Capital
LLC, which would operate on a business strategy founded on the following three premises: One, the venture capital and private equity investment

business had been consolidating in the hands of a shrinking number of competitors who controlled increasingly large investment funds, and it was becoming inefficient for those large funds to invest in smaller deals in the $1 million to $10 million range, so there was inefficiency in the pricing and quality of these smaller investments. It takes as much work to perform appropriate investment analysis and due diligence, and transaction pricing and structure negotiation, on a $10 million investment as it does for a $50 million transaction. But a $10 million investment doesn't move the needle for a $500 million investment fund (after all, it would be only 2 percent of assets), so larger funds tended to avoid these smaller deals. Less attention from larger investors meant more opportunities for mistakes by other potential investors competing with me in evaluating the quality of company business plans and management teams. Two, I had an extensive network of investment community relationships which would enable me to find and participate in attractive co-investment opportunities in this "lower-institutional" range of $1 million to $10 million deals. Three, I could be flexible and would not have to specialize in a specific narrow investment sector such as financial services because I could partner with experts to co-invest in any investment sector I thought attractive.

I rented an office for TWJ Capital in an executive office suite in downtown Stamford, a short commute from my home in New Canaan. Now I could work what is normally considered a full workday, but which to me felt like the equivalent of an undemanding part-time job compared to my previous experience.

"Click that light on, Tom," Addie said to me one night when she walked into the den and found me reading a novel on a Tuesday. I turned on the light and looked up at her and grinned. Ah, the pleasure of reading a book just for the hell of it! Of course, this was something she had been doing nearly every day of our thirty-year marriage. I had often seen her curled up gracefully in a chair, oblivious to the world around her because she was so deeply engaged in her reading. It was a habit our children had all inherited from her too. And now, finally, I was joining them in this lighter side of life. I found that I liked history, sociology, and economics best, and biographies of people who'd lived admirable lives. For the first time in years, I had time to read for pleasure and watch sports and late-night television. My best friend, Charles, was happy to find that I now knew what he was talking about football-wise. I felt comfort, and a sense of relaxation, creep into my bones and stay there.

I was pleased to be suddenly able to participate, too, in more of my younger daughter, Victoria's, high school activities. Intelligent, talented, and attractive, Vicky was co-captain of the girls' field hockey team and won the lead role of Sarah in her high school's production of the musical *Ragtime* in her senior year. As I sat in the audience on opening night, bowled over at her vivacity and talent up onstage, I realized that I had been so deeply engrossed in my own career, and away from home so much traveling for Citigroup, that I didn't really know her very well. I also realized, belatedly, that because I had been traveling and working long hours for most of the high school years of my older daughter, Evonne, who graduated in 2000, I had missed witnessing much of her education and personal triumphs. Evonne, an accomplished equestrian who had ridden competitively both locally and nationally, had almost never had her father watching her from the stands. I'd been at work. My younger son, Michael, who graduated from high school in 2003, had a passion for music. He'd formed his first band in fifth grade, which played mostly alternative rock and had performed after his middle school graduation ceremony. In high school his band was The Ort Phenomenon, playing instrumental jazzy electronic music and performing at Arch Street Teen Center in Greenwich and other teen venues around Connecticut and New York City. Over all, Mike probably played in six or seven bands. Again, I knew this more from talk around the house than from firsthand experience, as I was absent frequently during much of his high school years.

I tried to atone for my absences and lost time by communicating my life philosophy to my three younger children in various conversations, emails, letters, celebration cards, and whatever other opportunities became available. My major points of emphasis can be summarized as follows:

1. Learn personal discipline skills to manage time effectively and to feel good about how you've spent your time each day.
2. Learn personal discipline skills to always give 100 percent effort and perform to the best of your ability, and to feel good about your efforts to achieve your highest potential. Only you know in your heart if you're being all that you can be. Give 100 percent effort for yourself, because achieving your fullest potential is one of the greatest fulfillments possible in life.

3. Learn personal discipline skills to make good decisions about friends, and spend significant time only with positive and constructive people.

4. The only way to get and keep your life on track is personal discipline and hard work. Personal discipline means devoting each day to a healthy mix of work, physical exercise, spiritual reflection, and relaxation. Personal discipline also means being responsible to yourself and others, and doing whatever you are responsible for getting done every day. You will find yourself in a "loser's trap" if you think you can succeed by being slick and clever.

5. The only deep and lasting happiness comes from the joy and satisfaction of achieving difficult goals and feeling good about yourself. This applies to personal relationships, work and career, and your physical and spiritual self. It is the satisfaction of being rewarded for your discipline and hard work. It is the joy of living a "good life."

6. A book is a metaphor for life. If life as a book has around ten chapters for most people, you are only in the early chapters of your lives. Everybody has bad chapters in their lives; for some it comes in an early chapter, and for others it comes in later chapters. The difficult chapters you encounter do not define your life. Your life is defined by what you do to overcome adversity when you encounter trouble and failure.

7. Each of you has wonderful talents, you are smart, and you are attractive. God has blessed you in abundance. The weaknesses I see in you are primarily with regard to self-discipline. This discipline problem is fixable, but the commitment to fix it has to come from you.

8. The importance of self-discipline is a core determinant of success or failure for everybody. I learned as a young man to pray each morning for the discipline and strength to do the things I needed to get done each day, and to live that day in the right way. Our family would have suffered if I had failed to develop the discipline to do the right things every day, week after week, month after month, and year after year. When you look around the black community, you can see that many of the problems stem from lack of self-discipline—people lacking the discipline to do the things they could do each day to improve their own lives. Things they could

do in school to improve their skills, things they could do to avoid drugs and alcohol, things they could do to avoid pregnancies with people who are not able to function effectively as parents, things they could do to help improve their communities, and so on.

9. One of the most useful self-discipline tools is to have a plan to move forward so that every day you do something that helps you achieve the life you want. You will discover that when you live this way, you will feel good about yourself, and you will like yourself. You will also find that it is much easier to make friends, because people are attracted to people who feel good about themselves, and most people want to be around someone who is positive and happy.

10. My prayer discipline provides a solid foundation for my daily living and has helped me to not let my spirits get either too low in days of adversity or too high in days of triumph. You should consider building a similar spiritual foundation for your lives.

Soon after opening for business in April 2005, I was having lunch with a friend who mentioned that his firm had invested in a very promising retail flooring business, but the investors had grown the business too quickly, triggering bank loan covenant violations. The company was in technical default on the bank debt and needed $2 million in new capital to cure the default. His firm had already reached its maximum investment limit for any one company, so it could not provide the necessary capital itself. The business had only sixty days to cure the default before the bank called the loan and commenced collection actions, which could push it into bankruptcy. "Would this be an investment you might consider, Tom?" he asked me.

"I'll take a look," I told him, "and give you my decision in thirty days."

The company was Floor & Decor Outlets of America, and it qualified as a "category killer," a discount chain that has the potential to dominate a market by specializing in one narrow niche product. It was a superstore for hard surface flooring products such as ceramic and porcelain tile, stone tile, wood flooring, tumbled stone, and flooring accessories. It purchased its products in ocean shipping container quantities directly from manufacturers in over twenty-two countries, eliminating the markups of importers, distributors, and other middlemen. Its products were typically priced at 20 percent to 70 percent below competitors', but it still achieved approximately

40 percent gross margins. The target footprint for Floor & Decor stores was fifty thousand to sixty thousand square feet, which allowed it to boast the largest in-stock selection of hard surface flooring in the industry. My friend's firm had invested in 2003, when Floor & Decor had two only stores and a $25 million annual revenue run rate, and the company had grown to nine stores with an annual revenue run rate of $80 million in mid-2005. That rapid growth had triggered the loan violations because critical financial performance ratios and calculations were below the level required by the bank. Every time Floor & Decor opened a new store, it had to hire and train staff, rent the real estate, build out the interior amenities, and stock the store with inventory. From opening day to operating break-even was typically a ten-to-twelve-month period. Any negative variances from the revenue buildup model or the operating expense model could trigger cash flow deficiencies and operating losses greater than planned. And so, while the business was growing very well, operating variances had tripped-up Floor & Decor.

I immersed myself in due diligence analysis of the investment opportunity and quickly reached several conclusions. First, the build-out from two stores with $25 million revenue in 2003 to nine stores with $80 million in 2005 had enabled the company to refine its business model for store openings, and the management team was increasingly adept at executing against the model. Second, I determined that the company had developed an effective store format and marketing strategy, which enabled it to deliver a broad line of hard surface flooring products to consumers at substantially lower prices than the traditional fragmented and inefficient system based on small retail stores using distributors and importers. Third, the important components of the company's category-killer business model provided protective barriers against competitors, including a deep product assortment at low prices; unique products purchased in large quantities directly from international tile manufacturers and stone quarries; consistent purchases of large quantities, which allowed manufacturers to produce full runs and allowed quarries to produce "full block" quantities, maximizing their productivity and lowering costs. Fourth, the company was also able to make occasional "opportunity buys" from manufacturers and quarries that wished to clear certain products, which enabled Floor & Decor to offer high-value special sales to attract customers and create marketing excitement. Finally, the company was employing effective supply chain and inventory management techniques and had strong relationships with major suppliers. My research also confirmed that the U.S. hard surface flooring industry exceeded $14 billion annual sales, and the annual growth rate exceeded 10 percent. I met several times with Floor & Decor's senior management team and was impressed with them and their capabilities, especially Vincent West, the founder-entrepreneur and merchandiser, who was uniquely gifted in his understanding of flooring product styles and fashion merchandising opportunities.

As promised, I made my decision within thirty days and offered an attractive investment proposal. Instead of trying to take advantage of their distress by demanding superior economic investment terms relative to my friend's firm, I offered to invest $2 million pari passu with the terms of their last investment, but with one caveat: my investment would be in a separate class of securities that would have certain special rights in the event of violations of debt covenants, failure to achieve operating budgets, or decisions to raise new debt or equity capital. I was in effect requiring covenants that would enable me to exercise disproportionate influence in distressed circumstances, while accepting my pro rata share of the upside if things went well. I also requested voting rights to designate one seat on the seven-person board of directors, including positions on the executive committee and the compensation committee. They accepted my offer in July 2005. This confirmed to me that the speed with which I could perform due diligence, make investment commitments, and fund investments was a competitive advantage. Floor & Decor continued to grow but encountered adverse economic circumstances in the 2008 recession. I made additional investments amounting to $2.8 million in late 2008 and early 2009, bringing my total investment in the company to $4.8 million.

In late 2005 Floor & Decor opened two new stores, then six new stores in 2006, followed by six again in 2007 before being hit by the 2008 recession. Alert to the deteriorating economic environment, we did not open any new stores in 2008, and only one new store and one small-footprint prototype design center in 2009. We continued disciplined growth in 2010 with one new store and two more small-footprint design centers to increase market awareness and drive high-end sales in strategic locations where the company already had significant market presence. Our revenue run rate in 2010 reached $250 million, and EBITDA (earnings before interest, taxes, depreciation, and amortization) was approximately $31.7 million.

Floor & Decor's major shareholders agreed to launch a targeted sales process in 2010 to determine what exit value we could achieve, and we also analyzed status quo and recapitalization alternatives. Status quo meant maintaining the current ownership and capital structure and continuing to grow the business. The status quo alternative was rejected because it provided no near-term liquidity for shareholders, and shareholders would continue to bear all the risk of executing the company's growth plan in the still difficult economic environment. Recapitalization meant raising debt to pay a special dividend to shareholders, and continuing to grow the business under current ownership. Recapitalization was rejected after discussions with several banks indicated that debt leverage would be limited to paying a dividend in the range of $60 million to $80 million, and shareholders would continue to bear execution risk in a challenging economic environment while being additionally constrained by a less flexible balance sheet.

Our targeted sales process resulted in contacting forty-four prospective buyers, receiving eleven first-round indications of interest, and conducting eight first-round management due diligence meetings. The second-round process of management presentations and buyer due diligence resulted in four parties submitting letters of intent. We ultimately sold the company in November of 2010 for $340 million to Ares Management and Freeman Spogli & Co., large West Coast private equity investors.

After payment of amounts due on senior debt, employee compensation, and transaction expenses, and release of indemnification escrows, TWJ Capital Opportunity Fund received approximately $43.3 million, or over 900 percent return on invested capital and approximately 70 percent internal rate of return.

The buyers planned to accelerate the build-out of Floor & Decor's store count and geographic coverage. In November of 2014, they filed to go public with a footprint of forty-five stores, and their initial public offering occurred in in 2017.

While I was working to build my own business investing in startups and early-stage companies on the rise, I was still plugged into a behemoth of corporate America, Altria, as a member of its board of directors. I had been recruited by retired Citigroup co-CEO John Reed while I was still at Citigroup in 2002. Altria intrigued me primarily because of my curiosity about what went into its marketing wizardry, marketing that had made Marlboro one of the most iconic and valuable brands in America. One cigarette is pretty much like any other cigarette, after all, and so I was impressed that this corporation had managed to have its products rise above the throng, primarily through brilliant marketing.

In 2008 Altria Group spun off Philip Morris International (PMI) as an independent publicly traded tobacco company, enabling each of Altria's international and domestic U.S. tobacco businesses to focus exclusively on realizing its opportunities and addressing its challenges, and removing the international business from the risks of ongoing U.S. tobacco litigation. I was one of only three Altria Group board members who chose to go with the domestic U.S. business. Most of the board members and stock analysts thought the growth opportunities were primarily international, and the domestic U.S. business would be little more than a stable cash cow.

After the PMI spin-off, Altria assembled a new board of directors which proved over time to be very effective. I became chairman of the finance committee for the new Altria board. We encouraged the management team to focus on shareholder value creation and to bring a growth strategy to the board. Altria's new board embraced management's growth strategy, which encompassed product innovation, process innovation, marketing innovation, and cultural innovation.

Altria management developed a "Total Tobacco" strategic plan, and the board approved the acquisition of United States Smokeless Tobacco Company for $12 billion in 2009 to secure the Copenhagen and Skoal smokeless tobacco brands. In addition to supporting this product innovation by acquisition, the new Altria board also supported increases in research and development spending to create innovative and reduced-risk tobacco products, such as e-vapor, to meet changing tobacco consumer preferences. To achieve process innovation, Altria management reconfigured manufacturing and consolidated plants and other operations to reduce costs by over $2 billion. And to improve its marketing, Altria management developed a new Marlboro brand architecture which expanded its product lineup, revitalized its growth, and strengthened its brand equity. Altria management also innovated unique digital consumer engagement capabilities, which ranked with the strongest among consumer product companies. And regarding company culture, Altria's board encouraged senior management to emphasize employee engagement and a culture of innovation.

The result has been a remarkable economic performance by Altria. At year end 2008, Altria's market capitalization (total common shares outstanding multiplied by closing price per common share) was $31 billion, compared to PMI market capitalization of $87.3 billion. At year end 2016, my last full year on the board, Altria's market capitalization had increased 424 percent to $131.4 billion, while PMI market cap had increased 62.5

percent to $141.9 billion. Altria's share price increased from $15.06 closing price in 2008 to $67.62 closing price in 2016. In the five years from December 2011 to December 2016, Altria's cumulative total shareholder return (share price appreciation plus reinvestment of all dividends on a quarterly basis) was $286.61 on an initial $100 investment. This compares to $192.56 for Altria's peer group of consumer product companies (Campbell Soup, Coca-Cola, Colgate Palmolive, Conagra Foods, General Mills, Hershey Company, Kellogg Company, Kimberly-Clark, Kraft Foods, Kraft-Heinz, Lorillard, Mondelez International, Pepsico, and Reynolds American). The corresponding S&P 500 Index total shareholder return calculation for the period 2011–2016 was $198.09. It was fulfilling and enjoyable to be a core member of such an effective board, and to be part of the management and board team that delivered such extraordinary shareholder value creation. I retired from the Altria board in May 2017 as its most senior member after fifteen years of service.

There was a retirement dinner for me held at the Virginia Museum of Fine Arts in Richmond, and Altria's lead director, Thomas Farrell, chairman and CEO of Dominion Energy, Inc., honored me with a farewell speech that I appreciated deeply. I include some of his remarks that evening here:

> No doubt, in these sort of settings, the word "privilege" gets tossed around a little too easily—but I feel that way tonight. It is a privilege to say a few words on behalf of the Board about our colleague, Tom Jones.
>
> His demeanor and intelligence, his understated capacity for influencing the proceedings and shaping the outcomes—tells you why so many institutions have placed confidence in his judgement.
>
> One of our colleagues likened Tom to that old TV commercial.
>
> The one that always ended with, "When E. F. Hutton speaks, people listen."
>
> I listen; we all listen.
>
> And heed.
>
> Tom—along with George [Muñoz]—was here when Jerry [Gerald Baliles] and I joined the Board in 2008.
>
> Since that first day, I knew I should listen very carefully when Tom spoke. Always insightful; always wise; decades of experience in business. Since that day he has been a mentor and example for me—for all of us—to follow.

He chaired our Finance Committee for the last ten years—through the spin of PMI, the purchase of U.S. Tobacco, and the national financial crisis that followed.

More recently, he and Marty [Barrington, Altria CEO] guided the Board through the restructuring of our SAB Miller asset. His steady hand and thoughtful guidance took all the pressure off the rest of us. What a gift to Altria and all of us.

You know, this business of being a director, with all its technical, legal, and fiduciary components, can often sound like a science.

But it is very much an art. Between command and counsel lies an often uncertain space where people must lead and advise without fixed rules.

Still, there is a line out there and you have to know where and how to find it.

Which is a challenge, because you don't get a map—and fog tends to roll in at the most inopportune times.

There are many of us here who have seen how this works from both sides, from both perspectives—as those who govern—and those who are governed.

. . . The pressures are acute these days—from activist investors to a whole host of demanding constituencies, along with regulatory complexities, shifting public expectations—and on and on. Especially here at Altria.

. . . Never has there been a greater need for what someone has described as "pattern-recognition skills."

That's basically when you see disparate pieces combining, know what it means, and understand what might be made of it.

Tom—I think—may have invented pattern-recognition skills. He sees the interconnected flows of data, makes sense of them, and sees how they can shape the future of our joint enterprise.

Of course, you then have to make your insights persuasive to the other people in the room. He does that part, too, and brilliantly. He has been the one who has helped us maintain a comfort-level in the middle of potentially uncomfortable conversations. It all falls under the heading of skilled collaboration and I don't think I have seen anyone do it better than Tom Jones.

So, if you agree there is art to this work, then it is easy to see that Tom Jones is an artist of consummate ability. He has served this company for 15 years—and with him he brought us the additional benefit of Addie's delightful presence.

And so the story concludes—at least the Altria aspect of it, with Tom and Addie sitting here and all the rest of us feeling enormously grateful.

I believe a toast would be highly appropriate. Addie, Tom, thank you both for all you have brought to our deliberations. You have helped the company grow and prosper. You have taught us much about effective governance. And you have given us graceful and heartfelt friendship. To you both . . . thank you.

At the beginning of my second year running TWJ Capital, Nigel asked if there was any opportunity for him to come and work with me. He'd left Goldman Sachs in 2000 to join the private equity firm the Carlyle Group in Washington, D.C., as a member of its U.S. buyout team, where he'd risen to the rank of principal. His work took him frequently to countries such as India, where large firms like Carlyle were able to find opportunities to deploy their multibillion-dollar investment funds more readily than in more efficient developed markets like the United States. This travel routine was wearing on Nigel, who had married in 2001 and become a father in 2004. I thought about his inquiry and told him to wait a year until I could get a better feel for my business prospects. While it would certainly be a disappointment for me if TWJ Capital didn't succeed, it would be an absolute disaster if Nigel were to join me during the critical years of his career and be derailed by our failure.

By early 2006 I was confident that TWJ Capital's business model was viable, meaning that I could (1) identify sufficient attractive investment opportunities through industry contacts; (2) achieve competitive advantages through investment sector flexibility and speed of decision making and deal execution; and (3) exploit market inefficiencies at the $1 million to $10 million low end of the institutional investment space. So in early 2006 I agreed that Nigel could join me as a partner. He set up an office in Bethesda, Maryland, to provide broader geographic deal sourcing by covering the greater Washington metropolitan area.

On his birthday in January 2006, I wrote a letter to Nigel that read:

January 28, 2006

Dear Nigel:

Today is your 37th birthday, and I want you to know how proud I am of the fine man you have grown to be. You have excelled in college, excelled in the Marine Corps, and excelled professionally at Goldman Sachs and Carlyle Group. Most important, you have become a man of character, honor, and integrity. And you are now embarked on a new chapter of life with the opportunity to excel as a husband and father. I know that Papa, your Grandpa Jones, is at peace with God in heaven as he reflects on knowing that you are his legacy and lineage on earth.

I also want you to know how proud and pleased I am that you will soon be joining me as a business partner. In October 2004 when I was fired by Citigroup, I prayed to God for guidance. I told God that I believe all things work together for good to those who love Him, and I asked Him to help me understand what good could come from what had happened to me at Citigroup. It is now clear that the answer is that one good outcome is the opportunity to work together with you to build a business that will provide for our family, and protect our family, in this and future generations.

In addition to the legacy of building our business, it is also important to me to share with you my legacy of prayer. You need to understand how to communicate with God, and how to bring Him into your daily life. So I share with you my daily prayers, and I hope that you will develop your own personal prayers that bring you in touch with God every day.

I start each morning with the Lord's Prayer.

"Our Father who art in heaven hallowed be Thy name. Thy kingdom come, Thy will be done, on earth as it is in heaven. Give us this day our daily bread, and forgive us our trespasses as we forgive those who trespass against us. And lead us not into temptation, but deliver us from evil. For Thine is the kingdom, Thine is the power, and Thine is the glory forever and ever. Amen."

Then I say a second prayer which I composed many years ago after studying the Bible.

"Dear heavenly Father, we pledge to Thee that we will obey Thy commandments, turning aside neither to the right hand nor to the left. We will in all ways walk in the way that Thou has taught us, so that we may live and it may go well with us. We acknowledge our Father, that as a father disciplines a child, so Thou has disciplined us. We accept and appreciate Your discipline, and the love from whence it flows, and we ask Thee our Father to help us to have the discipline to always obey Thy commandments, and to achieve our highest potential in the context of Thy divine purpose. We affirm our belief our Father that all things work together for good to those who love Thee, to those who are the chosen instruments of Thy will. We commit ourselves to Thy service with a whole heart and a willing mind, and we seek Thee in prayer and in study so that we may know what Thou wouldst have us do, and so that we may do all such good works as Thou hast prepared for us to walk in. And we will not walk in fear our Father, because we know that Thou hast not given us the spirit of fear, but rather the spirit of power and of love and of sound mind. Amen."

And then I conclude with "May the words of our mouths and the meditations of our hearts be acceptable in Thy sight our Lord, our strength and redeemer. Amen."

I also end each day in prayer, each evening reciting the Lord's Prayer again and also the 23rd Psalm. "The Lord is my shepherd, I shall not want. He leadeth me beside the still waters, He maketh me to lie down in green pastures, He restoreth my soul. He leadeth me in the path of righteousness for His name's sake. Yea though I walk through the valley of the shadow of death, I shall fear no evil. For Thou art with me. Thy rod and Thy staff they comfort me. Thou preparest a table before me in the presence of my enemies. Thou anointest my head with oil, my cup runneth over. Surely goodness and mercy shall follow me all the days of my life, and I shall dwell in the house of the Lord forever and ever. Amen." I conclude with a prayer for each member of our family.

I give you this letter along with the Holy Bible and the Book of Common Prayer. Make time to read them cover to cover. You will find that they speak to you, and that you should listen to what they say. Then take the time to develop your own personal prayer discipline to bring God into your life every day. This advice is the most important legacy of all.

With my deepest love and affection,
Dad

Over the years after 2006, Nigel focused primarily on telecommunications software companies. One of these companies was NetNumber, which develops and delivers software addressing solutions and services to mobile operators, fixed-line carriers, and IP-based communication services providers. NetNumber is a leading provider of centralized signaling and routing controller solutions through its TITAN platform, which is a virtualized infrastructure for all signaling control, routing policy enforcement, and subscriber database services in the telecommunications network. NetNumber has won numerous awards for its innovative technology, and had an estimated market value of $150 million to $200 million in 2018. A second company, KoolSpan, developed TrustChip technology, which is a hardened microSD cryptocard specifically built for smartphone telecommunications security. KoolSpan addresses the problem of mobile voice and text intercept, and enables any two smartphones equipped with TrustChip to make secure encrypted calls and text messages end-to-end over public wireless networks. KoolSpan launched its software-based mobile voice and text encryption product in 2015. In 2014 Nigel was asked by the board of KoolSpan to step in as chief financial officer, and he was subsequently asked by the board to assume the chief executive officer position. And so our eight years as active partners at TWJ Capital had come to an end, but his career driving the growth of a high-profile startup company had begun, of which I am incredibly proud.

Addie and I suffered a rough four-year stretch of adversity from 2003 through 2006. Addie's mother, Yvonne Wright Knox, was afflicted with severe dementia and passed away, in 2003, at the age of eighty-three. On one moving occasion, during her last year, Addie's mother said to her, "I don't know who you are, but I know that I love you." I admired Addie's mother for her strength and courage in raising a close-knit and loving family after her husband's tragic death in his mid-forties, when Addie was only fourteen. Mrs. Knox was a regular part of our lives as the matriarch at Addie's family reunions, which we hosted for many years on the Fourth of July. Mrs. Knox had attended Spelman College in Atlanta, and after her death we established a scholarship there in her honor.

Our tribulations continued with my firing by Citigroup in 2004, the SEC's charging me with civil fraud in 2005, and the legal battle of 2006. In some ways this four-year ordeal drew Addie and me closer together. I gave Addie the following letter on her birthday in 2006.

January 30, 2006

Dear Addie,

Today is your 56th birthday, and I want you to know how blessed I have been to share the last thirty-one-plus years with you. When I think of you, I think of one of the inscriptions on the rotunda wall behind the altar at Trinity Church in Boston. It reads "God is Love." And I think of the lyrics to my favorite Erykah Badu song, "I See God in You." I do see God in you, because you are love, and God is love.

Your love has permeated my life, and engaged my heart, and lifted my spirit, and inspired me to become much more, in every way, than I ever could have been without your love. I thank you for the joy of knowing this depth of love in my life.

Your love touches all who share your life, especially our children. They are each good and happy and spiritually healthy people, in large measure because your love has shaped their lives. We are all blessed because you are in our lives.

I give you this letter, folded into the Book of Common Prayer, to symbolize my hope and faith that our spirits will remain together through eternity.

With eternal love,
Tom

Addie and I bought our summer home in Quogue, New York, in early 2002. Quogue, situated in the Hamptons on Long Island between Westhampton Beach and Southampton, is a low-key area often called the "un-Hamptons Hampton." It soon became a gathering place for our family and friends, and now it is rare for a summer weekend to pass without at least one of our children visiting, and often bringing friends. And that, after all, is one of the very best reasons to have a summer home.

Our dock, which sits on Quogue Canal near Shinnecock Bay, is what first inspired me to take up boating. Over the years, I progressed from a thirty-foot cabin cruiser, to thirty-four feet, then thirty-eight feet, and eventually a forty-seven-foot powerboat, which Addie named *Sugar Daddy*. Our cruising range extends as far north as Provincetown on Cape Cod, and as far south as Cape May on the southern tip of New Jersey. We are regular cruising visitors to Martha's Vineyard, Nantucket, and Newport. We take river cruises up the Thames River at New London, Connecticut, to the marina at Norwich, and stay overnight for dinner and entertainment at the Foxwoods and MGM Grand casinos. We cruise up the Connecticut River at Old Saybrook and stay overnight at the marina in Essex to enjoy some of the excellent local restaurants. We have a boat slip in Stamford on Long Island Sound, a few miles from our home in New Canaan, and cruise from there down Long Island Sound to the East River and around Manhattan, then up the Hudson River to West Point. We take day-trip cruises from Quogue to Greenport, Shelter Island, Orient Point, Sag Harbor, East Hampton, and Montauk. From Stamford, we take day trips to Huntington, Port Washington, Northport, and Oyster Bay. For several years I commuted most summer week-ends on my boat between New Canaan and Quogue, cruising east on Long Island Sound to Orient Point, through Plum Gut at Plum Island, south down Gardiners Bay, west around Shelter Island, and down Peconic Bay, through the Shinnecock Canal to the south shore of Long Island, and then west through Shinnecock Bay and Tiana Bay to Quogue. I love the sea and wind and sun, combined with the mental exercises of navigation and boat handling. I'm considering extending my cruising range farther north to Boston and perhaps Portland, Maine, and farther south to Annapolis and the Chesapeake Bay.

Our older daughter, Evonne, graduated from Georgetown University in 2004 and pursued a career in education. She returned to school and received a master's degree in education policy from Harvard University in 2009 and is now employed as a policy analyst with Democracy Prep Public Schools, a charter school operator. In July 2012 Evonne became engaged to a college classmate from Georgetown, and they were married on Saturday, June 22, 2013, in a beautiful wedding, with all their family and friends joining the celebration. The wedding was at the new Alvin Ailey Center for Dance at Ninth Avenue and West 55th Street in Manhattan, where Addie and I had gifted a rehearsal studio. This was fitting because Evonne and Chris's first date was an Ailey performance at the Kennedy Center in Washington. A special touch was that the wedding ceremony was performed by Father Michael Bird, a talented young Episcopal priest who had been youth minister for Evonne, Michael, and Vicky at St. Mark's Episcopal Church in New Canaan. Vicky was the maid of honor, and Michael was a member of the

Figure 19 / *Tom, Addie, Nigel's wife Diane, Michael, Evonne,*
Evonne's groom Christopher, Victoria, Nigel (rear left to right),
Nigel's children Isabella, Carter, and Logan (front left to right)
at Evonne's wedding, June 2013

groom's wedding party. Nigel's daughter Isabelle was the flower girl, and his two boys Carter and Logan were ring bearers.

Michael graduated from the University of Vermont, went on for a master's degree from the University of London in the United Kingdom, and has remained true to his passion for music. At the University of Vermont he joined the Student Activities Concerts Committee and was responsible for bringing a wonderfully diverse range of musical groups to campus. We had encouraged Michael to pursue his love of music but also to think more broadly about career opportunities in music. Very few people succeed as professional musicians; many more succeed in other aspects of the industry. He launched his career by working as a publicist with a start-up music-marketing company in Brooklyn. No longer in a band, he supplemented his income by DJing in his spare time at weddings, corporate events, private parties, and clubs. In late 2015 Michael was recruited to become director of publicity at Dim Mak Records and moved to Los Angeles. Mike and his wife, Rachel, an elementary school teacher, married in February of 2017. Michael has grown to be a wonderful young man—friendly, honest, caring, and hardworking. We are delighted that Mike pursued his dreams and found a career in music.

Our younger daughter, Victoria, always had a passion for fashion. She researched different aspects of the fashion industry, spent time working in high-end fashion retailing, and obtained an internship with OTEXA, the textile export and international trade program in the United States Department of Commerce. These experiences helped her to better understand the interesting possibilities in the fashion industry. Vicky graduated summa cum laude in the International Trade and Marketing for the Fashion Industries Program at Fashion Institute of Technology (part of the State University of New York), and also received an associate's degree of applied science in fashion marketing from Parsons School of Design–The New School. She has worked in merchandise planning at Century 21, Gap, and Under Armour, and is now a planning manager at Optoro, which is a startup technology company that works with retailers and manufacturers to manage their returned and excess merchandise.

One day in the spring of 2005, Addie's delighted laughter called me into the kitchen. She held a gilt-edged card in her hand. It was from Bennie and Flash Wiley, the couple who had introduced Addie and me in 1974. Composed by Bennie, it read:

May 15, 2005

Earl and Barbara Graves [the founder and former CEO of Black Enterprise magazine and his wife], Bob and Barbara Holland [the former CEO of Ben & Jerry's and his wife], Tom and Addie Jones

Re: L'Affaire Anniversairie

Dear Friends,

This note will confirm our "multi-anniversary" gathering (it sounds a lot better in French, doesn't it) at the home of Tom and Addie Jones (our gracious and generous hosts) on Wednesday June 15, 2005. Champagne toasts will begin at 7:00 pm; and dinner will be served at 8:00 pm. Attire will be "dressy casual"—mirroring the comfortable ease, elegance, and facile durability of the wonderful connubial relationships we gather to celebrate.

Please remember, at dinner each couple is expected to share stories on their lives together and formulas for building successful relationships. Those pithy observations will, of course, be subjected to the scrutiny and (where appropriate) derision of the others in attendance, so get your lies together!

Love,
Flash and Bennie

It was one of the most love-filled and funniest nights of our lives. As we were gathered in our living room enjoying champagne with our friends, Addie employed her wonderful sense of humor and recited a poem she had composed in honor of the occasion, titled "Ode to Tom." It was the hit of the party:

30 years ago in June I went to Boston to see
If I could start the grown-up part of being me
No more roommates, parties, road trips, strife,
I wanted to start the rest of my life

I didn't know where to begin,
So I asked my mother.
She said, "Go to Boston,
Sponge off your brother"

So off to Boston I drove with glee
My Plymouth Cricket, bad wardrobe, Unibrow, and me
I arrived very tired and wanted to crash,
"No," said my brother
"For a job go see Flash"

I arrived at his office,
Résumé in hand,
Flash said, "Don't be silly,
What you need is a man."

"Ring Ring" goes the phone, as if on script,
"Tom Jones calling, I need a date
Do you know anybody who might rate?"

"Yes, as a matter of fact I do,
Let me put her in touch with you"

"All arranged," said Flash,
But alas and alack,
The phone rings again—
It's Tom calling back
"I'm not sure I want to take a chance
And take an unseen to a big fancy dance"

I say to Flash, as he pondered,
"Your thoughts for a penny"
He replies,
"I'm calling the smartest person I know—Bennie"

So arrangements were made,
A meeting was planned,
All of this just to get Addie a man
So we met and I passed muster, we went to the dance,
And that was the beginning of this 30-year romance

The start was not smooth,
I'm the first to admit,
I got the hint when he showed up
With an Ann Taylor makeover kit

This was no problem because I knew from the start
This was a man I loved with all of my heart
I loved what was in his heart and his head,
I'd find out about the rest when I got him to bed

So using dinner as a lure
I cooked up a plan to seduce this man
So he arrives, this gentleman Jones,
Who up until now hadn't tried to jump my bones
I opened the door bright and gay,
Attired only in a green negligee
So three months have passed,
And Flash checks in—
"How's it going?" he asks with a grin
Having now seen me in the buff,
Tom responds, "She's a diamond in the rough."

So into his apartment I did move,
But not before signing a contract written by Mr. Smooth

"No marriage talk for at least a year," to which I replied,
"Of course, my dear"

The rest is history so they say,
30 years ago almost to this day
So now we are here with our good friends
As a new chapter of empty nesting begins
So all I have here are the words on this page
And pledge my continued love as we age

We are blessed with four children,
Who could want more?
Plus a grandchild whom we all adore
I love you, I love you
You have gifted me a great life,
And in return, I hope I have been a good wife

We've experienced some pretty high highs
And some pretty low lows,
What lies ahead really nobody knows

All I know for sure
Is I have you and you have me,
There isn't much more
As far as I can see

So light of my life,
My companion and friend,
There is no more to say
So this poem shall end
So let's toast to our friends and blessings all.

HAPPY ANNIVERSARY!!!!

I could not and cannot imaging loving a wife more than I love Addie. She is my best friend, my anchor, and my partner.

In quick succession, I lost three members of my family in the span of two years. My mother passed at age ninety-eight in May 2009. She had been in excellent health until falling and breaking her hip two years earlier, which started a pattern of physical decline that is common among the elderly. Near the end, it seemed like she simply made a decision that she was ready to leave this world. She refused to eat.

My mother had been very actively involved with our lives for many years. She'd taken care of Nigel for an extended period when he was young and was present at the birth of each of our younger children, always staying at our home to assist Addie after childbirth. She accompanied us on our winter vacations to Sanibel Island during the 1980s. She lived near us in an independent living apartment facility for the elderly in New Canaan starting in the early 1990s, and so was present with our family at all of our Easters and Thanksgivings and Christmas celebrations. My mother never asked for anything in return. All that she wanted was to be loved. Her heart was not exhausted by loving me, so she loved Addie as her own daughter, and loved each of my four children as much as she loved me. Her best friend once noted that my mother was "love never ending."

I handled the arrangements for Mom's funeral, and spoke at her funeral about her depth of love for me and for Addie and for our children. Addie wrote a tribute for my mother's funeral, but was too overcome with emotion to speak at the service. It read:

Remembering Mom

All of you know that the days after someone dies are filled with lots of tasks so it is only after things settle down that you have time to reflect.

After going through Mom's things and many pictures I had this gnawing feeling that I was missing something. At a moment of clarity, it came to me. Where is Mom's bag? There is no bag in her closets, no bag in with the pictures. In addition to her pocketbook Mom always carried a bag. A bag full of stuff, and as our family grew, her bag grew.

When traveling or babysitting she had the bag. With Nigel, Tom, and me, the bag had:

Food and books and other little home remedies, like cod liver oil. It always had a flashlight, with extra batteries. And in my heart of hearts I believe that flashlight doubled as a weapon, just in case anyone thought about bothering any of her grandchildren.

Evonne arrives and we add:

Hairbrush, clips, lotion, and lots of other things little girls need.

Michael arrives and we have all of the above plus:

Small tools because Michael likes to take things apart, like lamps and anything not nailed down, so there was repair work to do when we traveled with him.

Vicky arrived and we needed all of the above plus crayons and pencil and paper and lots of arts and crafts supplies. More medical supplies because the likelihood of someone getting hurt rose exponentially with each child.

Five years ago, Nigel got married in Washington, D.C. Tom and I arrived before Mom and when I looked out and saw Mom coming across the lobby of the hotel, her bag had turned into a rolling suitcase.

I now know why I could not find the bag. The bag has been emptied. The bag was not full of stuff but full of love. She emptied that love into our family and still had enough love for my brothers and their families, my mom and my sister-in-law Gail's mom.

So as the bag has been emptied into us, Mom's body has been emptied, but in each of us resides some piece of her generous and loving spirit.

We love you, Mom, we thank you for loving us, we will miss you terribly but we will never forget you."

My mother's passing weighed on my heart for a long time. To this day I continue to visit Long Island National Cemetery every Easter and Christmas to take flowers to my parents' grave, and to thank God for their lives, and to pray that He has redeemed their faith and received their souls into eternal life.

My oldest brother, Edward, died at age sixty-nine the very next year, in December 2010. Because we hadn't been close for a very long time, his death affected me much differently. Edward had never achieved significant success in his career, and he also failed in his personal life. He died alone after having been divorced twice, and I don't know how well he knew his two adult daughters, Sharon and Michelle, from his first marriage, or his grandchildren. I was not close to Ed because I did not think he was my friend. I had tried to help him by gestures such as buying him a new car in 2006. When he was hospitalized in mid-December 2010 after collapsing at his home, he gave my name as his closest relative. The hospital contacted me and said it was urgent for me to visit as soon as possible. When I arrived, the attending physician informed me that Ed's illness was probably terminal colon cancer.

I visited Ed several times in the next week, and counseled him that his illness could possibly be terminal so he should promptly attend to urgent matters such as writing letters to his children and preparing or updating his will. Ed ignored my advice and died intestate and without writing to his daughters.

When I was cleaning out his basement, I found our father's model trains stuffed into four boxes stacked in a dark corner, apparently never opened from the moment he had taken them on our father's death. The labels were spotted with mildew.

In March 2012 my second brother, James, died at age sixty-six. He also died alone, after three failed marriages and an unsuccessful career trying to follow in our father's footsteps in the ministry. Jim had purchased a burial insurance policy and named me as the person to contact for funeral arrangements in the event of his death. I traveled to Greeneville, Tennessee, and spent a week organizing his funeral and trying to close out his final arrangements, such as removing his belongings from his apartment. I was not close to Jim because we lived in two completely different worlds and I did not respect the way he lived his life, but I had always included him in our family occasions when he visited our mother in New Canaan. Over the years, I had also helped him financially with cash gifts at Christmas and on his birthday, and by giving him my used cars or buying cars for him.

I spoke at both Ed's and Jim's funerals, and prayed for their souls, but I did not feel deep grief for either brother because I did not feel that I had lost someone to whom I was really close and bonded in love. Their deaths brought to the forefront of my mind the realization that neither of my brothers or my father lived to age seventy. While I take much better care of myself and I'm in excellent health, I'm mindful that I'm not assured of living to a ripe old age.

My sister Marie, nine years older than me, seems to be in good health, so that gives me some optimism for longevity. She lives in Texas but traveled to attend the funerals for our mother and brothers. Her daughter, my niece Kim, lives in Manhattan with her husband and two boys, and we invite them to our family celebrations. Kim is quite successful and I'm very proud of her. She graduated from Radcliffe College and Columbia Law School and is a partner at Cleary Gottlieb Steen & Hamilton, one of the major New York law firms. I know that Kim is regarded as one of the top commercial real estate securitization attorneys in New York, because on more than one occasion New York real estate executives have praised her capabilities to me when they learned we are related.

As I'm sure many others do, I enjoy refreshing my memories over the years by rereading handwritten cards—from Father's Days, birthdays, anniversaries—given to me by my family. As I revisit the messages and sentiments, I am reminded that my life has overflowed with love, that my children have heard my advice and been guided and encouraged by it, that my wife adores me just as I adore her, that my friends and family feel the depth of my love for them, and that my mother was proud of the man I became—and I am thankful.

A Return to See How Far We've Come

In April 1969, there was no such day as this in sight. This is a
great day in Cornell history.

—*Cornell president emeritus Dale Corson, May 4, 1995*

In 1980, when I was thirty-one and living in Boston and working at Arthur
Young, I finally sat down to write a letter that I had been thinking of writing for quite some time. My life had evolved incredibly well since April
1969 at Willard Straight Hall, and I was thankful. I was successful, happily married, and healthy in mind, body, and soul. My thoughts sometimes
strayed to wondering what my life experiences might have been if I had been
arrested then or even imprisoned. Or—worst of all—what if I had died in a
gun battle? I believed that President James Perkins was the person primarily
responsible for the forbearance with which Cornell had acted in April 1969,
and I felt a moral obligation to thank him.

July 18, 1980

Dear Dr. Perkins,

It was nice to talk to you after so many years . . . I have thought of
you many times, and I have been pained and shamed that a friend
of Afro-Americans paid the highest price for that confrontation. As
one grows older one realizes, fortunately, that belated expressions of
apology and sympathy are perhaps still capable of rendering some
slight comfort; one knows, in any event, that such expressions must
be given to those to whom they are due. I give you my apology for

not having stood with you against the tide of emotionalism and racial fear, and for using my talents to mobilize forces which intimidated the faculty and, in turn, led the faculty to vent their anger and resentment upon you. My apology would have come earlier, but it is easier to evade and forget such responsibilities when one is younger.

I am confident that you are yet going to be extremely proud of me, and of your decisions which contributed to shaping me during those important Cornell years—most importantly, your decision to admit more black students (including myself) in the fall of 1965, and your decision not to crush us with police force (or criminal records) in the spring of 1969. I believe that I can make an important contribution to America during this ten to fifteen year period we are now entering—a period which may be decisive in the ultimate history of America's interracial relations . . .

Best wishes,
Thomas W. Jones

He must have replied immediately upon receiving it, because I got his return letter the same week:

Dear Tom,

Let me say immediately that your letter to me met my real expectations for you. Your basic intelligence and sense of fairness come through in full measure. Thank you for saying what you did, and the way in which you said it.

I suspected at the time that someday I would be proud of you and satisfied that the tough decision to admit the greatly increased number of blacks into American higher education was a social priority of the highest importance.

Sincerely,
James A. Perkins

It had nagged at my conscience for many years that I had been instrumental in creating a grievous wound at Cornell that had not healed. Some black students were so emotionally traumatized by the events of 1969 that they never completed their Cornell degree, and some never completed college at all. Faculty careers and families had been disrupted as some professors chose to leave Cornell in the wake of the takeover. President Perkins had become, in those months in 1969 and since, the primary scapegoat for the wrath of the faculty and the board of trustees, and he had resigned under pressure in 1970. I found his fate ironic, really, because it was he who had created COSEP to champion increased black student enrollment at Cornell in the first place, and he who had prevailed in negotiations with the AAS to prevent violence. In my mind, Perkins's commitment to black progress was further evidenced by his position as chairman of the United Negro College Fund when he became Cornell's president in 1963.

In 1987, former Cornell professor Allan Bloom published his book *The Closing of the American Mind,* a strong critique of events at Cornell and of higher education in general in the 1960s. I read his book and laughed at the irony of the title. From my perspective, the most perniciously closed minds had been those of Cornell professors Allan Bloom and Walter Berns and their like-minded colleagues who had ignored the ugly truths of American history. Professors Berns and Bloom were inspired by the noble themes and threads in American history, of which there are many, and their passion translated into masterly classroom presentations. Their courses were always very popular. But they tended to ignore or minimize historical themes and threads that didn't fit their noble narrative storyline. They didn't teach explicit falsehoods, but they lied by omission and they minimized historical realities that didn't fit their fairy-tale version of American history and government. For instance, they did not teach about the ravages of slavery inflicted on millions of African Americans. They did not teach about the genocide committed by American settlers and military forces against Native Americans, nor about the racial terrorism perpetrated by the Ku Klux Klan against African Americans from the post–Civil War Reconstruction era on through the 1960s. It was as though these ugly historical realities simply didn't exist in the academic courses taught by Berns and Bloom and most of their colleagues in Cornell's professorate.

And then what happened when students like me challenged their sanitized fairy tales? They became irritated. The African American, so integral to the American story, was simply and almost utterly excluded from the standard curriculum, which is one of the reasons why black students at Cornell and other universities had to fight for black studies. We had to insist upon an education that included us. On balance, the civil rights movement, antiwar movement, women's liberation movement, and gay pride movement have opened America's eyes to historical truths and contradictions about our country. Through this acknowledging of historical truth, and resolving to come closer to achieving America's noble founding ideals, America has become a better country.

I t became important to me, upon reflection, to remember those at Cornell who had lifted me up and to celebrate positivity and progress. In 1992 I made a gift to Cornell to endow a fund for planning programs in honor of Professor Barclay Jones, who had given me the time and friendship and guidance I'd needed all those years before. "This endowment," I told the university, "is dedicated to Barclay Jones in recognition that everybody stands on somebody's shoulders—and over the years, Barclay has willingly offered his shoulders to many of his students, including me." The fund supports work in the department Barclay led, the Department of City and Regional Planning, as well as the graduate planning field in general, which spans several departments in the university.

And then, two years later, I conceived the idea to endow an annual James A. Perkins Prize for Interracial Understanding and Harmony to honor President Perkins's legacy and sacrifice, and to foster a spirit of healing and reconciliation in the Cornell community. My gift was an atonement, a token of gratitude, a way to honor him, and a way to foster and support "activities that promote interracial respect, understanding and harmony on campus," as the official description of the prize states.

The A. D. White House is a lumbering, creaking old brick home in the Second Empire style, originally the official residence for Cornell's inaugural president, Andrew Dickson White. It sits up on a little hill on East Avenue, set apart from any other buildings. Today it houses the Society for the Humanities and hosts special gatherings, including the announcement of the Perkins Prize. That first announcement was a small affair, with some students and faculty and alumni, a few trustees, and some people from town in attendance. It was a quiet event but full of hope and affection. I made these remarks there that day:

> I am pleased to establish the James A. Perkins Prize for Interracial Understanding and Harmony, and to participate in this first annual award ceremony. The Prize is intended to convey three messages.
>
> First, a message of hope. Hope that America will continue to persevere to achieve our highest ideals. I believe our destiny is to be the

first nation in the world to successfully unite people of every race and culture in a free democratic society, with justice and equal opportunity for all. Hope encourages us to strive to be more tomorrow than we are today.

Second, a message of celebration. Celebration of how far we have come in our efforts to achieve racial equality and cultural acceptance. We have traveled a road carved through 375 years of adversity since the first African slaves landed in America. That road of progress has been carved in each generation by Americans of goodwill from all races. We should pause occasionally to celebrate how far we have come, even as we think of how far we have yet to go. Celebration encourages us to acknowledge how much we have achieved.

Third, a message of recognition. Recognition that enlightened individuals, institutions, and organizations help us to find the road to progress in each generation. President Perkins was an enlightened individual who led the way in opening the doors of our best colleges and universities in the 1960s to greatly expanded numbers of minority students. Cornell has historically been an enlightened institution in searching for racial progress—for example, it is noteworthy that Cornell had sufficient African American students to organize a black fraternity chapter in the early 1900s. Few American universities can make that claim. Recognition encourages enlightened individuals, institutions, and organizations to continue leading the way.

I hope that the winners of the Perkins Prize for Interracial Understanding and Harmony will continue to demonstrate this year, and in the years ahead, that love and goodwill can make a decisive difference in helping our country to overcome its racial difficulties.

After my remarks, the first-ever Perkins Prize was awarded, to the *Cornell Political Forum,* a student-published nonpartisan journal of respectful and impassioned intellectual debate. It was a respected forum for productive dialogue among a diverse set of viewpoints. The next year, at the ceremony to award the second annual Perkins Prize, the Festival of Black Gospel was recognized for its work in presenting annually an inspiring jamboree of choirs and individual artists, which attracts hundreds from campus and the town and surrounding region. Again, both President Perkins and I attended the award ceremony, and this time a local pastor, the Reverend Douglas Green of the First Congregational Church of Christ in Ithaca, was in attendance with

Figure 20 / *Tom and former Cornell president James Perkins at the inaugural Perkins Prize award ceremony, May 1995 (*Cornell Daily Sun *photograph by Aurianne Nappi, Class of 1996).*

his wife. They came up to speak with us afterwards, an encounter he was to recount later in a sermon to his congregation (which he was kind enough to mail to me). He concluded that sermon with these words:

> So at the end of that little ceremony, and as I said, there were no cameras, no crowds, no media, as there were at Willard Straight many years ago, I went up and talked to Perkins and Jones. I thanked them for what they had done, for what they had both said, and told them that this was one of the more hopeful and beautiful things I had seen in a long time. And Mrs. Perkins, who was standing there, and who, I imagine, suffered as much in the 60's as her husband, said with a smile, "Yes, this is very hopeful." And then she added, and this is where I almost cried, "And if this can happen, anything can happen." Amen.

My favorite Perkins Prize winner over the years was the Intergroup Dialogue Project, which won in 2014. It has as its mission and goal to raise the consciousness of all, develop a campus climate of understanding, build relationships across differences, and help people learn to work through conflicts.

The dialogues, which are given a new theme each semester, are focused on race and ethnicity, socioeconomic status, gender, religion, and sexual orientation. Thousands of Cornell students have taken the IDP course for academic credit, and enrollment is usually oversubscribed. Through this program, students are trained to make positive contributions to creating a more respectful and inclusive society in an increasingly diverse America.

I was surprised and very pleased with the reaction to the Perkins Prize. The May 5, 1995, *Cornell Daily Sun* front-page headline read "Former Straight Opponents Make Peace," and the story by Seth Stern read, in part,

> "I'm terribly proud to be part of this," said Perkins, who returned to Cornell yesterday for only the fourth time since leaving in June 1969. "I could not believe the University could fund a [prize] that so closely fulfilled the ideals I was groping for." . . . Perkins resigned two months after the takeover under pressure from faculty who criticized his performance during the standoff. . . . Although Perkins worked to increase the enrollment of minority students during his administration—raising the number of black students on campus from 10 to more than 250—it's the three-day takeover that will forever mark Perkins' tenure.

But the reactions to the Perkins Prize were not universally positive. An article in the *Philadelphia Inquirer* quoted a faculty member who had "left Cornell in disgust," describing both the 1969 and 1995 campus events as "obscene," and quoted Ed Whitfield, who "called Jones a sell-out."

When I was forty-three, members of the Cornell University board of trustees, along with senior staff in Alumni Affairs and Development, reached out to me and asked if I would consider being nominated for a seat on the board. My appearance on the nominee slate in 1993 stirred controversy and irritated the unhealed wounds from the Straight takeover. On April 7, a month before the board would vote to admit the nominated members, the *New York Times* ran an article about me titled "Evolution of a Protester: From Guns to Governing":

> Those who support Mr. Jones say he should be judged on his current qualifications . . . But some people argue that Mr. Jones should

not be forgiven, while those who consider the takeover symbolic of the struggle for minority rights complain that he has abandoned their cause. And some are disappointed that he has expressed regrets about his role in the takeover. It probably goes without saying that Mr. Jones no longer endorses the tactics and language he used in 1969. "Given the way things played out in that historical period, I made the best decisions I could under the circumstances, and I will not repudiate that 25 years later," he said in a recent telephone interview from his office in New York. "I regret that any incident of potential violence occurred in our society at the university then, and I wish it had not occurred."

I was graciously welcomed to the Cornell board by chairman Stephen Weiss, vice chair Patricia Stewart, and many other board members. One of my first duties was to serve on the presidential search committee charged with recommending a successor to President Frank Rhodes. In late 1994 our search and deliberations concluded with the appointment of Hunter Rawlings as Cornell's tenth president. My immersion in important board committees and decisions deepened my sense that I had unfinished business at Cornell, a feeling that had troubled my conscience for years.

The university was planning an event to commemorate the twenty-fifth anniversary of the Straight takeover. The organizers asked if I would be willing to speak at the event, since I was in the unusual position of being a member of the board and a key player in the takeover.

As I worked to draft remarks, I realized that I wanted to speak to the black students of today. I did not want merely to relay history or make something of an apology for behavior I no longer believed wholly correct. At the same time, I did want to convey something of the heat and necessity of the protest.

In April of 1994, I returned to the Straight to deliver my speech. I entered the building at its main entrance onto Ho Plaza, the same doors where we'd exited armed and triumphant all those years earlier. The podium was set up in the Memorial Room—a gracious room with a vaulted ceiling and high windows on three sides that flood the room with light. I faced a crowd of alumni, staff, and current students. My talk, which was titled "Reflections on the Sixties and the Nineties," read in part:

The April 1969 *Newsweek* cover photo of Cornell University black students armed with rifles, shotguns, and bandoliers of bullets probably ranks as one of the most vivid images of the sixties. Quite a number of years ago I was given a poster-size photo of myself leaving Willard Straight Hall at the end of the occupation, a rifle crooked in my left arm and my right fist in the air. The poster still hangs in my study at home and when I look at it I am most struck by the depths of anger and determination in my face.

Anger and determination. Those two words may reflect both the anguish and the hope of the sixties. "Anguish" because it was truly frightening, and a tragedy, that so many young Americans were so angry at our society that we did such things. Both anguish and anger were behind the Willard Straight Hall takeover, the "Days of Rage" at the Democratic Convention in Chicago, and the turmoil at Berkeley, Columbia, Harvard, and other universities. But *also "hope"* because it was in a spirit of self-sacrifice that we were determined to fight for beliefs and principles greater than ourselves. Our actions were not for personal gain. In April 1969, a month before my graduation, one of the few things I was not accused of was positioning myself for an auspicious career in the business world!

I want to talk to you about what caused that anger and determination, or anguish and hope. And I want to talk to you about how we might put the anger and anguish behind us, and move forward together with determination and hope to try to fulfill the great promise and destiny of this country. Let me develop these themes by addressing three questions that many of you have on your minds:

1. Do I have any regrets or apologies for being a leader of the "Guns at Cornell" incident in 1969?
2. Have I had to relinquish or compromise the ideals I used to care about in order to achieve success in the business world?
3. Has America become the kind of society that we of the 1960s wanted. If so, why is this what we wanted? If not, what should be different?

On the first question . . . the answer is both yes and no. Yes, I am sorry that the threat of violence racked this great institution which is dedicated to reason and truth, and for which I have great affection. Yes, I am sorry that I bear some of the responsibility for the failure to resolve our differences through reason and discourse. Yes, I am sorry that a fine man like Dr. James Perkins was the lightning rod for the reactive wrath of the faculty, trustees, and alumni. Yes, I am sorry that some black students were so traumatized and disoriented that they never completed their Cornell degrees, and some never completed college at all.

But no, I'm not sorry for standing up alongside my friends and fellows for what we believed in. No, I don't regret refusing to capitulate to those administrators and faculty who also contributed to the ingredients of the confrontation. They didn't pick up the guns, of course—they weren't "violent" in the literal meaning of the word. But violence is just the last stop on a line that also runs through ill will, arrogance, disregard, contempt, and intimidation. I will not cede the moral high ground to perpetrators of these things merely because they had no need at that particular moment to turn to force. Physical violence may be the most readily recognized and, even to many, the most frightening kind of threat, but it isn't the only kind, nor even necessarily the most damaging kind, nor the hardest kind to resist.

[. . .]

So we were prepared in 1969 to be the generation of African Americans that would draw the line. No more being treated with ill will, arrogance, disregard, contempt, and intimidation. Personally, I simply thought of it as being a generation fingered by the random wheel of history to shoulder an unusually difficult burden. I thought my life would be short, but I was not afraid. Death is not the worst thing that can happen to a person . . . Many generations and many individuals have had to summon the courage to shoulder unusually difficult burdens. So we were prepared in 1969 to meet our destiny in a struggle that was much bigger than any one of us, and even much bigger than all of us.

[. . .]

Let me turn to the second question I promised to address: Have I had to compromise my ideals to succeed in the business world? The answer is quite simply "No." I continue to care very deeply about social justice, and about our country. From my perspective, however, America has changed dramatically during the past thirty years. Let me give you just two simple but telling examples of how much America has changed.

Thirty years ago, it really was a problem for African Americans to be served at public facilities in many parts of the country. I remember as a child traveling through the South with my parents and stopping at gas stations where, before he would buy gas, my father would ask if we would be allowed to use the restrooms. Many of you can't imagine living under that kind of segregation. And thirty years ago, it was common for minorities and women to routinely be denied jobs and promotions in most American companies simply because of race or gender. Many of you can't imagine living under that kind of discrimination.

[. . .]

On the one hand, the petty discrimination of being denied access to public facilities was intended to dehumanize African Americans, and to proclaim every day that we were different and inferior. And on the other hand, the systemic institutional denial of economic opportunities was intended to ensure that African Americans remained poor and powerless. And as you step back through American history, each previous decade is typically more brutal in its treatment of African Americans.

But the purpose of reciting this history is not just to remind you of where we have been but also to focus on how far we have come. It is important to know history, and to understand how the world we live in today has been shaped by the past . . . But it is equally important not to be a prisoner of history. By that I mean there is no point in limiting our potential for today and tomorrow with the chains of the past. The burden is too heavy. We will never have a better world if each ethnic group or nation focuses solely on perpetual resentment and animosity for historical grievances and injustices . . . We must all be open to reaching accommodation and making progress in a spirit of tolerance, healing, and reconciliation.

I believe that the turmoil of the sixties was a major factor in convincing our governing institutions and elites, as well as many ordinary citizens, that the best hope for the future of America is for us to actually try to become what we say we are . . . And it also seems to me that it is undeniable that African Americans, other minorities, and women have economic, educational, and social opportunities available today which are unprecedented in American history. Does this mean that our country has overcome all of its problems? Of course not! The legacy of hundreds of years of slavery, abuse, and neglect created a scale of human misery and dysfunctionality which cannot be reversed in just twenty-five or thirty years. But do I feel that America is trying to become a better society, and that African Americans are welcome and can achieve a respected place in that society? Absolutely yes!

So from my perspective, I have not had to sacrifice my ideals in order to succeed. I always wanted to be part of America. But for most of American history, America wanted no part of me. That is the great change which has occurred in the past thirty years.

Now, let me move to the third question I promised to address: Do I think that America has become the kind of society that I and my 1960s compatriots wanted? So far, the "sixties generation" track record is that we're better at disrupting and dismantling than we are at creating and building. Let me cite a few examples.

We attacked rigid social standards and stereotypes regarding hair length, clothing, and social mores such as sexual abstinence before marriage. "Do your own thing" became the theme of the sixties. But while we rightly wanted freedom for personal lifestyle choices, did the "Me Generation" really intend to abdicate responsibility for defining and teaching basic moral standards of right and wrong essential for both the individual and society? When and how will my generation shoulder our responsibility to teach the eternal, enduring significance of values that celebrate personal responsibility, personal discipline, personal accountability, hard work, moderation, courage, and cooperativeness?

We attacked the compulsory military draft, and the seeds for an all-volunteer military were sown during the sixties. But while we rightly wanted freedom from military conscription, did we really intend to have the burdens of military service fall predominantly on the shoulders of low-income people who seek economic and educational opportunity in the military? When and how will my generation fulfill our obligation to teach the ideal that every young American is enhanced by service to the greater common good?

Perhaps most unfortunately, a missing element from this legacy of the sixties is what I earlier described as the hope of the sixties—that is, the spirit of self-sacrifice in which we were determined to fight for beliefs and principles greater than ourselves. When and how will my generation fulfill our responsibility to rekindle a sense of self-sacrifice in pursuit of noble ideals such as making America a better country?

As I look around the university today I wonder when students will realize that today's fight—the fight of the nineties, the fight which would engage me if I were a student today—is to build a society which respects and celebrates diversity while also affirming a greater sense of community, and transcends our diversity to unite us as one American people despite our various colors and cultures and creeds. All around the world this is the fight of the nineties. Call it Yugoslavia. Call it South Africa. Call it the Holy Land. Call it America. People all around the world are retreating into their racial and cultural enclaves. It is a virulent disease . . .

You, the students of the nineties, should rekindle the hope of the sixties. Shoulder your responsibility to fight this fight of the nineties. Strive to create a university community that provides leadership to our country and inspires hope and optimism. Struggle to create an America that is a beacon of hope to Yugoslavia, South Africa, and the Holy Land. Show the world that "E Pluribus Unum" is possible: out of many, we can build one community. Thank you.

Vestiges of a debate between me and some of the other students involved in the takeover lived on. On the thirtieth anniversary of the Straight takeover, the April 21, 1999, *Cornell Daily Sun* published an opinion column by Anthony Zuba, Class of 1999, which captured the essential elements of my alienation from the "blacker than thou" dynamics on the Cornell campus. The column, which was titled "A Straight Comparison," proceeded to compare my life and career to Ed Whitfield's, and also to compare current Cornell students' reception of us:

Tom Jones '69 and Ed Whitfield '71 are humble men, but differently so. Two weeks ago, Jones showed himself to be humble in the memory of the late James Perkins as he gave the fifth Perkins Prize for Interracial Understanding and Harmony. Famously remorseful for the way he and fellow members of the Afro American society intimidated Perkins during the Straight Takeover, he elevated the former University president to the status of martyr: "In our mutual anger, metaphorically, we killed the good shepherd . . . [I]t is the story of the New Testament. It is why it is written that "the anger of man does not work the will of God."

[. . .]

On Monday, during his keynote speech for the 30th anniversary of the Straight Takeover, Whitfield didn't deify anyone, but he professed humility in the presence of the activist students and educators on campus today. In a speech equally cadenced and articulate as Jones's, he also remembered the departed, but he paid homage to Robert Rone, John Garner '70 and Larry Dickson '70. Rone and Dickson were members of the radical faction of AAS; Garner was the leader of the black consciousness movement at Cornell. Whitfield did not praise Perkins or how far Cornell has come since the Straight.

During the 30 years since the Takeover, it has been customary to compare Jones and Whitfield like this . . . Their philosophical parting of ways since the Straight has been remarkable. Since 1969, Jones, now a corporate executive, has regarded his behavior during the Takeover as an aberration necessitated by the times, and has tried to accentuate the progress America has made . . . Jones clearly does not live in the same America as Whitfield, who, 30 years after fighting with Jones for a black studies program at Cornell, still crusades to secure an educational experience relevant to the lives of minorities. A community organizer in North Carolina, Whitfield said Monday that poor youth in rural and urban regions require effective educational institutions in order to "survive, transcend, transform, and transfer out" of their situation.

Jones talks about progress. Whitfield talks about survival. The disparity fascinates me. I wish Cornell could have brought the two together on the Straight Takeover anniversary so the community could learn why they disagree about the state of society. As time passes, I'm less optimistic such a meeting will ever occur . . . Both men have nearly become abstractions to each other and to the public. Introducing Whitfield Monday, graduate student Leslie Alexander said he is all too often portrayed as an icon; she encouraged people to get to know him as a person. But I doubt student activists are willing to do the same for Jones. They have chosen to caricature the contemporary man for renouncing his radical activities, branding him "Uncle Tom Jones" in 1997 during a protest of the Perkins Prize.

If such a "Jones-Whitfield debate" were ever to occur, I would say that I have no criticisms of the way that Ed Whitfield has lived his life, and I hope his community service endeavors have been successful. I would also say that Ed should acknowledge to the Cornell black community that I'm the person who stayed at Cornell in 1969 to ensure that the Africana Studies & Research Center actually materialized in the aftermath of the Straight, while Whitfield and a group of like-minded thinkers left Cornell that spring and summer and never returned. I would ask Ed to acknowledge to the Cornell black community that Africana probably wouldn't exist if it weren't for the work I did to get it approved, funded, and implemented. I would also say that I have drawers full of letters from people whose lives I have touched over the years in the companies in which I've worked, thanking me for promotions and compensation increases and for helping to create corporate environments conducive to their success. Many of those letters are from black men and women who are grateful for being better able to provide for their families. And I would say that I'm also appreciative of the letters I've received from whites I've worked with in corporate America thanking me for opportunities afforded to them, and thanking me for helping to renew their faith in America and the prospects for racial progress. I'm also proud of the letters and recognition I've received from the faculty and staff at St. Aloysius School thanking me for providing funding and technology resources which have had enormous impact on the education of hundreds of low-income black children in central Harlem.

I respect the life choices Ed Whitfield has made, and I hope that he and those who emulate him will someday learn also to respect the life choices that I and others like me have made. We both should be judged by the same standard, which is that success means that those whose lives have intersected with ours have been made better because we have lived and because they have known us. Finally, I would say to Ed that the day I will respect him most is the day when he publicly apologizes for calling me a "sellout," rebukes the Cornell black students who disparaged me by calling me "Uncle Tom Jones," and repudiates this type of name-calling in the black community.

When President Perkins died in 1998, I attended his memorial service in Princeton, New Jersey, and spoke at the invitation of his family. I was thankful that I had reached out to President Perkins while he was alive and that the Perkins Prize was a source of comfort to his family.

Seventeen years later Professor Walter Berns died, and his obituary, written by Sam Roberts, was in the *New York Times* on January 14, 2015. It read in part as follows:

Walter Berns, a distinguished constitutional scholar and government professor whose disgust with Cornell University's response to the armed takeover of a campus building by black students propelled him to become a leading voice of the neoconservative movement, died on Saturday.... It was not for nothing that Cornell was widely known as the Big Red during the 1960s, when passions over civil rights and the war in Vietnam provoked convulsive student radicalism. But the backlash to those campus revolutionaries also sparked the ascension of neoconservative intellectuals whose ideology has shaped the nation's political agenda for decades.... His embittered departure from Cornell in 1969 inspired a growing cadre of disaffected progressives and lapsed conservatives who blamed permissive liberalism for many social ills.

After the Cornell protest, one demonstrator, Thomas Jones, sent Professor Berns an apology, but he never responded, according to an account by Donald A. Downs, a professor at the University of Wisconsin. Mr. Jones acknowledged the other day, though, that years later, after he became the president of TIAA-CREF, ... he received a sardonic congratulatory note from his former professor. "First you wanted to kill me," the note from Professor Berns said. "Now you want to take care of me in my retirement."

In July 2014 I received an email from Cornell president David Skorton inviting me to participate in Cornell's 150th anniversary celebration, a year of events taking place worldwide.

Needless to say, I was pleased and proud to be invited to participate in this historic commemoration and committed immediately to participating in the first event, to be held in New York City. I drafted a script and shared it with Doug Bernstein, the freelance producer hired by Cornell to stage the event. Doug suggested judicious edits to sharpen the message and fit my allotted two-minute time slot. He also explained that during a portion of the program devoted to "community and tradition," I would be onstage with two professors discussing their research as examples of Cornell's impact on the broader world.

My final script read:

I am Tom Jones. Cornell's aspirational ideals of community and tradition were "radical ideas" in 1865—especially the notion that both men and women, and people of all races, should be able to pursue any field of study.

While the first Cornell class of 332 in 1868 was 100 percent white and male, the following year saw the first student of African heritage—and one year later the first woman. The founder's vision was off to a good start!

And yet . . . nearly a century later, when President James Perkins took office in 1963, Cornell had only four black students in an entering freshman class of 2,300.

What's more, Cornell's "community and tradition" included a long history of patronizing female students, ignoring fraternity restrictions against Jewish students, and allowing insensitivity toward Hispanics, American Indians, and LGBT students.

When I participated in the April 1969 takeover of Willard Straight Hall—a painful chapter sparked by issues surrounding academic and social accommodations for black students—it was clear that many in the Cornell community were ready to insist on *new* traditions.

Or perhaps it's better to say: we were ready to insist that Cornell return to its own original aspirational ideals.

In the years that followed, this pursuit delivered real results. And Cornell has grown stronger through the crucibles it faced.

Today, 51 percent of Cornell's undergraduates are female—and the class of 2017 is 16 percent Asian, 12 percent Hispanic, 7 percent African American, and 11 percent international.

Are all of Cornell's aspirations realized? Surely not. But the university's diversity initiatives demonstrate a commitment to students of every background.

As I spoke these words, names of these majors and centers scrolled on the large screen behind me:

Africana Studies & Research Center
American Indian Program
Asian & Asian American Studies
Center for Intercultural Dialogue
Jewish Studies Program
Latino Studies Program
Feminist, Gender & Sexuality Studies Program

Lesbian, Gay, Bisexual & Transgender Resource Center
Muslim Cultural Center
Program Houses:

Akwe:kon
Ecology House
International Living Center
Just About Music
Language House
Latino Living Center
Multicultural Living Learning Unit
Risley Residential College
Ujamaa Residential College

I salute and applaud Cornell's progress in moving ever closer to achieving the aspirational ideals of its founders.

The work continues—for students, faculty, administrators, and alumni—and *that* tradition is truly what makes our community strong.

My remarks were warmly received at both of the sesquicentennial programs held in New York City. Cornell was pleased with the audience feedback in the follow-up online survey and invited me to participate in as many of the upcoming presentations in other cities as I was willing to do. I agreed to speak at the next one, in Washington, D.C., in November 2014, and again received strong audience response. This success encouraged me to do all of the scheduled Cornell sesquicentennial events, except for the one in Hong Kong, so I eventually participated in presentations in Boston, Palm Beach, San Francisco, Los Angeles, and London. I did this because I thought it was important for the takeaway message from Straight Takeover/Guns at Cornell to be recorded in Cornell history as a message of racial reconciliation and community healing. Straight Takeover/Guns at Cornell is just one chapter in Cornell's continuing progress toward achieving its unique promise to be both an elite and an inclusive institution of higher learning.

April 2015 found me at Cornell again, for the Charter Day celebration that was the culmination of the sesquicentennial year. I sat for an hour on a sunny Saturday afternoon in the new Sesquicentennial Grove at the top of Libe Slope, directly behind the statue of Ezra Cornell. It is a beautiful spot, where winding gray walking paths bisect the green slope and below the paths are the residential halls and the Cayuga Lake glacial valley, dotted with far-away houses, everything spread out before you as if you were a bird in the sky. It is a spot where I must have sat fifty years earlier, maybe with Skip or Charles or Nigel's mother, when we were students. As I took in the view, I reflected on my long association with Cornell, dating from my freshman matriculation in September 1965 and making up one-third of Cornell's history.

The Sesquicentennial Grove is marked by benches, a path, plaques, and a timeline. I was impressed with the timeline's portrayal of Cornell's unique history as "the first truly American university," especially by the university's inclusion from the start of women and people of color, which was not the norm at other American universities at the time. This theme of inclusion is reflected in the stone carvings of Cornell founder Ezra Cornell's famous words "I would found an institution where any person can find instruction in any study" and in the stone carvings of Cornell's first president, Andrew Dickson White's, well-known description of Cornell as "a place where the most highly prized instruction may be afforded to all—regardless of sex or color."

The theme of inclusiveness is also reflected in the grove's stone carving of Cornell's historical timeline, which includes these two entries:

> 1964—President James Perkins creates a Committee on Special Education Projects (COSEP) to attract minority students to Cornell.
>
> 1969—During the decade of the civil rights struggle, over a hundred African-American students seize and occupy Willard Straight Hall for 33 hours, leading to the resignation of President James Perkins.

I mused to myself that it would have been even better if the timeline memorial designers had included the student demands during the takeover, the reason behind the action: the desire for a curriculum that included our own real part in history. I also thought it would have been a nice touch if they'd included one additional inscription:

> 1906—Alpha Phi Alpha, America's first black intercollegiate Greek letter fraternity, founded at Cornell.

As I sat at the edge of the grove, many other visitors paused to read the inscriptions and remark on the history. "I've heard about that takeover," I

**Figure 21 / *Tom, Rosa Rhodes, Frank Rhodes, and Addie
(left to right) at the Frank H. T. Rhodes Exemplary Alumni Service
Award ceremony, September 2017 (Cornell Alumni Affairs photograph
by Chris Kitchen for Cornell Brand Communications).***

overheard one woman say to her companion, who in turn replied, "I didn't
know all this Cornell history. This is great."

My Cornell story was capped in 2017, when I was honored with two
extraordinary awards, the Frank H. T. Rhodes Exemplary Alumni Service
Award, which is given out to just a handful of alumni each year who are
celebrated together at a tribute dinner, and then I was named a presidential
councillor by the board of trustees, the university's very highest honor. News
of both these distinctions came to me by way of letters from Cornell's new
president, Martha Pollack. Because I had expected neither award, I was at
once surprised, humbled, and grateful to have my service and financial support for my alma mater recognized in this way.

In September 2016, Addie and I attended the dedication ceremony for the
opening of the new National Museum of African American History and

Culture (NMAAHC) in Washington, D.C., which is part of the Smithsonian Institution. It will probably be the final addition to the National Mall. It is an extraordinary structure whose shape echoes a Yoruban crown, and the color varies in response to each day's unique light and color. The architecture is elegant and striking, and brings a new dimension to the National Mall by presenting a unique and powerful visual statement: this building is about a people whose story belongs to the American national story, and yet it's also about a people whose story is also decidedly different.

I came away from the dedication with newfound respect and appreciation for President George W. Bush and his wife, Laura. In 2003 President Bush signed the legislation establishing the museum, and Laura Bush has been an active member of the museum's advisory council. In his remarks at the dedication ceremony, President Bush said that NMAAHC is important for three reasons: (1) It speaks to America's commitment to truth; (2) it speaks to America's capacity for change; and (3) it showcases African American talent and greatness.

Bush's remarks caused me to reflect that NMAAHC answers the question posed by historian Nancy Isenberg: "Can we handle the truth?" I think NMAAHC answers, "Yes, we can." And our capacity for truth and our capacity for change have enabled us to become a better country, and will continue to do so far into the future. This is what is most exceptional about America, and the museum tells that truth to the entire world.

During much of the dedication ceremony I was overcome with profound gratitude. Tears of joy ran down my face—joy at being alive and present in person to participate in this extraordinary historic event. Congressman John Lewis spoke of how the museum means that "as long as there is America, the African American story will be told on the National Mall, and tell American history through an African American lens, . . . and describe the African American tributary which flows into the great river which is America."

President Barack Obama said, "This museum represents how we remake ourselves in accord with our highest ideals . . . and this commitment to truth is where real patriotism lies." I agreed with the sentiments expressed by Smithsonian secretary David Skorton, former president of Cornell University, who said that most of us are blessed with only a limited number of extraordinarily memorable days in our lifetime, and that the dedication and opening of NMAAHC was one of those days in his life.

The dedication ceremony concluded with the assembled thousands singing "Lift Ev'ry Voice and Sing," also known as the black national anthem. Written by James Weldon Johnson as a poem in 1899 and set to music by his brother, the lyrics fit this occasion so perfectly that it could have been written specifically for this NMAAHC dedication and celebration of the African American journey in America.

Lift ev'ry voice and sing,
Till earth and heaven ring.
Ring with the harmonies of Liberty;
Let our rejoicing rise,
High as the list'ning skies,
Let it resound loud as the rolling sea.
Sing a song full of the faith that the dark
past has taught us,
Sing a song full of the hope that the
present has brought us;
Facing the rising sun of our new day begun,
Let us march on till victory is won.

Stony the road we trod,
Bitter the chast'ning rod,
Felt in the days when hope unborn had died;
Yet with a steady beat,
Have not our weary feat,
Come to the place for which our fathers sighed?
We have come over a way that with tears
has been watered,
We have come, treading our path
through the blood of the slaughtered.
Out from the gloomy past,
Here now we stand at last
Where the white gleam of our bright star is cast.

God of our weary years,
God of our silent tears,
Thou who hast brought us thus far on the way;
Thou who has by Thy might,
Led us into the light,
Keep us forever in the path, we pray.
Lest our feet stray from the places, our God,
where we met Thee;

Lest our hearts, drunk with the wine of the world,
we forget Thee,
Shadowed beneath Thy hand,
May we forever stand,
True to our God,
True to our native land.

The choir wore formal black evening attire and entered the church in a measured procession one by one, each person carrying a lit candle that shone in the dimmed sanctuary. I studied their faces as they walked past my pew, and I could see pride to be part of the event, and I also saw in their faces the strength of people whose lives have not been easy but who have endured and overcome. Addie and I sat shoulder to shoulder in a crowded pew. It was a few days before Christmas 2016 at the Grace Baptist Church in Mount Vernon, New York. The choir was accompanied by an orchestra numbering about forty instrumentalists.

As they sang their repertoire of seasonal and gospel songs, I saw their faces become radiant with joy. These are descendants of slaves, I thought, like us. Their families have known hard times, and even now many probably have difficult struggles to make ends meet. But look at how they've taken their struggles and converted them, through internal spiritual strength, into the beauty and nobility reflected in their faces and in their dignified and worthy lives. Listen to the majesty they attain together as a choir in this extraordinary worship service of music. Their internal spiritual strength, I realized, is like the pressure of the earth that converts coal into diamonds.

I wish that the entire black community in Mount Vernon, especially the black men, could open their eyes and see how their neighbors have been transformed through faith, and say, "I want to be like them." And I wish that all of America could see this Grace Baptist Church Christmas concert and these radiant people, and understand and be proud that America is a beautiful mosaic, assembled from a long history of racial oppression and social injustice, a substance still in the process of becoming a diamond. This is America today, and all Americans should be proud of how far our country has come. We all should be inspired and reassured in our hearts that we can walk into the future together—many races, many religions, many nationalities, many ethnicities—confident that America will continue to become a better country with each successive generation.

Appendix

Excerpts from the *Wall Street Journal*'s
"Year-End Review of Markets & Finance," 2001–2004

The following bibliographic guide is drawn from *Wall Street Journal* "Year-End Review" features that include articles over the period 2001 to 2004 and the *Wall Street Journal* abstracts, lightly edited here, to the article content. References to events that impacted Freddie Mac or Citigroup are italicized for emphasis to help the reader better appreciate the atmosphere around the author at the time. This appendix is intended to give the reader an overview of coverage during this period. Full bibliographic references and texts of the articles are available at wsj.com.

February 2001

9 Lucent is under investigation by the SEC over possible fraudulent accounting practices. The inquiry focuses on how Lucent booked $679 million in revenue during fiscal 2000.

March 2001

1 Cendant's former chairman and vice chairman are indicted on criminal charges that they directed an accounting fraud that inflated earnings by several hundred million dollars.

May 2001

3 A grand jury indicts the former chairmen of Sotheby's and Christie's on charges that they masterminded a scheme to fix clients' commissions. Alfred Taubman and Sir Anthony Tennant are accused of colluding on how the auction houses

dealt with art sellers from 1993 through 1999, including agreeing to raise commission rates.

June 2001

20 The SEC fines Arthur Andersen and three partners more than $7 million in connection with audits of Waste Management's annual financial results. Arthur Andersen agrees to pay the fine in order to settle the case, one of the first fraud cases ever filed against a Big Five accounting firm.

October 2001

17 Enron takes a $1.01 billion charge, mostly connected with write-downs of soured investments, producing a $618 million third-quarter loss. One portion of the charge, connected with a pair of limited partnerships that were run by Enron's finance chief, is raising conflict of interest questions.

November 2001

1 Enron discloses that the SEC has elevated to a formal investigation an inquiry into the energy-trading concern's financial dealings with partnerships led by its former finance chief.

5 An Enron deal raises fresh questions about its financial interactions with management. The energy-trading giant's $35 million purchase from an entity run by a company officer appears to be one of a complex series of transactions that let Enron keep millions in debt off its balance sheet for the past three years.

8 Waste Management agrees to pay $457 million to settle a class-action suit alleging securities law violations.

9 Enron discloses in an SEC filing that it reduced its previously reported net, dating back to 1997, by $586 million, or 20 percent, mostly as a result of improperly accounting for its dealings with partnerships run by some company officers.

29 Enron's debt is downgraded to junk status by credit-rating agencies, and Dynegy calls off its planned merger following the announcements. Enron's stock price plunges 85 percent. A day later, Enron's European energy-trading unit files for protection from creditors.

December 2001

6 Alfred Taubman, former chairman of Sotheby's, is found guilty of conspiring with the ex-chairman of rival Christie's to fix fees charged art clients.

January 2002

10 *The Justice Department confirms it will pursue a criminal probe of Enron, focusing on possible accounting fraud.*

11 *Arthur Andersen says its employees destroyed many documents related to its work for Enron.*

16 *Arthur Andersen fires the partner who directed the destruction of thousands of emails and documents related to the Enron audit.*

17 *Enron's board fires Arthur Andersen as auditor amid a storm of recriminations between the companies.*

22 Three former Enron employees say documents were shredded in the accounting department of the company's Houston headquarters after federal investigators began an inquiry into possible illegalities at the energy concern.

24 Enron CEO Kenneth Lay resigns less than twenty-four hours after a bankruptcy court–appointed creditors committee seeks his removal.

25 Former Enron vice chairman J. Clifford Baxter, who quit the energy firm in May, is found dead, an apparent suicide.

29 Global Crossing files for Chapter 11 in the biggest telecom collapse so far.

February 2002

4 An internal Enron report finds various improper financial transactions and massive self-dealing by company officials.

5 Kenneth Lay says he is quitting Enron's board, and lawmakers announce they will subpoena him to appear before investigative panels.

8 In testimony before Congress, Enron's former CEO denies knowledge of improper activities by his subordinates and many of the details of the partnerships that brought the company down.

8 WorldCom's CEO says the company stepped in to cover a personal loan of $198.7 million. The long-distance firm cut its 2002 forecasts and said it expects a charge of $15 billion to $20 billion.

13 Enron's former chairman invokes the Fifth Amendment, declining to answer any questions from a Senate panel. Separately, remarks by Kenneth Lay to an investigative committee in January indicate that on at least two occasions he may have deliberately misled the public in order to keep the firm's problems from becoming known. Enron announces the planned resignations of six board members, including four who served on its audit panel.

20 CSFB (Credit Suisse First Boston) fines two executives and a top broker $500,000 apiece in the aftermath of a regulatory probe of alleged abuses in the way the firm handed out hot initial public offerings.

March 2002

4 Arthur Andersen agrees to pay $217 million to settle all pending litigation related to its audits of the Baptist Foundation of Arizona, which filed for Chapter 11 after its collapse in 1999.

12 Qwest and WorldCom say the SEC has launched inquiries into their accounting practices.

15 *Andersen is charged by the Justice Department with obstruction of justice over the destruction of documents related to its Enron audit. Anderson loses some forty clients in the wake of the Enron collapse, including Merck, Freddie Mac, and Delta Air Lines.*

April 2002

3 The SEC is looking into accounting methods at some of the largest U.S. companies, broadening the scope of its inquiry beyond the issues in the Enron probe.

8 An amended Enron lawsuit alleges that more than three dozen new defendants, including Merrill Lynch and J. P. Morgan Chase, participated in a scheme with the company's top executives to defraud investors.

9 *The Andersen partner fired by the firm for shredding Enron audit documents has agreed to plead guilty to obstruction and cooperate with U.S. prosecutors.*

10 The SEC widens its probe of alleged accounting fraud at Xerox, telling two former executives and KPMG, the firm's former auditor, that it may file civil charges against them.

23 Alfred Taubman of Sotheby's is sentenced to a year and a day in jail and fined $7.5 million for his role in a price-fixing scheme.

30 WorldCom's CEO Bernard Ebbers quits. He reaches his decision under pressure from outside directors frustrated by the company's sinking stock price, controversy over Ebbers's $366 million personal loan from the firm, and the SEC's investigation of the company.

30 Sotheby's ex-CEO Diana Brooks is sentenced to three years' probation instead of prison for her role in a price-fixing scheme.

May 2002

7 Enron energy traders manipulated California's power system to bolster profits during the height of the state's 2000–2001 energy crisis, documents released by federal regulators show. California officials call for a new criminal inquiry.

14 Reliant says it engaged in bogus power trades during the past three years to make its business appear larger. The company blames rogue traders.

16 CMS Energy says $4.4 billion of its electricity trading—most of its volume for 2000 and 2001—resulted from sham "round-trip" swaps with Dynegy and Reliant that had no economic value. Meanwhile, the SEC is conducting a sweeping probe across many industries into practices that pump up revenue.

16 Adelphia says its founder, John Rigas, has resigned and that it has launched a probe amid new allegations involving the Rigas family.

17 Adelphia is the subject of a probe by federal prosecutors into possible accounting irregularities.

17 Reliant and CMS announce management shake-ups, following admissions that managers had engaged in bogus power deals.

20 Federal authorities are trying to determine whether Computer Associates wrongly booked more than $500 million in revenue in its 1998 and 1999 fiscal years in a scheme to enrich the firm's senior managers.

22 Merrill Lynch agrees to pay $100 million and change how it monitors its stock analysts in settling the New York State attorney general's inquiry into allegations that it misled individual investors about the stock of its investment banking clients.

28 CMS's chief resigns following disclosures that the energy firm's trading unit had conducted transactions that artificially boosted volumes and revenue.

29 Dynegy's chief Chuck Watson resigns under pressure from the company's board. Watson's departure comes amid mounting questions about some of the energy concern's financial practices.

29 Halliburton says the SEC has launched a preliminary inquiry into its accounting treatment of cost overruns on construction jobs.

31 *Citigroup analyst Jack Grubman was instrumental in making management and business decisions at Global Crossing for two years after the firm went public in August 1998. The activities of the Salomon telecom analyst may lend support to New York State attorney general Eliot Spitzer's probe into conflicts of interest among research analysts.*

June 2002

6 New York prosecutors are looking into whether former Tyco CEO Dennis Kozlowski improperly used company funds to buy his $18 million New York apartment and whether he received interest-free loans from the company to purchase artwork.

7 Adelphia inflated the number of cable TV subscribers by 400,000 to 500,000 and kept two sets of books to inflate the amount it spent to upgrade systems.

10 Adelphia's board dismisses auditor Deloitte & Touche, accusing it of not informing the cable company about questionable accounting and self-dealing.

13 ImClone's former CEO is arrested on charges of trying to sell ImClone stock and tipping off family members after learning that regulators would soon reject his company's cancer drug.

13 The SEC reopens a probe of Tyco as part of a broader review of possibly questionable corporate accounting in the aftermath of the Enron meltdown. Separately, Tyco receives SEC clearance for a CIT share offer but is forced to take a $4.5 billion charge to reflect the unit's impaired value.

17 *Andersen is convicted of one felony count of obstructing the SEC's investigation into Enron's collapse. The verdict, which the accounting firm plans to appeal, gives the Justice Department a badly needed boost in momentum as it pursues indictments for more serious crimes at the energy trader.*

18 Enron discloses it made $745 million of payments and stock awards to executives in the year prior to its bankruptcy law filing.

24 Three former top Rite Aid executives are charged with masterminding an illegal accounting scheme that triggered the largest corporate earnings restatement in U.S. history.

26 WorldCom's audit panel uncovers what could be one of the largest accounting frauds ever, with the discovery of $3.8 billion in expenses improperly booked as capital expenditures. Without the transfers, WorldCom would have reported a loss for 2001 and the first quarter of 2002. The company fires its longtime chief financial officer Scott Sullivan.

26 Adelphia files for bankruptcy court protection amid probes into some of the largest self-dealing in U.S. corporate history.

27 The SEC files a civil suit alleging WorldCom engaged in a fraudulent scheme to pad earnings.

27 Former Tyco chief Dennis Kozlowski is charged with two new felony counts of tampering with evidence in connection with an alleged tax evasion scheme.

28 A new Xerox audit finds that the company improperly accelerated far more revenue during the past five years than the SEC estimated in an April settlement. The total amount of improperly recorded revenue from 1997 through 2001 could be more than $6 billion.

July 2002

1   Xerox overstated its pretax income by 36 percent, or $1.41 billion, in the past five years, showing bookkeeping misdeeds more severe than the SEC estimated.

5   The Justice Department begins a criminal probe into Qwest, the latest blow for a telecom firm struggling with $26.6 billion in debt and steep declines in local and long-distance businesses.

12 Bristol-Myers confirms the SEC is probing whether the drug maker improperly inflated revenue last year by up to $1 billion.

22 WorldCom files for Chapter 11 in the largest bankruptcy case in U.S. history.

25 Adelphia founder John Rigas and two of his sons are arrested and charged with looting the cable television company.

29 Qwest says it expects to restate financial results for 2000 and 2001 and to withdraw previously reduced financial projections for 2002.

31 President Bush signs a bill to fight corporate fraud. At an elaborate ceremony to give his approval to legislation he initially resisted, the president promises "no more easy money for corporate criminals, just hard time."

August 2002

8   ImClone's Samuel Waksal is indicted for insider trading; he pleads not guilty. ImClone soon files suit against its founder and former CEO, alleging he deliberately impeded continuing probes of the biotech firm.

9   WorldCom expects to expand its planned financial restatement to $7.2 billion from $3.85 billion as a result of additional accounting irregularities.

16 *Citigroup analyst Jack Grubman resigns from Salomon Smith Barney. The tele-communications analyst had faced mounting pressure from regulators, who say he hyped stocks to help the firm win investment banking deals. The move comes as Salomon faces an NASD (National Association of Securities Dealers) inquiry into whether it directed shares of hot initial public offerings into clients' personal brokerage accounts at below-market prices. Salomon later acknowledges that it directed thousands of shares of hot IPOs to executives of WorldCom. Nearly 1 million shares of those IPOs went to Bernard Ebbers, WorldCom's ex-CEO, documents show.*

22 Former Enron executive Michael Kopper names Andrew Fastow, Enron's ousted chief financial officer, as an unindicted co-conspirator as he pleads guilty to money laundering and fraud. A onetime aide to Fastow, Kopper was a key player in several off–balance sheet partnerships. His plea agreement is the first by a former Enron executive.

23 *Salomon Smith Barney is being investigated by New York's attorney general over how the securities firm won a lucrative deal from AT&T and what role Citigroup CEO Sanford Weill may have played. Salomon was picked as lead underwriter for the April 2000 stock offering only after telecom analyst Jack Grubman upgraded his rating of AT&T to a "buy."*

29 Prosecutors win an indictment against Scott Sullivan, WorldCom's former top finance executive, accusing him of orchestrating the telecom firm's $7.2 billion fraud. The federal grand jury also indicts Buford "Buddy" Yates, a midlevel accounting official. The two are charged with securities fraud and making false filings to the SEC.

September 2002

5 Credit Suisse First Boston's Frank Quattrone pushed for greater IPO allocations for investment banking clients, according to email records and people familiar with the firm. The allegations against the star technology industry investment banker thrust Credit Suisse Group's CSFB into the spotlight of regulatory scrutiny regarding IPO allocation practices. It soon emerges that CSFB analysts felt pressured by the firm to avoid writing negative reports on investment banking clients, according to evidence in a Massachusetts probe.

9 *Citigroup ousts Michael Carpenter as head of its global corporate and investment bank amid allegations of questionable practices at its Salomon unit.*

13 Tyco's former CEO and ex–finance chief are charged with stealing over $170 million. Prosecutors accuse Dennis Kozlowski and Mark Swartz of running a "criminal enterprise" aimed at defrauding investors, saying the executives siphoned off company funds for their own use. Mark Belnick, the former general counsel, is charged with falsifying business records.

16 Prosecutors are investigating alleged fraud by Enron in the manipulation of power prices in three western states during the California electricity crisis. They are examining whether two former top executives, Jeffrey Skilling and

Greg Whalley, were aware of the questionable trading practices or sought to conceal them.

19   WorldCom prepares a further revision of its financial results that could add about $2 billion to the $7 billion in accounting problems it has already disclosed. The move marks the second time the long-distance firm has added large amounts to its earnings revision.

19   Merrill fires Thomas Davis, one of two vice chairmen, for his refusal to testify in an investigation of several Enron deals.

20   *Citigroup agrees to pay $215 million to settle FTC allegations that Associates First Capital engaged in deceptive and abusive lending.*

24   Xerox is facing a criminal inquiry by federal authorities related to the copier company's massive misstatement of earnings. FBI agents and prosecutors recently questioned James Bingham, a former assistant treasurer, who said he was fired for trying to rein in unethical accounting.

24   *Salomon agrees to settle civil charges levied by the NASD that analysts touted Winstar while privately questioning the stock. Winstar, a telecom company, filed for bankruptcy court protection in 2001.*

24   Adelphia founder John Rigas, two of his sons, and two other former executives are indicted on charges of looting the firm.

26   Merrill employee Douglas Faneuil agrees to plead guilty to a misdemeanor charge and provide testimony against Martha Stewart and others over their sales of ImClone stock in 2001.

27   WorldCom's ex-controller David Myers pleads guilty to fraud, claiming he manipulated accounts at the behest of management.

30   New York prosecutors are examining whether Tyco's outside auditor PricewaterhouseCoopers knew about secret bonuses paid to former Tyco executives and accounting that regulators say hid the payments.

30   *Citigroup offers to create a separate research arm as part of a global settlement with regulators probing allegations of stock hyping at its Salomon unit.*

October 2002

1   *New York attorney general Eliot Spitzer sues five telecom executives, demanding that they return to investors the $1.5 billion that the suit says was obtained from the sale of stock in their own firms and $28 million in profits from the sale of Salomon IPOs.*

11   Two former WorldCom employees plead guilty for their role in the $7.2 billion accounting fraud.

16   ImClone's Samuel Waksal pleads guilty to insider trading and other charges.

18   The former head of Enron's western energy-trading desk admits he conspired to manipulate California's electricity market to maximize profits.

24   AOL Time Warner says it will restate financial results for the past two years because of more questionable advertising transactions at America Online. The restatement will reduce revenue by $190 million and is likely to deepen uncertainty about accounting issues.

25 Eliot Spitzer and the SEC unveil a plan for a panel to oversee independent stock research that brokerage firms would be required to provide to individuals.

25 Bristol-Myers says it will restate sales and earnings for at least the past two years because of a wholesale inventory-stocking issue.

30 *Citigroup plans to break out its research and retail brokerage operations into a new unit, amid pressure on the firm from regulators to tackle stock analyst conflicts.*

November 2002

1 Former Enron official Andrew Fastow is indicted for fraud, conspiracy, money laundering, and coercing his lieutenant to destroy documents.

6 WorldCom discloses that its false profits could top $9 billion. The SEC slapped the firm with more fraud charges and said the deception goes back to 1999.

13 *Jack Grubman indicates Citigroup CEO Sanford Weill pushed him to upgrade AT&T's stock rating as part of Weill's power struggle with Citigroup's former co-chairman John Reed.*

December 2002

23 *A stock research settlement unveiled by regulators requires ten firms, including Citigroup, to pay $1.4 billion, including $900 million in penalties, $450 million for independent research over the next five years, and $85 million for investor education.*

January 2003

3 J. P. Morgan says it will take a $1.3 billion charge for the fourth quarter, largely to settle litigation over its involvement with Enron.

23 *Freddie Mac will restate its earnings higher for at least the past two years after its auditor recommends accounting changes.*

February 2003

5 Sprint forced out its two top executives last month as part of a dispute over their use of a questionable tax shelter.

7 The SEC will require Wall Street analysts to certify that they believe what they put in research reports and public statements.

25 Ahold ousts its CEO and chief financial officers and says it will have to lower its earnings for the past two years by at least $500 million. Federal regulators later open inquiries into accounting at the Dutch supermarket owner's U.S. Foodservice unit.

March 2003

4 ImClone founder Samuel Waksal pleads guilty to criminal charges related to evading $1.2 million in sales taxes on art purchases.

5 Frank Quattrone is forced to resign from CSFB after he fails to provide testimony to regulators investigating his activities.

7 The NASD charges Quattrone with several civil violations, describing conduct that benefited wealthy individuals at the expense of small investors. Quattrone denies wrongdoing.

11 Bristol-Myers concedes that its accounting has been "inappropriate" and that sales from 1999 to 2002 were inflated by up to $2.75 billion.

20 The SEC accuses HealthSouth and CEO Richard Scrushy of accounting fraud, alleging that they overstated earnings by $1.4 billion since 1999 in order to meet Wall Street estimates. According to the complaint, Scrushy personally profited from the scheme. Weston Smith, the former finance chief, pleads guilty to four criminal charges.

24 *Citigroup CEO Sanford Weill withdraws his nomination as a director to represent public investors on the board of the New York Stock Exchange.*

24 *The NYSE is under fire for its corporate governance in the wake of its nomination of Citigroup's Sanford Weill to be a director. A few days earlier, Weill withdrew his nomination.*

27 HealthSouth's finance chief pleads guilty to falsely certifying financial statements.

28 Lucent agrees to a $568 million settlement to resolve shareholder suits that alleged the telecom firm engaged in financial fraud and aggressive sales practices.

April 2003

1 HealthSouth dismisses CEO Richard Scrushy and moves to replace its outside auditor, Ernst & Young.

24 Frank Quattrone is arrested and charged by prosecutors with obstructing justice and witness tampering in connection with the probe of IPO practices at CSFB. He denies wrongdoing.

28 Former Merrill analyst Henry Blodget pays $4 million and is barred from the securities industry for life as part of a settlement over his research calls.

29 *Ten securities firms including Citigroup agree to pay a record $1.4 billion to settle government charges that they issued overly optimistic stock research to win investment banking business. The pact also settles charges that at least two firms improperly doled out IPOs to executives.*

30 Tyco finds roughly $1.2 billion in fresh accounting problems. The new problems come on top of $265 million to $325 million in charges announced in March.

May 2003

2 Prosecutors file new charges against Enron's former finance chief Andrew Fastow and indict his wife and seven other ex-officials for fraud and other violations. Fastow denies the allegations that he helped engineer a massive financial fraud and stole millions from his employer.

8   *Securities regulators missed "systemic" problems on Wall Street, lawmakers charge at a Senate Banking Committee hearing into the $1.4 billion stock research settlement. Senators also allege the agreement doesn't go far enough to punish wrongdoers and prevent future abuses. Regulators look into the actions of investment bankers in their stock research probe, focusing on Salomon.*

9   The SEC is in talks with Qwest to settle potential fraud charges stemming from the phone company's swaps of fiber optic capacity with other telecom firms. Qwest says the deals had a business purpose, a claim the SEC contests.

13 Frank Quattrone is indicted on criminal obstruction of justice and witness-tampering charges. Later this month, he pleads not guilty to the charges.

14 Ahold ousts the chief executive of U.S. Foodservice, the unit whose accounting problems have forced the retailer to restate earnings. Later in the week, two executives resign in the wake of the scandal involving supplier rebates that were inflated to boost earnings.

20 MCI agrees to pay investors $500 million to settle fraud charges that the company, formerly WorldCom, misled investors in the biggest accounting scandal in U.S. history.

June 2003

5   Martha Stewart is indicted on criminal charges of securities fraud, conspiracy, and making false statements to federal agents. In a separate civil case, the SEC accuses her of insider trading related to her ImClone share sale. Stewart relinquishes her posts as chairman and CEO of Martha Stewart Living.

6   The SEC forces six former and current Xerox executives, including two ex-CEOs and a former finance chief, to pay $22 million in fines and other penalties to settle civil fraud charges related to overstated revenues and profits. The agency says the executives profited from bonuses and stock sales based on false financial results.

6   A report on accounting fraud at WorldCom concludes for the first time that former CEO Bernard Ebbers played a role in efforts to improperly boost revenue. A week later, two external probes find that Ebbers conspired with top officials and employees beginning in the late 1990s to carry out a massive fraud.

10 *Freddie Mac fires its president and asks its chairman and CEO and its finance chief to resign. The firm reiterates plans to restate three years of earnings. The moves send Freddie's stock down 16 percent.*

11 Samuel Waksal is sentenced to seven years and three months in prison for insider trading, obstructing justice, and tax evasion.

12 *Freddie Mac's ex-CEO will receive a $24 million severance package, despite being asked to resign in the wake of accounting problems. In addition, both Leland Brendsel and David Glenn, the former chief operating officer, will be able to exercise stock options valued at $14.2 million for Brendsel and $5.3 million for Glenn. The U.S. attorney and the SEC have opened probes of the firm.*

18 Rite Aid's ex-CEO pleads guilty to two conspiracy counts in a massive accounting fraud. Under the plea deal, Martin Grass agrees to pay $3.5 million in fines and forfeiture.

26 *Freddie Mac says it understated past earnings by as much as $4.5 billion after taxes, blaming lax accounting controls.*

July 2003

29 *Citigroup and J. P. Morgan Chase agree to pay a total of $305 million to settle actions related to loans and trades made with Enron and Dynegy, ending nineteen months of intense regulatory scrutiny. They also agree to overhaul the way they vet their most complex financial deals. Regulators say the settlement involves $8.3 billion in loans improperly accounted for by Enron.*

August 2003

22 *The NYSE fines Salomon Smith Barney for failing to supervise brokers dealing with WorldCom employees.*

25 *Freddie Mac bowed to pressure from its federal regulator Friday and agreed to remove chief executive Greg Parseghian, a former head of Freddie Mac's $600 billion loan portfolio who was tapped to be CEO just two months ago in a management shake-up.*

September 2003

4 At a hearing, WorldCom ex-CEO Ebbers pleads not guilty to fifteen felony charges of violating Oklahoma securities law.

11 Enron's former treasurer pleads guilty to one count of conspiring to commit fraud and is sentenced to five years in prison.

17 New York's attorney general files criminal charges against Theodore Siphol, a former Bank of America broker, over allegedly improper fund trading. Siphol has denied committing any illegality.

18 Merrill accepts responsibility for the role of some employees in the Enron scandal as part of a deal to avoid prosecution. The brokerage firm agrees to a wide-ranging set of changes and restrictions in exchange for not being prosecuted by the Justice Department. Three ex-officials are criminally charged.

October 2003

6 Merrill Lynch fires three brokers who allegedly helped hedge fund Millennium improperly trade more than five mutual funds.

17 A former executive at Alger pleads guilty to New York State criminal charges of obstructing a probe of improper mutual fund trading. The SEC also brings civil charges against the executive, James Connelly, saying he let select customers rapidly trade some funds.

27 The case against Frank Quattrone ends in a mistrial, an outcome that could give prosecutors pause about how they try future financial cases.

29 Massachusetts regulators and the SEC charge Putnam and two fund managers with securities fraud over market timing.

November 2003

3 Richard Strong steps down as chairman of Strong Mutual Funds in the wake of allegations he engaged in improper trading.

4 Putnam's CEO is ousted in the wake of civil charges against the firm. The SEC said it found widespread fund industry abuses.

5 Richard Scrushy is indicted on eighty-five counts related to the HealthSouth accounting scandal, including fraud, money laundering, and violations of the Sarbanes-Oxley corporate crime law. The indictment says the former chairman pursued plans to keep the $2.7 billion fraud from being revealed as pressure from a federal probe mounted.

5 Prosecutors announce plans to retry Frank Quattrone on obstruction charges, but lawyers agree to a delay in setting a retrial.

14 Investment firm Pilgrim Baxter's two founders quit after it was disclosed that they were connected to market timing trades.

24 *Freddie Mac releases a restatement showing it understated earnings by almost $5 billion and revealing new accounting troubles.*

December 2003

2 Boeing's Philip Condit resigns as chairman and chief executive in the wake of scandals that tainted the aerospace giant's relationship with the government.

3 Richard Strong quits as chairman and CEO of Strong Financial amid allegations that he engaged in short-term trading at the mutual fund company he founded.

3 Securities regulators file civil fraud charges against Invesco and its CEO, alleging they allowed market timing by some investors in at least ten funds.

12 Regulators bring civil charges against the former Prudential Securities for an alleged late-trading scheme and accuse Heartland executives of insider trading.

16 Alliance agrees to reduce its mutual fund management fees by 20 percent for the next five years as part of an agreement with Eliot Spitzer to settle allegations that it allowed improper fund trading. The reduction would come on top of a record $250 million fine Alliance is expected to pay to settle civil fraud charges it could be facing.

17 Putnam says that an additional nine employees engaged in short-term market-timing trades of its mutual funds are being fired. The Marsh & McLennan unit previously disclosed that six of its fund managers had engaged in timing trades.

22 Parmalat plans to seek bankruptcy court protection in Italy after disclosing that an account it reported at Bank of America allegedly holding billions of

dollars doesn't exist. Prosecutors later find more money missing, widening the scope of the alleged fraud to over $8 billion.

January 2004

14 Former Enron finance chief Andrew Fastow and his wife agree to plead guilty to criminal charges for their roles in the energy concern's collapse. Fastow later agrees to serve ten years in return for his cooperation.
27 Parmalat hid nearly $16 billion of debt and reported earnings more than five times their actual size, an initial report finds.

February 2004

18 Five NYSE specialists tentatively agree to pay about $240 million to settle civil charges that they stepped ahead of customer orders.
20 Jeffrey Skilling is indicted on an array of charges stemming from an alleged plan to manipulate Enron's financial statements. The indictment of the fallen energy company's former president and CEO leaves former chairman Kenneth Lay as the highest-ranking Enron figure who hasn't been charged with criminal wrongdoing.

March 2004

3 Bernard Ebbers, the former chairman and CEO of WorldCom, is indicted for allegedly helping to orchestrate the largest accounting fraud in U.S. history. After a two-year probe, prosecutors got their break as Scott Sullivan, WorldCom's former finance chief, pleaded guilty to three charges and agreed to cooperate in the case.
8 Martha Stewart is convicted of obstruction charges related to the sale of ImClone stock and vows to appeal.
16 Bank of America and Fleet Boston agree to $675 million in fines and fee cuts to settle civil fraud charges in the mutual fund scandal. The penalties bring to more than $1.65 billion the total to be paid by fund industry participants to settle allegations of improper trading.
26 Former Dynegy executive Jamie Olis is sentenced to more than twenty-four years in prison in an accounting fraud case that fell under tough federal rules.

April 2004

5 The case of former Tyco chief executive Dennis Kozlowski and former chief financial officer Mark Swartz ends in mistrial.
8 Computer Associates' ex–finance chief Ira Zar and two other former finance officials agree to plead guilty to at least two criminal charges, including securities fraud and obstruction, in the federal probe of the software maker's accounting.

22 Computer Associates' Sanjay Kumar steps down as chairman and chief executive amid fears that he might be charged in the company's accounting probe. The company soon restates more than $2 billion in revenue.

29 Nortel Networks fires chief executive Frank Dunn and other senior officials, as the firm's accounting problems spread to its top ranks. The telecommunications equipment maker also warns of a sharp downward revision of 2003 results.

May 2004

4 Frank Quattrone, the ex-head of technology investment banking at Credit Suisse First Boston, is found guilty after a retrial on charges he interfered with a U.S. investigation at the investment bank in 2000.

7 The wife of Enron ex–finance chief Fastow is sentenced to a year in prison after pleading guilty to a tax charge arising from the Enron scandal.

11 *Citigroup agrees to pay $2.65 billion to settle a lawsuit brought by investors of the former WorldCom who lost billions of dollars when the telecommunications operator filed for Chapter 11. The suit alleges Citigroup and other investment banks that underwrote WorldCom bonds didn't conduct adequate due diligence.*

21 Richard Strong and his Strong Funds agree to a $175 million settlement of allegations that he took part in and allowed rapid trading.

25 Eliot Spitzer sues former NYSE chairman Dick Grasso and compensation committee ex-chairman Kenneth Langone, seeking to recover more than $100 million of Grasso's $200 million compensation package. The civil suit alleges that the two men misled directors about the size of the package and that Grasso intimidated them into approving the payouts.

25 Bernard Ebbers is charged with six new counts accusing the former World-Com CEO of making false filings to the SEC.

28 Former Rite Aid CEO Martin Grass is sentenced to eight years in prison for his role in accounting fraud at the drugstore chain.

June 2004

22 Goldman and Morgan Stanley tentatively agree to pay a total of $80 million to settle accusations over their handling of IPOs.

24 The SEC approves a rule requiring fund firms to have independent chairmen, a move that will displace most funds' heads.

30 Bank One agrees to a $90 million settlement with the SEC and New York attorney general Spitzer over charges the firm's mutual fund group entered deals to allow short-term trading.

July 2004

8 Kenneth Lay is indicted for his role in Enron's collapse. The energy giant's former CEO, charged with being part of a wide-ranging scheme to defraud investors, denies any wrongdoing.

9   Prosecutors win criminal convictions against Adelphia founder John Rigas and his son Timothy, former CFO, but fail to convince a jury the looting at the cable company involved the firm's former assistant treasurer.

9   MCI sues former CEO Bernard Ebbers in a bid to collect more than $300 million that he owes on $408 million of loans from the company.

28   The government brings civil and criminal charges against four former executives of the U.S. Foodservice unit of Ahold NV, alleging they inflated earnings to reap big bonuses.

August 2004

5   Bristol-Myers agrees to pay $150 million to settle SEC charges of accounting fraud involving $1.5 billion of inflated revenue.

19   *The SEC staff warns Freddie Mac that the company is likely to face civil charges involving alleged securities law violations.*

20   Nortel fires seven finance officials as it strives to clean up accounting problems.

September 2004

1   A probe of Hollinger International finds former CEO Conrad Black and ex-president David Radler siphoned off more than $400 million through "aggressive looting" of the publishing company, in what amounted to a "corporate kleptocracy." The two executives quit in 2003 when the company alleged that they and other officials had received $32 million of unauthorized payments.

9   Frank Quattrone is sentenced to eighteen months in prison for obstructing a government probe into how CSFB allocated IPO shares.

13   Qwest Communications International agrees to a preliminary $250 million settlement with the SEC over improper accounting, while ex–chief executive Joseph Nacchio soon may face civil charges.

21   The regulator of Fannie Mae (the Federal National Mortgage Association) outlines the results of its accounting probe, finding a pattern of decisions aimed at manipulating profit.

23   Sanjay Kumar is indicted for allegedly helping to orchestrate a widespread accounting fraud at Computer Associates and then lying to investigators. The software maker's ex-CEO, along with its former sales head, faces charges including securities fraud and obstruction.

23   Fannie Mae's regulator accuses the mortgage finance giant of a wide range of improper accounting practices in a report that follows an eight-month probe.

October 2004

15   Marsh & McLennan is accused of cheating corporate clients by rigging bids and collecting fees from insurers for throwing business their way. The allegations are contained in a civil suit filed against the insurance broker by New

York State attorney general Spitzer. The suit also names insurers American International Group, Ace, Hartford Financial, and Munich-American Risk Partners as participants.

22   The SEC alleges that Qwest Communications engaged in pervasive fraud by top management. The telecommunications company agrees to pay a $250 million penalty.

26   Jeffrey Greenberg quits as Marsh & McLennan's chairman and chief executive officer under pressure from prosecutors in the bid-rigging case.

November 2004

4   A jury finds four former Merrill bankers and an Enron ex-executive guilty of conspiracy and fraud in connection with a scheme to inflate the energy firm's 1999 earnings. The verdicts in the first Enron criminal trial involve the purported sale by Enron to Merrill of an interest in barges off the coast of Nigeria.

16   Fannie Mae estimates it will have to post a $9 billion loss if the SEC finds it has been accounting improperly for derivatives. Regulator OFHEO says Fannie incorrectly applied accounting rules in a way that let the mortgage company spread out losses over many years rather than taking an immediate hit.

December 2004

22   Fannie Mae's CEO Franklin Raines and chief financial officer Timothy Howard step down amid growing pressure from regulators over accounting violations. The mortgage company's board also dismisses KPMG as outside auditor.

Permissions